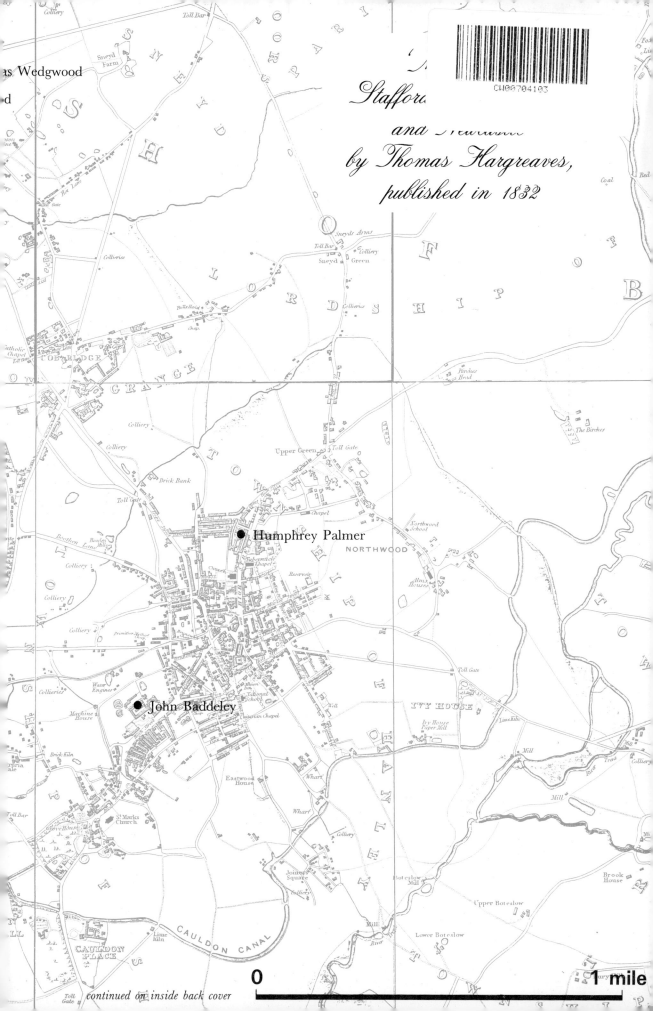

Stafford...

and Newcastle

by Thomas Hargreaves,

published in 1832

● Humphrey Palmer

● John Baddeley

0

1 mile

continued on inside back cover

WILLIAM GREATBATCH

a Staffordshire Potter
by
David Barker

Foreword by Arnold Mountford C.B.E.

Published by
Jonathan Horne

© David Barker 1990
First published in 1991 by
Jonathan Horne Publications
66c Kensington Church Street
London W8 4BY
ISBN 0 951 2140 3 9
Designed by Jonathan Horne
Printed in Great Britain by
Grillford Ltd., Granby, Milton Keynes

CONTENTS

ACKNOWLEDGEMENTS

In the production of any publication such as this, the end result will have come about only through the support, help and active interest of countless people, of colleagues, friends and people who have come to be friends on the basis of shared enthusiasm. There are many people who deserve my most sincere thanks, and many who will, of necessity, be omitted in so short a piece; I can only hope that I may be forgiven my preference for brevity.

That there was ever an opportunity to carry out the excavations of the Greatbatch site is due entirely to the interest of Linden Evans, who not only 'discovered' the site, but also recognised the initial finds for what they were. Permission to excavate was granted by the landowners, Mills and Allen Ltd., and the work was undertaken, in fair weather and foul, by members of the Stoke-on-Trent Museum Archaeological Society. I would like to acknowledge their enthusiasm both during the excavation, and in the years which followed. The vast quantities of excavated pottery have required washing, sorting and piecing together, and the efforts of Society members have made a major contribution to this work. Acknowledgement is also due to Mrs. Evelyn Heath who, over a period of almost ten years, has single-handedly washed by far the greatest proportion of the excavated pottery.

Much of the pottery illustrated in this volume has been drawn by Diane Baker and by Roy Fern. Their help has been invaluable. Also, at this stage, I would like to acknowledge financial support from the Wedgwood International Seminar which has enabled me to attend to the many drawings needed for this and subsequent reports. Various photographers are acknowledged in the volume, but in particular I should mention the work of Richard Weston, of the City Museum & Art Gallery, Stoke-on-Trent.

Throughout the excavation of the Greatbatch site, the research into the ceramics, and in the eventual preparation for publication, I have received constant support from the City Museum & Art Gallery, Stoke-on-Trent, and its staff, and in particular from Pat Halfpenny, Keeper of Ceramics, and from Arnold Mountford, the Museum's former Director. Their patient encouragement over the years has been appreciated by this relative newcomer to the world of ceramics.

In addition, I would like to thank all those individuals or institutions who have, over the years, brought Greatbatch pieces to my attention, supplied photographs or information, or who have allowed me access to their collections. Many, if not all are acknowledged in the text of this volume, but I would like to single out the following: Gaye Blake Roberts of the Wedgwood Museum; Myra Brown of the Liverpool Museum; Alison Cowling of the Central Museum and Art Gallery, Northampton; David and Gwen Drakard; Robin Emmerson of Norwich Castle Museum; Lindsay and Leslie Grigsby; Rodney Hampson; Paul Holdway; Jonathan Horne, my publisher; Mr. & Mrs. Jacobs; John Mallet, formerly of the Victoria and Albert Museum; Robin Price; Sheila Tabakoff and Vera Watts of the Mint Museum, Charlotte, North Carolina; Olive Talbott; Tom Walford; Peter Walton of the Bar Convent Museum; and Henry H. Weldon.

Greatbatch's correspondence is quoted by courtesy of the Trustees of the Wedgwood Museum, Stoke-on-Trent, Staffordshire, England. I acknowledge, also, Keele University Library, where the manuscripts are deposited, and would like to thank Dr. Ian Fraser for his help in making these available to me. Extracts from Greatbatch's will are reproduced by courtesy of the Staffordshire County Archivist.

The final stages on this publication would not have been possible without the constant support, and editorial eye of Miranda Goodby; thanks alone do not suffice.

Finally, I wish to acknowledge the major contribution made to the field of ceramic research, by the late Donald Towner who, more than any one else, has brought the name of William Greatbatch to the attention of the ceramics world. It is fitting that he should have been involved in the initial identification of pottery from the Greatbatch site and I am pleased that he was able to see some of the early results of the excavation.

FOREWORD

During the term of my Directorship of the City Museum & Art Gallery, Stoke-on-Trent, which lasted for more than a quarter of a century, I was a priviledged witness to many fascinating archaeological discoveries in North Staffordshire, most, as one might expect, relating to ceramics. When, in 1978, the creamware specialist Donald Towner identified some wasters submitted to him from Fenton as having been manufactured by William Greatbatch, it sparked off a great deal of interest in an 18th century potter known principally through his business connections with Josiah Wedgwood. A small-scale trial excavation by members of the Stoke-on-Trent Museum Archaeological Society began the following year under the direction of David Barker and, from the outset, it was obvious that this was not going to be an ordinary, run-of-the-mill 'dig'.

There was excitement enough during the first few days, but the prodigious amount of pottery sherds, saggars, kiln furniture, bricks, ash and other refuse led the archaeologists to discount an earlier report that they were working on the site of the Greatbatch factory; rather, they were recovering waste material dumped into an exhausted marl hole sometime during the second half of the 18th century. As each week went by, the surprising variety of pottery types coming from the ground held the attention of the digging team, but, back at the Museum, the task of washing, sorting and endeavouring to piece together the countless fragments produced a growing awareness that this was to become the most important site of its kind and date ever to be uncovered in the Staffordshire Potteries.

The end result was the recovery of several tons of pottery wasters which included hundreds marked with the initials of William Greatbatch, together with several pieces which were signed. At the Museum, every sherd had to be handled time and time again in the frustrating exercise leading towards restoration. As one might imagine, the task took several years to complete, but as matching fragments slowly developed into partially completed pots, the news that David Barker had directed a major archaeological excavation of immense value to the ceramic world stimulated collectors and museum colleagues in England and the United States to descend on Stoke-on-Trent to share in the excitement. For the first time, it was now possible to identify wares as Greatbatch by direct comparison with the excavated material.

This one site has caused many to re-assess the state of ceramic history, and to ponder upon what else lies buried in Stoke-on-Trent. The value of this mass of excavated material towards future ceramic studies cannot be over-stated; already many pots in private and public collections have been re-attributed by direct comparison with the sherds and without doubt this new publication will accelerate further changes.

Everyone agreed that a book was called for with a minimum of delay and the archaeological and documentary evidence here presented will ensure the acceptance of this volume as the standard work of reference. The author has at long last drawn William Greatbatch from the shadows, and for this we are grateful.

Arnold R. Mountford C.B.E.

PREFACE

The name of William Greatbatch is well-known to students of English ceramics. A contemporary of the pre-eminent potter of the eighteenth century, Josiah Wedgwood, Greatbatch has, over the years, been referred to in many works of ceramic history. However, he has always been something of a mystery and those few wares attributed to him by different writers have remained problems, thorns in the side of the serious researcher. The simple fact is that there is insufficient documentary evidence to allow positive attributions and early errors in print have lived on to become accepted truths.

The present volume describes the results of a major archaeological excavation undertaken in Fenton, Stoke-on-Trent, between 1979 and 1981, on a site which was intimately associated with William Greatbatch. This was not the site of Greatbatch's factory but, more important than this, the waste tip of that factory. Pottery production is an extremely wasteful process and, as a result, the identification of factory waste tips, and the recovery of the pottery from them, have a potential for ceramic research which is unmatched by any other form of evidence. The excavation of the Greatbatch site has exposed the enormity of this potential.

The excavation recovered a vast quantity of waste pottery which can be positively attributed to Greatbatch, and which can be shown to span virtually the whole of his twenty year career as an independent potter. This site has produced examples of almost every type of ware produced by Greatbatch, evidence which is of more potential value to students of ceramics than contemporary shape books, written records or pieces which have survived in collections. This body of material is unique and forms the most complete record of the products of any eighteenth century pottery factory. This is an extremely valuable resource for the ceramic historian, with far-reaching implications for a wider understanding of the development of the pottery industry in North Staffordshire in the eighteenth century.

The excavation of the Greatbatch site proved to be a massive undertaking; the research, analysis and writing up of the finds were even more involved and time-consuming. Indeed, the writing up of the excavation and all the finds from this is still far from complete. The final report, which will be produced by the City Museum & Art Gallery, Stoke-on-Trent, will provide a detailed account of every type of pottery found, with every vessel form, every type of decoration and every feature of the vessels being illustrated in full. Clearly, this level of detail would be impossible in the present volume — the aim in producing this study is very different.

My aim in this book is to make available, at the earliest opportunity, and to as wide a public as possible, the latest research into Staffordshire ceramics. This is not in any way a preliminary presentation, nor is it simply an examination of one potter or one factory. This book sets out to provide an in-depth analysis of the evidence for this one potter's wares and of the wider implications for the future study of English ceramics. A detailed understanding of the products of one factory and the chronological developments of different types, styles, bodies and technology will have an important bearing upon the way in which other, contemporary factories and their products are assessed. In short, the detailed study of the pottery of William Greatbatch has underlined the need for a complete re-assessment of the evidence upon which the present state of knowledge of English ceramics is based. Something of this re-assessment will be attempted in this volume in the light of the evidence from the Greatbatch site.

David Barker

INTRODUCTION

The Development of the 18th Century Staffordshire Pottery Industry

The 18th century witnessed dramatic changes in the nature and scale of pottery production in North Staffordshire. These changes transformed not only the pottery industry and its products, but also the landscape and the whole social fabric of North Staffordshire. The 17th century had seen a growing preoccupation with the manufacture of pottery as a means of existence, the consequence of the unsuitability of the local land for agriculture or for pasture. Pottery production became an important part of the local economy, but was based, in the 17th century, largely upon local raw materials: coal and clay were readily available in the area, with the lead and salt needed for the glazing of wares being brought only short distances, from Derbyshire and Cheshire respectively. The importance of Staffordshire wares to the market grew as the century progressed, with slipwares, mottled wares and other coarse earthenwares traded ever further afield by road, river and sea. However, the transformation to a full industrial economy was not yet complete.

Changes in the market in the early years of the 18th century provided the stimulus for innovation within the Staffordshire pottery industry. Growing consumer demand for finer ceramics led to the introduction of new wares involving new techniques. Changes within the factories were needed to accomodate these new techniques, with the workforce becoming progressively more specialised as division of labour resulted. Long before the construction of the canals in the 1770s made the easy movement of goods and raw materials possible, the potters developed an effective distribution network, based upon merchants, warehouses and specialist china and glass dealers, which enabled wares to be shipped abroad. By the middle of the century, Staffordshire earthenwares and stonewares were ubiquitous at the tables of the English middle classes, while the opening up of the overseas markets saw English fine pottery pre-eminent in the North American colonies and beyond, surpassed for quality and desirability only by Oriental porcelain.

The social climate of the 18th century dictated many of the changes which occurred within the pottery industry. The potters received much of their impetus from the growing popularity among the fashionable classes of chocolate, coffee and, especially, tea-drinking. Early in the 18th century tea-drinking became firmly established amongst the nobility of England and tea parties became a feature of life in the great houses. The growing popularity of tea-drinking amongst the lower social classes as the century progressed did nothing to lessen its popularity amongst the nobility and gentry, but did serve to widen the potential market for the potters.

Tea-drinking brought with it the need for an extensive range of items, teapots, tea canisters, cups, slop bowls, milk jugs and sugar bowls. These requirements had at first been met by the use of imported Oriental porcelain whose very high price made it inaccessible to all but the most wealthy. Home-produced tea and coffee wares did not appear in any quantity until the 1720s — the wares available prior to that time were generally not of a standard to satisfy the potential well-to-do customer.

The Staffordshire potters responded to the new fashions by the introduction of white salt-glazed stoneware, which was both hard and durable, and of a sufficient similarity in colour and finish to Oriental porcelain to deceive the eye, at least from a distance. Tea, coffee and chocolate wares also appeared in earthenware at the same time, with glazed red earthenware and agate ware offering an alternative to the grey-white of the salt-glazed stoneware.

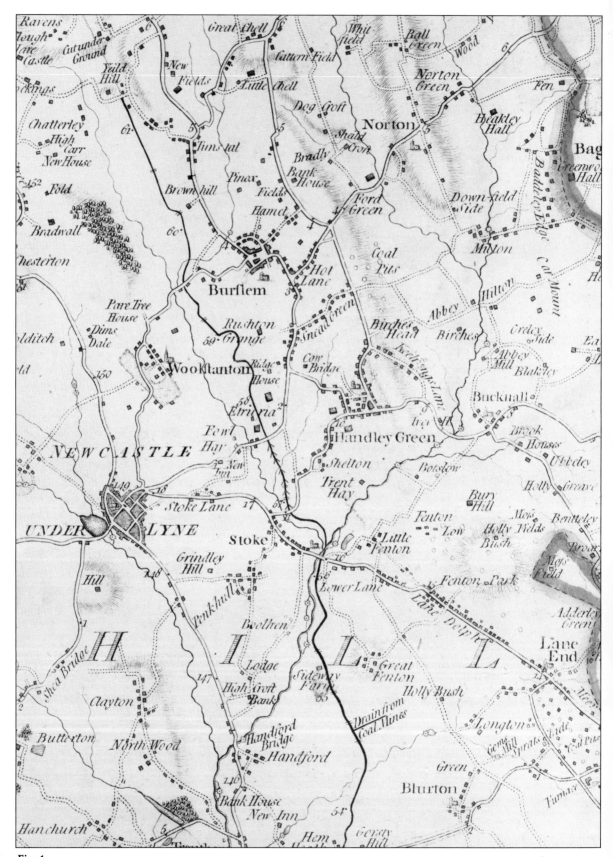

Fig. 1
North Staffordshire in 1775. (William Yates' *Map of the Countie of Stafford from an actual survey, 1769 — 1775,* engraved by John Chapman 1775)

Nothing like these wares had been known before in Staffordshire, or indeed in England; they were new developments in every sense. However, neither the earthenwares nor the white salt-glazed stonewares could compete with porcelain for elegance and desirability, although their relatively low price did bring ceramic tea wares and, eventually, table wares within the reach of the less affluent. Only from the 1740s could home-produced soft-paste porcelain challenge the Oriental porcelain at the tables of the nobility, and yet their cost made them even less affordable than the imported wares and, hence, beyond the reach of most. Consequently, the English earthenware and stoneware potters had every incentive to compete with the manufacturers of porcelain at Bow, Chelsea and Worcester.

*   *   *

North Staffordshire is central to any discussion of the ceramic developments of the 18th century. Not only was there a greater concentration of potteries and potters here than in any other part of the world, with the exception of China, but most of the innovations of stoneware and earthenware manufacture during the century seem to have taken place in this area. The way in which the Staffordshire potters adapted to the needs of a new era was remarkable and resulted in the complete integration of an ever-increasing local population into an industrial economy which revolved around the manufacture of pottery.

The first of the significant innovations of the 18th century was white salt-glazed stoneware. The early development of a pure white-bodied ware by the North Staffordshire potters was impossible due to the absence locally of good quality white-firing clays. The majority of the Staffordshire clays fire to an orange or red colour and are rich in iron oxide. This was a major drawback. Only the clays used in the manufacture of clay tobacco pipes were white-firing, and these were in too short a supply within the area, and not of a sufficiently high quality, to have a significant effect upon the manufacture of ceramics.

Brown salt-glazed stoneware had been manufactured by the North Staffordshire potters at least prior to 1693[1] using local clays which were tempered with sand. Numerous surviving mugs and jugs attest to the very limited range of vessel forms produced[2]: cups are rare, while teapots, as one would imagine, are virtually unknown.

At some time within the first decade of the 18th century, white dipped salt-glazed stoneware appeared as an alternative to the brown, with the iron-bearing local clay body of the vessels hidden by the application of an engobe, or coat of slip, which was prepared from white-firing clay. Shaw states that white dipped wares were first made by John Astbury of Shelton and that the white slip coat used in their manufacture was of *Pipe Clay, from Biddeford, mixed with water*[3]. Surviving white dipped wares can be recognised by the crazing of the salt-glazed surface which was the result of the different rates of shrinkage of the body and the slip coat which occurred during the firing.

White salt-glazed stonewares are sometimes seen as a development of the white dipped wares of the early 18th century, but, in fact, they mark a complete departure both from traditional methods and from traditional forms. Unlike the white dipped wares, whose bodies were of local clays, their production was entirely dependent upon the use of imported clays. The *ball clays*, so-called because they were transported in balls of about a half-hundredweight each, were brought into Staffordshire by sea, river and road from Devon and Dorset. These clays are found in three separate areas, all accessible by sea: one around Poole, Dorset; one around Bideford, in north Devon; and one to the north of Newton Abbot, in south Devon. In writing of these clays, Shaw states that they were *extremely white when fired, owing to being scarcely impregnated with oxide of iron*[4]. It has not been possible to identify from contemporary sources when clay was first brought into Staffordshire from the south-west but there is no reason to doubt that shipments were being received by 1710.

A second non-local material was essential to the manufacture of white salt-glazed stoneware — flint. At the end of the 17th century, the London stoneware potter, John Dwight, had been aware that, when calcined and crushed, flint could be mixed with the potter's clay to act as a temper in the high temperature firings which were necessary in the production of stoneware[5]. Flint had the added properties of making the pottery more durable and of whitening the body.

The date at which flint came to be widely used in the production of stoneware is not known but it certainly pre-dates 1720, the date traditionally given for its accidental discovery by John Astbury[6], for in 1719 a partnership was formed between two Staffordshire potters, John Fenton and Thomas Hill, specifically for the manufacture of *fflintware*[7]. In 1777, Josiah Wedgwood gave his opinion that the use of flint had been introduced into North Staffordshire by Mr. (Joshua) Heath[8], although subsequently he was to give credit for this to John Astbury[9]. According to Shaw, it was Astbury who *first employed the flint, (after it had been calcined and pounded in a morter,) in a mixture with water to a thick pulp, as a wash or dip, which he applied to give a coating to the vessels, some time before he introduced it along with the clay into the body of his ware*[10]. Whether or not Shaw's information is wholly correct, tests have shown that flint was indeed a constituent of the white slip coats of a sample of early white dipped wares, but that it was not present in the clay bodies of the vessels which were presumably, therefore, tempered with sand[11].

The use together, of flint and white firing clay for the clay bodies[12] allowed the potters to produce a strong, durable ware, resistent to heat, and of a tolerable off-white colour — white salt-glazed stoneware. This first appeared shortly before 1720 and continued to be made throughout the remainder of the 18th century, exerting a considerable influence upon the market and spreading the reputation of Staffordshire wares abroad. The earliest known dated piece of white salt-glazed stoneware is a posset pot which is dated 1720[13], while vessels of this type were being advertised for sale in North America in 1724[14].

A much greater variety of vessels was produced in white salt-glazed stoneware than had been previously available. Now, for the first time in North Staffordshire, tea and coffee wares came to supplement the mugs, jugs, porringers and posset pots which had hitherto been the staple products of the Staffordshire potters. The earliest white salt-glazed wares were comparatively simple in form, invariably thrown, and decorated, if at all, with turned or rouletted bands.

The salt-glazed stonewares — brown, dipped and white — were fired to high temperatures of 1200 degrees C. or more, but, significantly, they were fired only once. At the time that white salt-glazed stonewares made their appearance, innovations were effected locally in the manufacture of earthenware vessels. Perhaps the most important development in earthenware production was the introduction of two firings — a biscuit and a glost firing. The products of the 17th century pottery industry in North Staffordshire, the slipwares, mottled wares, blackwares and other coarse-bodied earthenwares, had received just one firing, with the glaze applied to the leather hard vessels immediately prior to this. This practice probably continued for some time into the 18th century in the manufacture of coarser earthenwares, but for the production of fine earthenwares something different was necessary. Two firings gave the potters much greater control over their products, with the possibility of achieving a very high quality, and, in addition, losses during the difficult glost firing could be significantly reduced.

The earliest known twice-fired wares in North Staffordshire are glazed red earthenwares of the type produced by Samuel Bell at his Pomona factory in Newcastle-under-Lyme between 1724 and 1744. Examples of his wares have been excavated on the site of his factory[15] and these include the earliest known agate wares. These latter include both solid agate, produced by mixing together clays of different colours, and inlaid agate, whereby a band cut out of the body of a red earthenware vessel is filled by a thin band of mixed clay. Bell's agate wares, and presumably those of the many other Staffordshire potters who came to produce them, must post-date a patent taken out by Bell in 1729 for *red marble stoneware*[16].

The earthenwares of Samuel Bell and his contemporaries were further enhanced by the use of a liquid glaze. Liquid glazes were not new and had been used on once-fired slipwares and other earthenwares in the later 17th century. However, when a liquid glaze is applied to an already-fired biscuit surface, the potential for a really finely finished product, which would be both durable and resistent to crazing, is great. The development of a liquid glaze was dependent upon the use of lead oxide, which had been noted as early as the 1680s for its superior quality[17].

Shaw credits the potter Enoch Booth of Tunstall with the introduction of liquid glazes used on biscuit wares in about 1750. According to Shaw, it was he who: *first united the clays of the neighbourhood carefully levigated, in union with those from the south of England, and a certain proportion of flint, on Mr. Astbury's method, but with this difference: Littler dipped the clay ware into his liquid; but Mr. Booth fired his once, and dipped the biscuit ware*[18]. The evidence from excavation has been able to prove that this was not the case, and that the biscuit firing was in fact practised much earlier. Shaw is full of tales such as this and, if there is any truth in this particular story, what he is probably referring to is an improvement in glazing. For example, the use of calcined flint in the glaze recipe, which he mentions, would have been an important improvement, but when this improvement took place, and whether it can indeed be credited to Enoch Booth is not known.

The most influential pottery type of the 18th century was cream-coloured earthenware, or creamware as it has come to be known in recent years. The term 'creamware' is likely to bring to mind the fine earthenwares which were typical of Josiah Wedgwood's production and made popular — or rather *fashionable* — by him under the name of *Queensware* from the mid-1760s onwards. This was creamware at its most elegant, but it was also, by this stage, a refined and perfected ware. Creamware had been in production for many years before the 1760s under the name *cream colour*. The technical developments outlined above — the use of flint, the use of imported white-firing clays, biscuit firings and liquid glazes — made creamware a possibility. However, in the absence of contemporary evidence for the date and manner of its introduction later writers have allowed their imaginations free rein.

Inextricably linked with the story of early creamware manufacture — for the present, at least — is the potter Enoch Booth of Tunstall. What part, if any, might have been played by Booth in the development of creamware has not been documented by any contemporary writer, although Shaw states that he made *'Cream Colour; and its quality excels any then made*[19].' Booth has been drawn into the story on the evidence of Shaw's account and an extremely tentative and unprovable link with one of the earliest dated pieces of creamware to survive.

There is, in the British Museum, a bowl of cream-coloured earthenware which is inscribed and dated *E.B. / 1743*[20]. The bowl is a splendid piece, decorated under the glaze with a sponged manganese-speckled ground, into which are set panels painted in blue which depict flowers and animals. That such decoration was possible was a direct result of the introduction of biscuit firings, for now the potter, or rather the decorator, had the opportunity to apply painted or sponged decoration to the unglazed vessel. The colours used in the decoration are of metallic oxides prepared as liquids — manganese for the brown colour and cobalt for the blue. There are a few other vessels of this type, decorated in this manner, which have likewise been attributed to Enoch Booth because of the similarity of their decoration to the dated bowl[21].

Generally seen as part of this same group, and consequently also attributed to Booth, are a handful of pieces whose most important representitive is in the City Museum & Art Gallery, Stoke-on-Trent[22]. This, too, is inscribed and dated: *W.G. 1743*. The painted decoration, although still under-glaze, is however, rather different in style to that of the British Museum bowl and is without a coloured ground. The design comprises a mounted gentleman, animals and classically draped ladies. The figures are painted mainly in out-line, but rather more skilfully executed than the wares just described. Additional oxide colours are used in the decoration: iron for the yellow and copper for the green. The significance of the initials of the inscription is not known.

Although apparently of the same date, these two small groups of creamwares are sufficiently different for their attribution to the same factory to be questioned. Of course, painted decoration can only rarely be used as evidence for attribution, as painters may have worked for any number of potters. The style of decoration represented on these early creamwares was not native to Stoke-on-Trent at this early date: no other class of locally produced ware was decorated in this way. Indeed, the style of their decoration is very much reminiscent of that of contemporary tin-glazed earthenwares from the factories in London, Bristol and Liverpool. That decorators from these factories moved to North Staffordshire during the middle years of the 18th century is almost certain. Writing in 1817, William Pitt tells us that the newly developed white-bodied wares of the Staffordshire potters *soon attracted the enamellers from the china and Dutch-tile manufactories then established in different parts of the kingdom*[23].

So, what of Enoch Booth? It is apparent that the only evidence for a link with these early creamwares is a single piece inscribed with initials which could have belonged to anyone, manufacturer or customer. This is far from conclusive and, indeed, there is at present not one shred of evidence that these vessels were even made in Staffordshire. Booth certainly was a leading manufacturer of his day: after an apprenticeship which commenced in 1717, he went on to work as a potter in both Hanley[24] and subsequently Tunstall. However, not a single pot can be positively attributed to him. There is a well-known salt-glazed stoneware mug in the Fitzwilliam Museum, Cambridge, which is decorated in scratch-blue and inscribed *Enoch Booth 1742*[25], but even this may be considered a commemorative piece and need not have been made by him. The question regarding Booth's involvement in the development of cream-coloured earthenware remains open.

These early creamware pieces are exceptional and quite unlike anything which followed them. Closest to them are the well-known tortoiseshell wares, first referred to in 1749 in Thomas Whieldon's Account and Memorandum Book[26]. These are effectively creamwares, using the same mixture of imported white-firing clay and flint for the body recipe, but decorated under the glaze with metallic oxides. The oxides are applied as liquids by sponging or painting on to the surface of the biscuit vessel and during the glost firing the colours flow to produce the 'tortoiseshell' effect.

Although in the past often referred to by writers on ceramics as *Whieldon ware*, or *Whieldon-type*, tortoiseshell was the term used by the 18th century potters, and it is now abundantly clear that Thomas Whieldon was but one of many involved in its manufacture. For example, in 1750 two Staffordshire men, Richard Mountford and John Shaw, entered into a partnership to produce, amongst other types, *Torterter Shell ware* (*sic*) at Mountford's Shelton factory[27]. Moreover, examples of tortoiseshell wasters have been recovered from the ground from numerous sites over virtually the whole of Stoke-on-Trent. Nonetheless, not one single piece of tortoiseshell ware could be positively attributed to any Staffordshire potter before archaeological excavations on the site of Whieldon's factory at Fenton Vivian produced the first pieces with a known provenance[28]. Using these pieces as a reliable basis for comparison, it has since been possible to attribute a number of extant vessels to Whieldon[29], as well as to discredit a large number of previous attributions to him.

The partnership referred to above, between Richard Mountford and John Shaw, confirms what is now becoming abundantly clear from a study of both documentary sources and archaeological evidence: that numerous Staffordshire potters were producing an extremely wide and varied range of pottery types. Mountford and Shaw, for example, were intending to produce *Brown China, Black, White* and *Red* wares in addition to tortoiseshell wares[30]. The *White* is white salt-glazed stoneware which, by 1750, was probably being produced by the majority of the Staffordshire potters. The *Red* is the glazed red earthenware mentioned above (page 15) in connection with Samuel Bell from as early as 1724, but which went on to become one of the most popular earthenware types produced during the decade 1750 — 1760, in the repertoire of almost every potter of the period. Equally popular during this decade was the *Black,* blackware or the so-called 'Jackfield-type' ware, characterised by its lustrous glazed finish. Both the *Red* and the *Black* were made out of local red-firing clays, with just the minimum of imported white-firing clay being used in relief decoration which was applied prior to the biscuit firing. Such relief decoration was common on the glazed red earthenwares, but on the blackwares reliefs in the same local clay as the body were the more usual. *Brown China* is red stoneware which, although never a very common type, became increasingly popular around 1760 — 1765.

The potters Mountford and Shaw are unknown apart from this partnership agreement, but the same wide-ranging and varied output was equally typical of the leading potters of the time, such as Thomas Whieldon. Whieldon's Memorandum Book, already referred to in connection with tortoiseshell ware, contains several specific references to his products, references which are now supported by archaeological evidence. It is clear that Whieldon, like his peers, was producing the full range of contemporary wares.

The Memorandum Book shows that Whieldon was producing creamware, or *cream colour*, by 1749 at the latest[31]. The development of creamware in the years following 1743 is poorly understood and pieces which can be attributed to factories are few. It would appear, however, that by the mid-18th century cream-coloured earthenware was available to consumers at home and abroad, for there is a reference to *cream-coloured* ware in an advertisement appearing in *The Boston Evening Post* on 11th March, 1751[32]. The early creamwares are unremarkable: they are identical in form to contemporary tortoiseshell wares and are decorated in the same manner, with applied reliefs which are sometimes themselves coloured underglaze with metallic oxides. Of the few creamwares of this period which can be attributed to a known manufacturer, perhaps the most important is a jug in the City Museum & Art Gallery, Stoke-on-Trent, which is inscribed and dated *RH / 1757*[33]. The applied relief-moulded decoration of this jug is matched exactly by sherds excavated on Whieldon's factory site and, consequently, production by Whieldon is almost certain.

A further important innovation had been made in pottery production at some time around, or before 1740. This was the introduction of plaster of Paris, a vital prerequisite to the mass-production of elaborate shapes based upon the use of porous moulds. Shaw credits the potter Ralph Daniel of Cobridge with the introduction of plaster of Paris in about 1740[34], but this cannot yet be confirmed. Moulds of fired clay had already been in use for many years, in the manufacture of slipware dishes for example, and by the potter Samuel Bell of Newcastle-under-Lyme, at some time between 1724 — 1744. Fragments of clay moulds excavated on Bell's factory site were associated with slip-cast teapots of glazed red earthenware whose poor quality was striking[35]. The rapid saturation of clay moulds during the slip-casting process made their widespread adoption impractical. Even with plaster of Paris moulds, which dried more quickly than clay moulds, slip-casting was not an economical process until the introduction of deflocculents in the 19th century and was reserved during the 18th century solely for those vessels which could not have been produced by any other method.

Perhaps the earliest wares to have been produced with plaster of Paris moulds are the white salt-glazed stonewares which are well-known from the 1740s, from elaborate hollow wares — teapots, jugs and sauce boats — to the more simple flatwares — plates, stands and trays. Although slip-cast vessels are known in salt-glazed stoneware, by far the majority of the moulded shapes were press-moulded, a technique which demanded a great deal more skill from the workman, but which in terms of time was far more cost-effective. By the 1750s moulded wares are found in a wide variety of bodies and it is likely that the tortoiseshell plates noted in Whieldon's Memorandum Book under the year 1749 were press-moulded.

The variety of moulded wares which survive today bear witness to their importance amongst the potter's output in the middle of the 18th century. The growing popularity of moulded wares saw the rise in importance of a new skilled workman — the modeller, or block maker. The plaster of Paris moulds were the working moulds, the 'negatives' from which the wares were made. The moulds were themselves taken from blocks or master moulds. These latter were formed of clay which was normally fired to a stoneware and often salt-glazed to give them greater durability.

It is unfortunate that very few of the 18th century modellers are known, either by name or by the survival of their work. Those who are best known are the members of the Wood family. Aaron Wood is said to have worked for all the major potters of the day[36], including Thomas Whieldon[37], while his elder brother, Ralph, worked for John and Thomas Wedgwood of the Big House,

Burslem, for over twenty years. The work of the two brothers, and of Ralph in particular, is known through the survival of a large number of blocks, preserved by Aaron's son, the potter Enoch Wood. Many of these are initialled, some dated, and some few both initialled and dated. The earliest of the dated pieces is associated with Ralph Wood, and is dated *17489 (sic)*[38], while the latest is dated 1770[39]. William Wood, Aaron's eldest son, was apprenticed to Josiah Wedgwood and later became the premier modeller of *useful* wares at Wedgwood's Etruria factory[40].

The use of moulds became widespread in the production of almost every type of fine pottery. The mid-18th century saw a proliferation of earthenware and stoneware types in production by the Staffordshire potters, as well as short-lived ventures for the production of soft paste porcelain at Newcastle-under-Lyme (1746) and Longton Hall (1751 — 1760). By 1760, a potter's repertoire was likely to include white salt-glazed stoneware, blackware, glazed red earthenware, tortoiseshell, agate ware, red stoneware, and lesser types which included plain creamware.

Josiah Wedgwood gives us some useful information about the wares produced during his partnership with Thomas Whieldon at Fenton Vivian, which lasted between 1754 — 1759. On 23rd March, 1759, he wrote:

At this time our Manufacture was in a very unimprov'd state, & the demand for it decreasing, so that the trade was universally complain'd of as being bad, & in a declining condition.

White stoneware was the staple Article of our Manufacture, but this had been made a long time, & the prices were now so low that the Potters could not afford to make it as good in any respect, or finish it so high as the ware would otherwise admit of, & with respect to elegance of form, that was a subject very little attended to.

The next staple Article in the pottery was an imitation of Tortois-shell, but as there had been no improvement in this branch for several years past, the Country was grown weary of it, & though the price was lower'd from time to time, in order to increase the sales, the expedient did not succeed & something new was wanted to give a little spirit to the business.

I had already made an imitation of Agat which was esteem'd very beautiful, and a considerable improvement, but the Country had been surfeited with variegated colours as a sort of blue & green had already been mixed with the Tortois-shell, & this induced me to try for self colour'd Glaze[41].

It is not difficult to appreciate Wedgwood's comment that something new was needed, and indeed something new there was. By the early 1760s creamware was becoming the rising star, taking a variety of forms. For example, the increased reliance upon moulded wares gave manufacturers the ability to produce an impressive range of elaborate, ornate shapes which could be coloured under-glaze with metallic oxides, as in tortoiseshell ware, or with coloured glazes.

The application of coloured glazes to a biscuit creamware body, marked a departure from the long tradition of clear lead glazes. Coloured glazes have always been associated with Josiah Wedgwood, and the green glaze, in particular, with the partnership between Whieldon and Wedgwood. For this association, we have the evidence of Wedgwood's own words, describing the well-known experiments which he undertook in 1759. One of these experiments is indeed concerned with the production of a good quality green glaze — *A green glaze, to be laid upon Common white (or cream color) Biscuit ware*[42]. He was successful in this and wrote of this glaze: *This is the result of many experiments, which I made in order to introduce a new species of color'd ware to be fired along with the Tortois-shell and Agat ware in our common Gloss Ovens to be of an even self color, & laid upon the ware in the form of a color'd glaze*[43]. He continues: *This number has been used several years very successfully in a Great Variety of Articles, both for home & foreign consumption*[44].

In consequence of this, all green-glazed wares have been dated to the years after 1759 and the term *Whieldon-Wedgwood* has been much used in describing the moulded green-glazed cauliflower wares. It can be shown, however, that coloured glazed wares were being produced before this date by Whieldon, if not by other potters. *Green leaves* are referred to in contemporary documents[45] and excavation has shown that moulded cabbage wares, cauliflowers were amongst the green-glazed types produced by Whieldon. Consequently, Wedgwood's green glaze experiment must be seen, not as an innovation, but rather as an improvement of an existing glaze. Surviving green-glazed wares — leaves, cabbages, cauliflowers, etc. — certainly exhibit a wide range of colour variations, many of which suggest the need for improvement, and many others reflecting the perfection of the glaze. Green-glazed wares were a great success, for they were produced by many Staffordshire potters during the 1760s and beyond.

Wedgwood's first wares, produced after the termination of his partnership with Whieldon, continued to be much the same as had been produced during the partnership. However, his experiments did not cease, and in 1760 he perfected a yellow glaze of the kind found on pineapple and melon wares[46]. This has led to the assertion that yellow-glazed wares cannot have been produced by the other Staffordshire potters before this time. We must consider, however, that once again Wedgwood's success may have been nothing more than a perfection of an existing colour, and the possibility must exist that pineapples and other coloured wares were produced by Wedgwood's contemporaries in the years before the experiment recorded in 1760.

Whatever, the situation regarding the introduction of cauliflowers, pineapples and the other coloured glazed wares, the 1760s certainly saw a massive increase in their popularity and documentary sources attest to their production by numerous potters. These coloured and moulded wares maintained their popularity into the 1770s, although Wedgwood tired of them much more quickly: in 1766 he wrote that he was clearing his warehouse of coloured ware and was *heartily sick of the commodity*[47]. By 1774, he was able to write that *the agate, the green, and other colour'd glazes, have had their day, and done pretty well*[48]. However, in expressing this opinion Wedgwood was atypical — while he led the way, other potters continued to produce and to find a market for these types.

If Wedgwood is best known for his creamware, ironically it was with his green-glazed ware that he achieved his first great breakthrough which subsequently enabled him to promote his creamware. This breakthrough came in 1765 when he accepted an order from Queen Charlotte for *a service of Staffordshire ware*[49]. The order came to Wedgwood, not because of any reputation of his for quality, but because no other potter would accept the order. The order was for a tea set in green, with applied relief decoration, and covered with in gold; as well as melons and green fruit baskets and stands, edged with gold. Wedgwood recognised the potential importance of this order and worked hard to please, having particular difficulty with the perfection of the gilding. He wrote of his intention of including with the order, as a gift to Her Majesty, *two setts of creamcoloured Vases, engine turn'd & printed*[50].

Queen Charlotte was clearly impressed by his work, for by June, 1766, we learn that *Mr. Josiah Wedgwood, of Burslem, has had the honour of being appointed Potter to Her Majesty*[51]. Wedgwood's skills as a potter are beyond question, but his success was due as much to his skills in promotion. The prestige of royal patronage secured for Wedgwood the position of leading potter of the time. This was a position to be capitalised upon and in 1767 we hear of *Queensware* for the first time. Wedgwood wrote, in September, 1767: *The demand for this sd. Cream colour, Alias Queen's Ware, Alias Ivory, still increases. It is really amazing how rapidly the use of it has spread almost over the whole Globe and how universally is it liked*[52]. Royal patronage and active promotion aimed at the nobility and at people of taste and discernment, ensured Wedgwood's success and other royal orders followed.

The cream-coloured earthenware which came to be known as *Queensware* was not new. The cream-coloured wares of the 1750s had been improved considerably in both body and glaze, but it is unlikely that Wedgwood was solely responsible for these improvements. It is unfortunate that there is little evidence available beyond Wedgwood's own writings and, as a result, Wedgwood becomes central to any discussion of ceramic developments.

The 18th century consumer was ready for creamware — a good quality, affordable alternative to porcelain. The development of such an alternative had provided the motivation for the potters' improvements in fine earthenwares and stonewares, and the creamware of the 1760s rewarded their endeavours. The earlier cream-coloured and tortoiseshell wares had been no substitute for porcelains and had served a less affluent market. The later wares were to appeal to royalty and nobility alike and were to become fashionable and desirable. Commodities which were embraced by the leaders of fashion soon filtered down the social scale and, by this means, fine ceramics, and creamware in particular, eventually became available to a much wider consumer public.

Wedgwood described his *Queensware* in the following manner: *In 1763, Mr. Josiah Wedgwood, who had already introduced several improvements into this art, as well with respect to the forms and colours of the wares, as the composition of which they were made, invented a new species of earthenware for the table, quite new in its appearance, covered with a rich and brilliant glaze, bearing sudden vicissitudes of heat and cold without injury: it was accompanied also with the advantage of being manufactured with ease and expedition, was sold cheap, and as it possessed, with the novelty of its appearance, every requisite quality for the purpose intended, it came into general estimation and use. To this manufacture the Queen was pleased to giver her name and patronage, commanding it to be called Queen's Ware, and honouring the inventor by appointing him Her Majesty's potter*[53]. This ware had many advantages over others, most notably the suitability of its smooth, glazed surfaces for on-glaze decoration, both painted and printed.

Salt-glazed stonewares had received enamel-painted decoration since the early 1750s[54], and similar decoration came to be applied to creamware from the early 1760s. Enamel painting is first found on the red stonewares produced by the Elers brothers in the late 17th century, and also on early English brown salt-glazed stoneware tankards, but examples are few. The wider application of enamel painting as a method of pottery decoration came about with the production of soft paste porcelains at Chelsea and Bow during the 1740s and 1750s. The manufacturers of white salt-glazed stoneware were swift to adopt this method and enamel painted wares of the 1750s and later survive in abundance.

Mystery surrounds the introduction of enamel painting into North Staffordshire, a situation not much helped by Shaw, who tells of the secrecy in the early days of its use. He credits its introduction to *some Dutchmen, in Hot Lane* (Burslem); *who, to preserve their operation's secret, had their muffle in a garden at Bagnall...Mr. Daniel, of Cobridge, was the first native who practised enamelling. Workmen were soon employed, from Bristol, Chelsea, Worcester, and Liverpool...*[55]. The sudden proliferation of enamel painting on pottery is no surprise and it need not be assumed that there was any shortage of talented artists able to undertake this work. Enamel painting had long been employed in a variety of crafts and the techniques used were equally applicable to pottery as they were to, say, copper. Shaw tells us that: *For some years the branch of enamelling was conducted by persons wholly unconnected with the manufacture of Pottery; in some instances altogether for the manufacturers; in others on the private account of the Enamellers; but when there was great demand for these ornamented productions, a few of the more opulent manufacturers necessarily connected this branch with the others*[56].

The employment of specialist decorators by the manufacturers of creamware during the 1760s is well-known. A great deal has been written about perhaps the best known of these decorators, Jasper Robinson and David Rhodes, of Leeds, and the work that they undertook for Wedgwood[57], and many pieces have been attributed to Wedgwood on the evidence of painted decoration *in the style of* Robinson and Rhodes. However, such attributions must be extremely suspect, for it is virtually impossible to make a positive attribution solely on the evidence of a painted design[58].

The newly developed technique of transfer printing was also used as decoration on some salt-glazed stonewares, from about 1755[59], but the ware's lightly dimpled surface made it unsuitable for fine printed detail; consequently, relatively few printed pieces were produced. The same was not the case with the earthenwares.

The technique of printing on pottery had been developed during the early 1750s by John Brooks and came to be widely used on the soft-paste porcelains of the Bow, Worcester and, later, the Derby factories. However, the application of printed decoration to earthenware, rather than porcelain, may be credited to John Sadler of Liverpool. On 27th July, 1756, Sadler and his partner Guy Green swore a joint affidavit that they had, in six hours, printed over twelve hundred earthenware tiles in different patterns[60]. Sadler and Green continued to experiment with printing on porcelain, enamels and earthenware, and by September, 1761, they were trying the technique on Wedgwood's creamwares[61]. Within six months they had perfected over-glaze printing and Wedgwood received his first delivery of printed creamware in March 1762[62].

Sadler and Green were successful to the extent that business between them and Wedgwood increased from £30 per month in 1763 to £650 per month in 1771[63]. They undertook to print only on Wedgwood's creamwares, but were soon in competition with others, some of whom were their former employees. Sadler and Green were printers, not engravers, and consequently employed engravers, either on a free-lance basis or on their staff, several of whom subsequently left to set up in business on their own. Shaw notes John Robinson of Burslem, who left Sadler and Green to print for Wedgwood, and afterwards *commenced business as a Printer in Black or Red, on the glaze, and also as Enameller, for any of the manufacturers*[64]. He also mentions Harry Baker of Hanley, said to have been the first *black printer* in North Staffordshire, who again *offered his services to any of the manufacturers in the district, as a printer on the glaze of cream colour, in Black, Red, & c. and soon was fully employed*[65].

Clearly, by no means all early black printed designs are by Sadler and Green; during the 1760s the number of engravers and printers who were available to undertake work for the pottery manufacturers proliferated. As early as 1763, James Albernethy complained to Wedgwood: *I imagined that you was the only person that printed that sort of ware — but it seems that there are others that put up with smaller profits*[66].

This comment underlines the fact that Wedgwood was not unique in his production of fine quality creamwares: he was simply one of many local potters who were adapting to a changing market, introducing new wares and new styles, and developing new attitudes towards the marketing of their wares. What Wedgwood offered the customer was no different to what could be obtained from other local potters. His great success was due to his marketing ploys and to the fact that, as *Potter to Her Majesty*, he had become fashionable.

There is abundant evidence for the improvement of creamware during the 1760s. The earliest creamwares were of a dark, almost butter colour, but despite improvements during the 1750s, the colour of the creamwares of the early 1760s was little changed. The development of a lighter coloured ware seems to have been a priority with Wedgwood and by October, 1764, John Sadler was able to write to Wedgwood: *We have unpack't the 18 crates we recd. and the Ware is very good. It's of a paler colour, in general, which is lik'd vastly better by every Body than the deep Yellow, and will be better in every respect*[67]. A general lightening of the colour had been achieved by the majority of Staffordshire potters by about 1770, but not even Wedgwood was able to please every customer. In response to a complaint he wrote, in 1768: *With respect to the colour of my ware, I endeavour to make it as pale as possible to continue it cream-colour and find my customers in general, though not every individual of them, think the alteration I have made in that respect a great improvement, but it is impossible that any one colour, even though it was to come down from Heaven, should please every taste, and I cannot regularly make two cream colours, a deep and a light shade, without having two works for that purpose*[68].

By the end of the 1760s, Wedgwood had produced a light-coloured ware which could be marketed as a fashionable alternative to porcelain. Royal orders for his ware, from the Prince of Wales in 1769, and from the King and Queen in 1770, must have greatly enhanced his reputation. Queen Charlotte chose plates in the old barleycorn pattern, but without the seeds[69] — this came to be known as the Queen's shape. The King chose a similar plate, but with the divisions into segments removed, the shape which came to be known as King's. Successful amongst the nobility, fashionable with the middle classes, and the subject of royal orders,

Wedgwood's creamware had, by 1770, become sought after over most of the civilised world. Even greater success was to follow, with orders in 1770 and 1774 from Catherine the Great, Empress of Russia.

The story of the early Staffordshire pottery industry is dominated by just a few individuals. This is a result solely of the evidence which has survived. The position of Wedgwood in this story cannot be challenged, and it is clearly a reflection of the extent of his success that the name *Queensware* came to be used by every Staffordshire potter. But Wedgwood was not alone — the majority of his contemporaries may be little more than names to us, but their contributions to the developing pottery manufacture are totally overlooked.

Just as Wedgwood cannot be credited with the introduction of creamware, neither can he be said to have been responsible for the introduction of that type of ware known today as pearlware. Many writers have claimed that Wedgwood introduced pearlware in 1779, under the name *pearl white,* but an extremely convincing argument has been presented by George Miller which suggests that pearlware was being produced by Staffordshire potters before this date under the name *china glaze*[70]. This new development dates to about 1775, and was apparently regarded at the time as an improvement of existing creamware, but of a whiter colour. In fact, the improved ware was essentially creamware whose lead glaze had been modified by the addition of minute quantities of cobalt, giving a finished appearance which was not wholly unlike Oriental porcelain, having a slight blue tint.

It was the growing popularity of this new ware, and the wishes of his customers, which forced Wedgwood to turn to its production, although apparently with considerable reluctance. His correspondence with his partner Thomas Bentley betrays his reluctance to proceed with the production of a whiter ware and it was not until 25th February, 1779, that Wedgwood was able to write to Bentley that he had *Settled my white body and glaze (pray give me a name for it...)*[71]. On 6th August, 1779, Wedgwood wrote to Bentley: *Your idea of the cream color having the merit of an original, & the pearl white being consider'd as an imitation of some of the blue & white fabriques, either of earthenware or porcelain, is perfectly right, & I should not hesitate a moment in preferring the former if I consulted my own taste and sentiments.... The pearl white must be considered as a change rather than an improvement, & I must have something ready to succeed it when the public eye is pall'd, or it comes upon the town*[72].

The man credited with the development of *China Glaze applied to Cream colour* was John Greatbatch[73], but who this Greatbatch was and when the glaze was developed is not known. This is one of but two names which can be linked with the early china glaze, or pearlware. The other is James Tidmarsh of Cobridge, who can be linked with the earliest known dated piece of pearlware in existence. This is a large jug inscribed under-glaze in blue *Tidmarsh's Original Staffordshire Warehouse N 1775*[74] which, it has been suggested, was produced by James Tidmarsh for members of his family who were London-based dealers in pottery[75]. No other manufacturers of pearlware at this date are known to us, although by the next decade it had become one of the staple products of the Staffordshire pottery industry.

We have now looked at the major developments in pottery production in the 18th century, or at least at those developments which provide the background necessary for an understanding of the wares discussed in the present volume. It is important to place into context those wares which which were current during the formative years of our potter, William Greatbatch. In doing so, we should be able to appreciate the extent of the changes which occurred within the industry during the decades 1760 — 1780, the period during which Greatbatch worked as a successful independent potter.

1. Mountford 1971, 5.
2. *ibid.*, plates 6 — 12, and 15 — 18.
3. Shaw 1829, 126.
4. *ibid.*, 125.
5. Entry of 6th April, 1698, in John Dwight's Notebook, page 58. Copy made by Lady Charlotte Schreiber (British Museum). Reproduced in Haselgrove and Murray 1979, page Biv.
6. Shaw 1829, 128 — 129.
7. Weatherill 1971, 23.
8. Wedgwood MSS: E18772-25.
9. Wedgwood's contribution to Aikin 1795, 526 — 527.
10. Shaw 1829, 129.
11. Mountford 1971, 36.
12. Ascribed by Shaw to Daniel Bird of Cliffe Bank, Stoke (Shaw 1829, 157), and by Josiah Wedgwood to Joshua Heath or John Astbury who *made white ware with the addition of flint the first there* (i.e. in Shelton). *And Mr. Thomas Wedgwood of Red Lyon and Richard Wedgwood of the Overhouse, Burslem, made it first there* (Account given January 5th, 1765, by —·· Steel, aged 84, which is given in Josiah Wedgwood's Commonplace Book, Volume I, page 219. Wedgwood MSS: E39-28408).
13. The Burnap Collection, Nelson-Atkins Gallery, Kansas City, Missouri, Cat. No.: B675. See Taggart 1967, 75 no. 182.
14. In this year William Randall of Boston advertised for sale *white stone tea cups and saucers, bowls, plates, salts, milk pots, etc.* See Noel Hume 1970, 248.
15. Bemrose 1975.
16. *ibid.*, 295 — 297. Patent of 9th May, 1729: PRO, C66/3577.
17. Plot 1686, 123.

18. Shaw 1829, 176.
19. *ibid.*, 177.
20. Franks Collection, Cat. No.: H41.
21. For example, a teapot in the City Museum & Art Gallery, Stoke-on-Trent, Cat. No.: 14P 1969 (Towner 1978, 25 plate 2A), and a teapot decorated in a similar style which employs a Chinese lion as both knop and feet (Horne 1989, no. 236).
22. Cat. No. 117P 1989. Other pieces of this type are a vase in the Victoria and Albert Museum, Cat. No.: 2270-1901, and a teapot at Colonial Williamsburg, in the De Witt-Wallace Decorative Arts Gallery, Cat. No.: 1975-178 (Towner 1978, 25 plate 2B).
23. Pitt 1817, 419.
24. In 1735 he is described as *earth potter* of Hanley. Deed (SCRO).
25. Glaisher Collection, Cat. No.: Gl. 507.
26. City Museum & Art Gallery, Stoke-on-Trent (unpub.).
27. Richard Parrott's Book, 219 — 226 (Newcastle-under-Lyme Museum & Art Gallery).
28. Mountford 1972b, plates 122 — 124 and 129.
29. For example, Barker & Halfpenny 1990, 41 — 43 nos. 22 and 23.
30. Richard Parrott's Book, 219 — 226 (Newcastle-under-Lyme Museum & Art Gallery).
31. Thomas Whieldon's Account and Memorandum Book. City Museum & Art Gallery, Stoke-on-Trent (unpub.).
32. Advertisement of Henry Barnes, quoted in Dow (ed.) 1927, 98.
33. City Museum & Art Gallery, Stoke-on-Trent, Cat. No.: 3859. Illustrated in Barker & Halfpenny 1990, 42 no. 23.
34. Shaw 1829, 163.
35. Bemrose 1975, 298 and plate 195.
36. E.Wood, quoted in Faulkner 1912, 80; also inscriptions by Wood which appear on the reverses of busts of himself, such as City Museum & Art Gallery, Stoke-on-Trent, Cat. No.: 639P 1937. The inscription reads *My father Aaron Wood...made the models for all the potters, during the time the Salt Glaze was in general use.*
37. Shaw 1829, 155 — 156.
38. City Museum & Art Gallery, Stoke-on-Trent, Cat. No.: 1752.
39. City Museum & Art Gallery, Stoke-on-Trent, Cat. No.: 422.
40. Shaw 1829, 189.
41. Wedgwood's Experiment Book, page 71. Wedgwood MSS: E.26-19115.
42. *ibid.*, page 71, Experiment No. 7, dated 23rd March, 1759.
43. *ibid.*
44. *ibid.*, continuation on page 73.
45. John Wedgwood's Sales Ledger, page 54, sale of 29th August, 1758. City Museum & Art Gallery, Stoke-on-Trent (unpub.).
46. Wedgwood's Experiment Book, page 92: Experiment 93, dated 10th March, 1760; page 94: Experiment 100, not dated. Wedgwood MSS: E.26-19115.
47. Wedgwood MSS: E.18123-25.
48. *ibid.*: E.18521-25.
49. *ibid.*: E.18073-25.
50. *ibid.*: E.18080-25.
51. Aris's Birmingham Gazette, 9th June, 1766.
52. Wedgwood MSS: E.18167-25.
53. Wedgwood's contribution to Aikin 1795, 528 — 529.
54. Mountford 1971, 55 — 56.
55. Shaw 1829, 178 — 179.
56. *ibid.*: 179.
57. For example, Towner 1959.
58. Lockett 1986a, 56 — 57; Barker & Halfpenny 1990, 10 — 11.
59. Mountford 1971, 61.
60. Affidavit quoted in Williams-Wood 1981, 102.
61. John Sadler's Notebook. Quoted in Price 1948, 34. Also Reilly 1989, 210.
62. W/M: 1431.
63. Reilly 1989, 211 & 234.
64. Shaw 1829, 193
65. *ibid.*
66. Wedgwood MSS: E.30554-5.
67. W/M: 1431.
68. Quoted in Mankowitz 1953, 44. Presumably in the Wedgwood archive but not located by the author.
69. Enoch Wood: handwritten comments in Wood's own annotated copy of Aikin 1795. Private collection.
70. Miller 1987.
71. Wedgwood MSS: E.18878-26.
72. *ibid.*: E.18914-26.
73. Shaw 1829, 184.
74. City Museum & Art Gallery, Stoke-on-Trent, Cat. No.: 46P 1970.
75. Adams 1977.

CHAPTER 1

WILLIAM GREATBATCH

The Staffordshire Advertiser of 1st May, 1813, carries the following obituary:

A few days ago, at Etruria, in this county, in his 78th year, Mr. Wm. Greatbatch, an old and faithful servant to the late and present Mr. Wedgwood, in the extensive manufactory at that place.

The burial of the old man had taken place on 29th April in the churchyard of St. Peter ad Vincula in the parish of Stoke upon Trent[1].

*   *   *

The name of William Greatbatch is well-known today to both ceramics students and collectors. Indeed, it would be true to say that Greatbatch is very much better known to us than many of his fellow potters of the later 18th century. Two short references to Greatbatch in Simeon Shaw's *History of the Staffordshire Potteries* have guaranteed his place in history[2], but it was his business relationship with the most eminent potter of the day, Josiah Wedgwood, which has guaranteed the attention of later scholars. This scholarly interest has been aided by the fortuitous survival of a sizeable body of contemporary documentary evidence which has, until the present, served as the basis for all study of Greatbatch and his wares.

Nearly two hundred letters, notes, invoices and statements of accounts survive in the Wedgwood archive of manuscripts, housed at the University of Keele. These were written by Greatbatch to Josiah Wedgwood or his colleagues, Thomas Wedgwood and Thomas Byerley, and document a close and mutually beneficial business association between the two potters. Such detailed evidence is invaluable in any study of the 18th century ceramics industry, although many later writers have failed to recognise either the true value of the evidence or its limitations. The limitations are significant, but have been largely overlooked.

The limitations of this documentary evidence arise partly from the fact that this is business, not personal correspondence. Greatbatch had no need here to engage in idle chit-chat nor to discuss his family life, except where this interfered with business[3]. Indeed, he gives little away about his circumstances, either of his private life or of his business. He leaves unsaid much that we today might wish to know. Another limitation is the one-sided nature of the correspondence: we have Greatbatch's remarks and queries, but not Wedgwood's suggestions or complaints, although these can sometimes be inferred. Consequently, it is rather difficult to determine the exact nature of the relationship between the two. The greatest limitation, however, is the short time span covered by the documents. The bulk of the correspondence covers just three years, 1762 to 1765, and the seventeen years from 1765 to the end of Greatbatch's career as an independent potter are a complete documentary blank. For evidence of the greater, and most productive part of Greatbatch's career we must to turn to other sources.

Contemporary sources, therefore, simply do not provide adequate detailed information on either Greatbatch's career or his private life and family background. For this, we may look to other, later sources, although these too have their limitations and must, as with all non-contemporary sources, be scrutinised for bias and the innaccuracies which come with the passage of time. Sadly, the picture is far from complete.

28

The best-known account of Greatbatch is that of Simeon Shaw, which was published in 1829, sixteen years after Greatbatch's death. In two separate passages of his *History of the Staffordshire Potteries* Shaw writes:

Of the four apprentices to Mr. Whieldon, three commenced business, and were eminently successful; Mr. Josiah Spode (the first), Mr. Robert Garner, Mr. J. Barker, (and his brothers we believe,) — but Mr. William Greatbatch, a person of great ability, (mentioned again hereafter,) was ruined by a bad debt. The father of William Greatbatch, was a farmer, at Berryhill; and he supplied coals to the manufacturers at Fenton, from Botteslow and Coalamoor; and among others, to Mr. Whieldon, and Mr. Daniel Bird, on the backs of horses, the roads being then so bad that had a horse stumbled, or missed a step into the holes, he certainly would have fallen, and with difficulty would have been again raised. He received his money every journey, because fearful of the parties[4].

He continues:

Another excellent modeller, and in fact a general workman of first rate abilities, was Mr. William Greatbatch, some time employed by Messrs. Whieldon and Wedgwood; and who had commenced business on his own account at the manufactory at Fenton, now a small part of the extensive establishment of Messrs. Bourne, Baker and Bourne; where he produced numerous articles, of improved patterns and kinds; and for some time had a most rapid sale of teapots, on which was printed, in black, by Thomas Radford, the history of the Prodigal son. But heavy losses at length ruined him. His well known abilities caused him to be consulted, and to form the plan, for the New Field Manufactory, then being erected by Admiral Child; from whom he was to have received a third share of the profits for managing the establishment. Mr. Wedgwood, aware of the talents of his former servant, engaged him, for life, at the very high wages of five shillings a day, whether at work or play, and a house rent free; which sum was regularly paid him, to the time of his death, tho' he survived his master; by whom he was so much respected, that most of his sons, and many of his relations, were employed at Etruria[5].

By contrast, the most important contemporary reference to William Greatbatch is contained in a letter written by Thomas Byerley, Josiah Wedgwood's nephew, to Josiah Wedgwood II, on 25th May, 1807, twelve years after the death of the great potter. The account given by Byerley is rather less favourable than that of Shaw, clearly displaying an element of bias against Greatbatch, but it does contain important information and corroborates some of Shaw's statements. Byerley writes:

William G. came to Etruria in 1788 — when Thomas Wedgwood declared his intention of settling at Hill House with his family — W.G. and all his family were at the time in Turner's employ — who, upon the old man going away sent all the rest after him — and they all came to Etruria — W.G. was an app. at Fenton during my late uncle's partnership there, and when he first set up at Lower Lane for some years he made biscuit ware only — for the new work at Burslem where it was sent to be coloured and glazed. I never heard that any engagement or promise was made him to continue the whole or part of his salary during life — indeed at one time he would have quitted unless his wages had been raised £25 p. ann. — which went under the name of extra 1/2 (illegible) in order to conceal that such high wages were given to anyone. This was when W. Bent had been tampering with him, & offered him higher wages. I think that he should certainly be made easy and comfortable in his circumstances for the remainder of his days — but that it is not necessary to make his present salary the basis — I think it should be limited to a sum that he and his wife can live comfortably upon in their condition of life, and I think too what they possess of their

own should not be entirely left out of consideration in fixing the annual sum to give him —
they have 2 or 3 houses at Lane Delf what else I know not — the late W. Wood had been
his entire life with you from his first working day to the day of his death — but in W.G.'s
case there is not a great deal to distinguish it from that of many persons in the potteries, who
cannot indulge expectations of this kind. W.G. has many hangers on who will urge him to
scramble for all he can get — but as it is possible that principles & precedents now established,
may, in the course of your life, be often quoted it is proper to proceed with caution and whatever
is granted not to do it lightly as a matter of course — I suppose all good & sound reasoning
would be on the side of our saving our money on such occasions, but I am not inclined to
deny my feelings the gratification of a share in these discussions .... [6]

There is little else to contradict these references to Greatbatch, but their agreement on a number of points is both interesting and significant. For example, both Shaw and Byerley mention Greatbatch's employment at Etruria on a very high salary. It would seem quite clear from this that Josiah Wedgwood thought highly of Greatbatch. Byerley, however, does not share his late uncle's enthusiasm for Greatbatch and resents the size of the salary being paid to him. This biased reference to Greatbatch's period of employment at Etruria may be balanced by other evidence which consists of letters and notes written by him in connection with the business of the Etruria factory. Some fifty-seven separate documents survive in the Wedgwood archive, spanning the years 1786 to 1807, which show that Greatbatch's position was that of general manager or similar (see below, page 64).

Shaw and Byerley also both refer to Greatbatch's apprenticeship at Thomas Whieldon's factory which was in Fenton Vivian, one-quarter of a mile to the south-east of Stoke. This is important, as there is no independent evidence for Greatbatch's apprenticeship at Fenton Vivian: no records of the apprenticeship survive. There is, however, a potentially significant entry in Thomas Whieldon's Memorandum Book, which survives in the collection of the City Museum & Art Gallery, Stoke-on-Trent. This entry, under the year 1753, reads:

Augst	*hired Daniel Greatbachs son*		
29	*if he trims he is to have*	— 2	4
	but if load wk	— 2	6 [7]

Whieldon's entry does not explain further the identity of the Greatbatch who is being hired, which may, or may not be William. Perhaps it is significant that, here, the reference is to hiring, not to an apprenticeship. In 1753, William Greatbatch would have been in the region of eighteen years old, of an age to be taking up employment. An apprenticeship, however, would last for seven years, normally from the age of fourteen to the age of twenty-one, although some variations might be expected.

However, this is pure speculation. We have no knowledge whatsoever as to the identity of William Greatbatch's father and the abundance of Greatbatchs who appear in the parish registers of Stoke-on-Trent and the neighbouring parishes offers many candidates. Indeed, another Greatbatch, Isaac, appears in Whieldon's Memorandum Book on a number of occasions. Entries for 1749 show Isaac Greatbatch being paid for carrying loads of sand and brick for Whieldon[8], while in 1751 and 1752 an Isaac Greatbach (*sic*), possibly the same, is paying rent to Whieldon as is shown in the following entry:

March 25th	*Set the above 3 Crofts to*		
1751	*Isaac Greatbach for 3 years*		
	for six pounds p. Yr.	*6 — 0 —*	
	& the large ox lesower		
	& 2 acers for	*14 — 0 —*[9]	

Mystery surrounds the early years of William Greatbatch. Exhaustive searches of the registers of baptisms for the parishes of Stoke upon Trent and its neighbours[10] for the years around 1735, the probable year of Greatbatch's birth, have revealed nothing. There were many Greatbatchs in the Potteries towns in the 18th century, but William does not appear to have been a popular christian name amongst them before the 1760s.

No supporting evidence has been found for Shaw's statement that Greatbatch's father was a farmer at *Berryhill*[11] (Berry Hill, in the Township of Little Fenton), which lies a mile and a half to the north-east of Stoke upon Trent, although the parish registers do record Greatbatchs from that area. On 26th January, 1737, one Elizabeth Greatbatch, daughter of Isaac and Elizabeth Greatbatch, *of Buryhill*, was baptised[12], and it would appear to be the same Isaac and Elizabeth whose sons Isaac and John were baptised on 23rd February, 1728, and 7th March, 1730, respectively[13], although no place of residence is given in these earlier records. On 22nd October, 1740, Thomas, son of Isaac and Ann Greatbatch, *of Bury Hill*, was baptised[14]. This may be a second family of Berry Hill Greatbatchs, but it is equally not inconceivable that these Isaacs are one and the same man.

Little more can be deduced from these references. Clearly the possibility exists that one of the Isaacs recorded in the parish registers is that Isaac referred to in Whieldon's Memorandum Book. Indeed, Shaw's statement that William Greatbatch's father *supplied coals to the manufacturers at Fenton, from Botteslow and Coalamoor* (areas in the immediate vicinity of Berry Hill); *and among others to Mr. Whieldon...*[15] leads one to wonder whether there has not been some confusion here with that Isaac Greatbatch who was making deliveries of sand and brick to Thomas Whieldon. A final reference to an Isaac Greatbatch occurs in the Rate Book of 1740 for Fenton and Longton. Here we see Isaac Greatbatch paying one of the largest rates in the area at £2.2.4[16]. This is clearly no pauper.

The first of the modern writers to enquire about Greatbatch's family was Donald Towner. He concluded that it was Daniel Greatbatch who was William's father; subsequent writers have accepted this without reservation[17]. However, Towner's hypothesis is based solely upon the evidence of the entry in Whieldon's Memorandum Book cited above. There is, at present, no supporting evidence to provide proof for this assertion.

The parish registers offer no evidence for a connection between William Greatbatch and any Daniel. The parish registers do, however, preserve records of a Daniel Greatbatch. On 25th December, 1729, Daniel *Gratebach* (sic) married Mary Clews at Leek, a moorland market town some ten miles to the north of Stoke[18], while on 2nd June, 1733, Daniel and Mary Greatbatch *de Bagnall*, almost certainly the same couple, had their two sons, Joseph and Isaac, baptised[19]. Bagnall is a small village four and a half miles to the north-east of Stoke upon Trent. Other entries in the parish registers refer to Daniel and Mary Greatbatch of *Little ffenton*, whose daughter Mary was baptised on 1st January, 1735[20], and whose son Daniel was baptised on 2nd April, 1738[21]. Amid the confusion of Greatbatchs in North Staffordshire at this time there are no further references to Daniels, and I am inclined to conclude that Daniel and Mary *de*

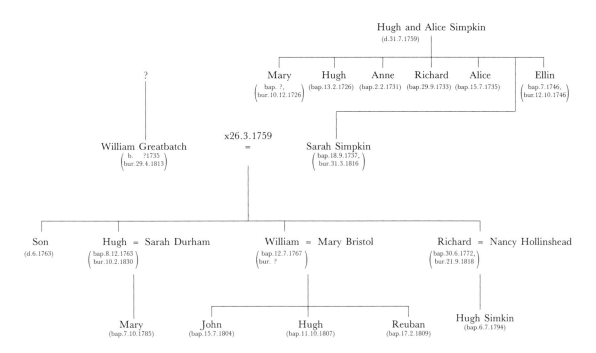

Fig. 2 The Family of William Greatbatch

Bagnall, and Daniel and Mary of Little Fenton, are one and the same couple. This leaves few people who could be the *Daniel Greatbachs son* who was hired by Thomas Whieldon in 1753. Sons Joseph and Isaac would have been twenty or more years old in 1753, while son Daniel would have been fifteen or more, allowing for the fact that baptism need not have taken place within the first year of a child's life.

Towner was of the opinion that there was a Daniel Greatbatch working as a potter in Stoke-on-Trent in the mid-eighteenth century[22]. His evidence for this hypothesis is the existence of a tea canister, now in the collection of the Mint Museum of Art, Charlotte, North Carolina, which is inscribed on the base *Daniel Great / Batch / 1755*[23]. This is a rectangular canister with relief-moulded geometric decoration, which is coloured with metallic oxides beneath a lead glaze (Plates 1a & b). The limited references to Daniel Greatbatchs in the parish registers suggest that the Daniel Greatbatch of this canister is either the father or son referred to above.

It is impossible to know whether this inscription was added by a proud workman marking a first, or otherwise special piece with his name and date, or perhaps by a young man completing his apprenticeship with a signed piece, or whether the canister is a commemorative piece destined for a customer by the name of Daniel Greatbatch. Certainly no credence can be given to the idea of the master potter taking time to mark his wares with carefully executed signatures and dates. In an extremely competitive business such efforts would have been unnecessary and wasteful.

Those pieces of pottery of this period which are inscribed or dated are generally quite clearly commemorative in nature. However, the identification of a potter by the name of Daniel Greatbatch lends a little weight to Towner's suggestion

that the inscription of the canister was added by the maker. The documented Daniel Greatbatch was not a master potter; he appears to have been one of Josiah Wedgwood's workmen at Burslem and is listed regularly in Wedgwood's notebook of payments made to workers during the year 1762[24]. This Greatbatch was paid for producing a variety of wares, most of which appear to have been press-moulded.

The connection between the inscribed canister of 1755 and the Daniel Greatbatch employed by Wedgwood in 1762 is tentative. Nor can it be known whether the Daniel Greatbatch working at Burslem is either the father or son of that name mentioned above. The significance of the canister is a mystery and the question of its relevance to the present study will remain unanswered until further evidence is forthcoming.

Plates 1a & b
Tea canister decorated with under-glaze oxide colours. Inscribed on base *Daniel Great / Batch / 1755*. (Delhom Collection, The Mint Museum of Art, Charlotte, North Carolina)

It has been impossible to learn anything of William Greatbatch's family background from the local parish registers, although there is sufficient evidence for his own children. The fortunate survival of Greatbatch's will, in which his children are named, enables the evidence of the parish registers to be confirmed. Greatbatch does, however, make two early appearances in the parish registers. The first is on 11th February, 1757, when a William Greatbatch is witness to the marriage of James Lowe, hatter, and Tamer Coxon, spinster, both of Newcastle-under-Lyme[25]. His second appearance is on 26th March, 1759. This is the record of the marriage, at Newcastle-under-Lyme, of William Greatbatch and Sarah Simpkin, both of Stoke[26]. The entry in the marriage register shows that the couple were married by licence and that both signed the register[27]. This tells us a great deal about the couple. Not only were both literate, but they also had the means to be able to afford the more expensive method of marriage, by licence. Greatbatch would have been twenty-four years old at this time and this union must have occurred at an opportune moment in the young man's career. He must have had money, land or expectations; Sarah, for her part, is most unlikely to have married beneath herself.

Little is known about Sarah Greatbatch. She was baptised on 18th September, 1737, the daughter of Hugh and Alice Simpkin, of Lane Delph[28]. The baptisms of other older children of Hugh and Alice are recorded — Hugh, Anne, Richard and Alice[29]. The burial of possibly another child of Hugh and Alice, Mary Simpkin, infant, is recorded in 1726[30], while another late child, Ellin, was buried on 12th October, 1746, aged just three months[31]. Sarah survived her husband by three years, to be buried in the churchyard of St. Peter ad Vincula at Stoke on 31st March, 1816[32].

William Greatbatch's will was drawn up on 24th April, 1813, a day or so before his death. The signature is extremely shaky — the old man must have been very weak indeed. Sadly, the will sheds no light on Greatbatch's earlier career as a potter. The beneficiaries of the will are his wife, Sarah, and his three sons, Hugh, William and Richard. Hugh and William were appointed executors of the will whose main business is contained in the few lines:

I give, devise and bequeath all my messuages, tenements, hereditaments and premises and real estate, and also the use and enjoyment of all my household goods and furniture and other personal estate and efforts unto my dear and loving wife Sarah Greatbatch for and during her natural life, and from immediately after her decease I give, devise and bequeath unto my two sons, Hugh Greatbatch and William Greatbatch, all and singular my messuages, dwellings houses or tenements and real estate with their respective appurtenances to the same belonging situated at Lane Delph in the County of Stafford or elsewhere and also my household goods and furniture and other personal estate and effects whatsoever[33].

After Sarah's death, Hugh and William are required to:

...sell and dispose of the said buildings and premises and personal estate for the most money and best price that can or may be had or obtained for the same and by public auction and do and shall pay, apply and dispose of the monies by such sale in the manner and for the purposes hereinafter mentioned. Subject to the payment of my debts, funeral expenses and incumbrance affording my real estate, I give and bequeath unto my son Hugh Greatbatch the sum of forty pounds, I give and bequeath unto my son William Greatbatch the sum of one hundred pounds, and I give and bequeath unto my son Richard Greatbatch the sum of eighty pounds, and as to all the rest, residue and remainder of my personal estate and effects I give and bequeath unto my said three sons Hugh, William and Richard to be equally divided to and amongst them, share and share alike ...[34].

Although Greatbatch's property is not listed, here, at least, is confirmation of Thomas Byerley's statement that the family owned *two or three houses at Lane Delph*[35]. Greatbatch did not die a pauper.

The will was published at Newcastle-under-Lyme on 28th October, 1813. The executors, the two sons, are both described as potters: William being *of Woolstanton* (Wolstanton), a village two and a half miles to the north-west of Stoke, and Hugh *of Etruria*[36].

Greatbatch's eldest son, Hugh, was baptised on 8th December, 1765, at Lane End; he is listed as the son of William *Greatback (sic)*[37]. On 25th June, 1788, Hugh Greatbatch was married to Sarah Durham[38], and on 7th October of the same year, a daughter, Mary Ann, was baptised[39]. Hugh Greatbatch is listed in the Etruria Rent Book for 1797 — 1810 at House No. 82, paying a rent of £3.13.6 *per annum*, which was raised in 1805 to five pounds[40]. In the 1818 Trade Directory of Staffordshire he is described as a warehouseman at Etruria[41]. Hugh died in 1830, aged sixty-five, and was buried at Stoke on 10th February of that year; again he is described as of Etruria[42].

Greatbatch's second son, William, was also baptised at Lane End, on 12th July, 1767[43]. On 5th July, 1791, he was married to Mary Bristol *of Woolstanton*[44]. Ann, the daughter of William and Mary Greatbatch, was baptised on 13th January, 1792[45], and although no place of residence is given, this is certainly our couple on account of the absence of any other William and Mary Greatbatchs in the registers at this time. Thereafter, the couple appear in the parish register of Wolstanton. On 15th July, 1804, a son, John, was baptised; on 11th October, 1807, a second son, Hugh, was baptised; and on 17th December, 1809, a third son, Reuban[46].

William junior also worked at Etruria, and a William Greatbatch is listed as an overlooker there in the 1818 Trade Directory[47]. This William is stated to have a house at Wolstanton. Despite his Wolstanton connection, William also appears to have a house in Etruria village as No. 44 is listed as being occupied by William Greatbatch junior; the rent in 1797 was £3.12s *per annum* in 1797, rising the next year to £4.5.6[48].

It is difficult, however, to trace William junior beyond this time as confusion arises over the identity of individuals. Another William Greatbatch appears at Etruria in the early years of the 19th century, but this William is married to Elizabeth[49]. By this time William has become a very popular christian name in the area. Indeed, the 1818 Directory mentions, under Lane End and Lane Delph, a William Greatbatch, earthenware manufacturer, who had a house at George Street[50], but his identity cannot be ascertained.

The third, and youngest son, Richard, was baptised on 30th June, 1772, again at Lane End[51]. On 6th August, 1792, he married Nancy Hollinshead at Norton-in-the-Moors, a small village four miles to the north of Stoke[52]. The first of the couple's children, Hugh Simkin, was baptised at Wolstanton on 6th July, 1794[53]. The child has not been named after its great grandfather, Hugh Simpkin, but rather after its great uncle, Hugh Simpkin junior. The elder Hugh Simpkin was by this time deceased[54]. This naming of children after relatives was a well-known practice at this time and, indeed, it is possible that Richard Greatbatch was himself named after his mother's brother, Richard, as there is an R.S. Greatbatch listed as a clerk at the Etruria works in the 1818 Trade Directory[55]. Richard, too, lived at Etruria: on 25th March, 1800, he rented House No. 84 for £3.13.6 *per annum*[56], but his previous whereabouts cannot be ascertained. Richard Greatbatch died in 1818 at the age of forty-six and was buried at Stoke on 21st September[57]. He is described as of Etruria.

The Etruria Rent Book and the 1818 Trade Directory both support Byerley's remark that the whole of Greatbatch's family moved to Etruria[58], and the latter suggests that all three of the sons worked at the Etruria factory, even after their father's death. There is other evidence for this in the form of a letter written by William Greatbatch junior to his brother Richard in April, 1813, requesting him to visit H. Greatbatch on a matter of business: a strain in the brothers' relationship is apparent[59].

William Greatbatch had at least one other child who cannot be identified from the entries in the local parish registers. A son, who is not named, is referred to in Greatbatch's correspondence with Josiah Wedgwood. On 30th May, 1763, Greatbatch writes to Wedgwood:

I intended to have come over to Burslam on
Friday next, but my little boy is so very ill that
I am doubtful I cannot come, but in case I do not
shall send a lad. So Remain Sr. Yr. Most Oblg'd
& Hble. St.

Wm. Greatbatch
Lowr. Lane May the 30th 1763 [60]

On the day of the intended visit to Burslem, he writes:

Lane Delph Friday at noon

Sir,

Desire you'l will Remit what cash is
is Convenient for you by the bearer hereof.
I could not possible come over myself for
my Dear wife was taken so ill this morning
that she was oblig'd to take her bed
and our Dear boy is extream bad which
leaves us but small hopes for his recovery.

If you want anything in particular Desire you
will send a Note by the Bearer for I cannot
possible tell when I shall come over to Burslam. [61]

The following day, Greatbatch writes:

Saturday Morning

Sir.

Desire you'l Remit me some cash by the
bearer on the present occasion, for the Lord
has been pleased to take my Dr. Boy this
morning. [62]

The name of Greatbatch's son has not been found, despite extensive searches of the local parish registers and other records[63]. There is, quite simply, no surviving record of either the baptism or the burial and the likely situation is that the infant was never baptised at all. Baptisms in the 18th century were regularly not coincidental with the year of birth, and it would not be unusual for a considerable time to pass before baptism took place.

There is no shortage of documentary evidence relating to Greatbatch and his family, but it is not sufficient to answer all the questions; there still remain many mysteries. Not least of these is the date and place of his birth. Baptism records have been examined for all the neighbouring Midlands counties, as well as for the counties around the ports of London, Bristol and Liverpool[64]. This has revealed nothing. Greatbatch was an extremely common family name during the 17th, 18th and 19th centuries, but was almost entirely restricted to North Staffordshire and, to a lesser extent, Shropshire; it is barely represented elsewhere. Students may make what they will of the available evidence but we may, at least, consider North Staffordshire as the most likely place for William's birth. We must content ourselves with the fact that his is one of the many baptisms which have not been recorded, if indeed he was baptised at all.

1. Stoke upon Trent Parish Register (unpub.).
2. Shaw 1829, 156 & 190.
3. For example note, Wedgwood MSS: 30113-30. Below, page 35).
4. Shaw 1829, 156.
5. *ibid.*, 190.
6. Wedgwood MSS: 121-23528.
7. Thomas Whieldon's Account and Memorandum Book. City Museum & Art Gallery, Stoke-on-Trent (unpub.).
8. *ibid.*: 12th June, 1749; 13th June, 1749.
9. *ibid.* Also entries for 30th September, 1751; 15th April, 1751; and 26th March, 1752.
10. Parishes covered include: Stoke upon Trent, Burslem, Newcastle-under-Lyme, Trentham, Keele and Wolstanton. In addition, the Mormon Records, the International Genealogical Index, have been checked for the following counties: Staffordshire, Cheshire, Shropshire, Worcestershire, Gloucestershire, Warwickshire, Leicestershire, Derbyshire, Lancashire, Yorkshire, as well as the southern counties of Middlesex, Surrey, Kent, Essex, Hertfordshire, Buckinghamshire and Somerset.
11. Shaw 1829, 156.
12. Stoke upon Trent Parish Register III.
13. *ibid.*
14. *ibid.*
15. Shaw 1829, 156.
16. Rate Book, Fenton and Longton. Staffordshire County Record Office, bundle D(w) 1742/46.
17. Towner 1963, 180.
18. Leek Parish Register II.
19. Stoke upon Trent Parish Register II.
20. Stoke upon Trent Parish Register III.
21. *ibid.*
22. Towner 1963, 180.
23. Delhom Collection, Mint Museum of Art, Cat. No.: 65.48 DC. EPy, W706.
24. Wedgwood MSS: E.31-24107.
25. Stoke upon Trent Parish Register IV.
26. Newcastle-under-Lyme Parish Register II.
27. Register of Marriages, entry no. 65. SCRO, Cat. No.: D3251/1/14.
28. Stoke upon Trent Parish Register III.
29. On 13th February, 1726, 2nd February, 1731, 29th September, 1733, and 15th July, 1735, respectively. Stoke upon Trent Parish Register II — III.
30. Stoke upon Trent Parish Register II.
31. Gravestone in St. Peter's churchyard, Stoke upon Trent.
32. Stoke upon Trent Parish Register (unpub.).
33. Lichfield Joint Record Office.
34. *ibid.*
35. Wedgwood MSS: 121-23528.
36. Lichfield Joint Record Office.
37. Lane End Parish Register (unpub.).
38. Stoke upon Trent Parish Register IV.
39. Stoke upon Trent Parish Register III.
40. Wedgwood MSS: 28683-43.
41. Parsons and Bradshaw, 1818.
42. Stoke upon Trent Parish Register (unpub.).
43. Lane End Parish Register (unpub.).
44. Stoke upon Trent Parish Register IV.
45. *ibid.*
46. Wolstanton Parish Register II.
47. Parsons and Bradshaw 1818.
48. Wedgwood MSS: 28683-43.
49. Stoke upon Trent Parish Register III, entry for 1st May, 1803.
50. Parsons and Bradshaw 1818.
51. Lane End Parish Register (unpub.).
52. Norton-in-the-Moors Parish Register II.
53. Wolstanton Parish Register II.
54. On 31st July, 1759. Gravestone in St. Peter's churchyard, Stoke upon Trent.
55. Parsons and Bradshaw 1818.
56. Wedgwood MSS: 28683-43.
57. Stoke upon Trent Parish Register (unpub.).
58. Wedgwood MSS: 121-23528.
59. *ibid.*: 25607-129.
60. *ibid.*: 30113-30.
61. *ibid.*: 22395-30.
62. *ibid.*: 22336-30.
63. See note 10 above.
64. Besides Staffordshire, Cheshire, Shropshire, Worcestershire, Warwickshire, Derbyshire and Leicestershire.

CHAPTER 2

GREATBATCH THE POTTER

William Greatbatch's potting career lasted for over half a century. For twenty years he worked as an independent manufacturer until bankruptcy apparently forced him to quit. Following this, he found an extremely lucrative position at the Etruria factory of Josiah Wedgwood, where he spent the remainder of his working life.

Simeon Shaw and Thomas Byerley have both given us important information about Greatbatch's career, and, indeed, their accounts still remain the most complete, and most reliable references to the man. Subsequent passages in works of ceramic history have added little of substance to these and have served, largely, to confuse. It is clear that these two accounts are far from sufficient to permit a detailed understanding of a lengthy career and it is essential to have alternative evidence, documentary or otherwise, to support them. Thomas Byerley was, after all, writing to Josiah Wedgwood II with a clear motive, to save some of the money which was then being paid to Greatbatch as a salary, and he seems intent upon undermining his position at Etruria. Shaw, by contrast, was writing fifteen years after Greatbatch's death and some seventy or more years after his supposed apprenticeship to Thomas Whieldon at Fenton Vivian. The evidence from such sources cannot be taken at face value and must be corroborated.

Both men agree upon Greatbatch having been an apprentice at Whieldon's factory, but more than that they do not say. In the absence of any evidence to the contrary, it would be unwise to seriously dispute this event in Greatbatch's career but, as we have seen (above, page 29), there is no surviving contemporary evidence of Greatbatch's apprenticeship. Moreover, there is no evidence to link William Greatbatch with the Daniel Greatbatch's son who was hired by Whieldon on 29th August, 1753. Apprenticeships, or at least formal apprenticeships, were the exception in the pottery industry during the eighteenth century. Many potters had been hired as youths to learn their trade, but those who were apprenticed tended to be those individuals who became master potters in later life and those who came from a good family. Family support was absolutely necessary, to pay for the apprenticeship and subsequently to provide the financial backing for any business venture.

An apprenticeship to Thomas Whieldon, one of the most prolific and influential potters of his day, would have given Greatbatch a very useful start to his career as a potter, and it is presumably during his time at Fenton Vivian that he learned the not inconsiderable skills of a modeller, referred to by Simeon Shaw in his account[1] and discussed in more detail below (page 56). Moreover, it was most probably at Fenton Vivian that Greatbatch came to know Josiah Wedgwood, during the latter's five year partnership with Thomas Whieldon, an acquaintance which was to prove a benefit to Greatbatch for the rest of his life.

Further light is shed on this early period of Greatbatch's career by the text of a little known unpublished biography of Josiah Wedgwood which survives in the Wedgwood archive[2], two drafts of which seem to have been written by Thomas Byerley shortly after Wedgwood's death in 1795. The drafts vary slightly in detail, but essentially tell the same story. The first and earliest of these reads:

He (Josiah Wegdwood I) *had other difficulties to encounter arising from the novelty of his works. Workmanship of the pottery was at this period in a very low state as to its stile* (sic) *— The whole country and those in the habit of forming common vessels made in white stone ware enjoyed only three professed modellers — one of these was brought up under Mr. W. in the partnership we have spoken of* (with Thomas Whieldon) *and had just left him to establish a separate work for himself, in which, however, he worked only for Mr. W. during some years; a second was employed in Mr. W's manufactory, and the third was the modeller of the country at large*[3].

The text of the biography here echoes Wedgwood's own words in describing the wares produced during his partnership with Whieldon and the state of the market at that time (above, page 19). We can clearly recognise William Greatbatch as the first of the modellers. The second modeller is most probably William Wood who, after serving an apprenticeship with Wedgwood, became the leading block maker for useful wares at Etruria[4]. The third modeller is most likely to be Aaron Wood who is said to have *made the models for all the potters, during the time the Salt Glaze was in general use*[5].

Byerley's second draft adds further detail to the picture:

At this time (first six months with Whieldon) *he* (Josiah Wedgwood) *had only the assistance of an ingenious young man who had acquired a small knowledge of modelling during his apprenticeship and Mr. W. therefore must have modelled these things himself and indeed he seems to have given birth, or at least STILE ornament to the art of modelling in this manufactory, and has diffused it throughout having instructed many. (This was when he designed new green e'ware in forms of leaves, plates, moulded fruits, agate snuff boxes & c.)......*

He had other difficulties to surmount arising from the novelty of his works. The workmanship of the pottery was at that period in a very low state as to its STILE. They had only three professed modellers in the whole manufactory. One of these was brought up under Mr. Wedgwood at Fenton, and had left him a little before to establish a separate works for himself. The wares he made, however, were all for the use of Mr. Wedgwood on an engagement that lasted some years, and they received their last finish at his own manufactory in Burslem; — another of the three was altogether in his (Josiah Wedgwood's) *employment, and the third was the modeller of the country at large*[6].

Byerley's reluctance to name the individuals described was doubtless intended to avoid any detraction from the achievements of Wedgwood but this does present difficulties for the present-day researcher. For example, we cannot be absolutely certain who the *ingenious young man* is, although the context suggests that this is William Greatbatch. On the other hand, both drafts provide a clear picture of Greatbatch's business involvement with Wedgwood: after leaving Fenton he set up in business for himself, and then worked solely for Wedgwood for some years. These details are wholly in accordance with the text of Byerley's letter of 1807 to Josiah Wedgwood II (quoted above, pages 28-29) and we might assume that Byerley was well-placed to know the facts.

Although Shaw does not mention Greatbatch's early business dealings with Josiah Wedgwood, they are well known, mainly through the work of later writers, such as Luxmore[7], Mankowitz[8], and Towner[9]. These, and others, have all drawn extensively, and some rather selectively, upon the correspondence between Greatbatch and Wedgwood which gives an excellent first-hand account of business

Fig. 3
Wedgwood's Brick House Works, Burslem (after Meteyard).

between the two potters. Byerley, too, tells us something of the nature of this business, when he writes: ...*when he* (Greatbatch) *first set up at Lower Lane for some years he made biscuit ware only — for the new work at Burslem where it was sent to be coloured and glazed*[10]. The 'new work' here referred to is surely the Brick House works, Burslem, rather than Wedgwood's first factory[11] which he rented from his distant cousin, John Wedgwood, on 1st May, 1759, immediately following the termination of his partnership with Thomas Whieldon, and continued to occupy it until the New Year of 1764[12]. The date upon which Wedgwood leased the Brick House works from William Adams is not known, although it has been generally assumed that he took possession upon vacating his first factory[13]. This assumption needs to be questioned and the possibility that Wedgwood was, for a time at least, operating two factories must not be overlooked. Indeed, to our knowledge, Wedgwood was operating more than one factory for much of his career, for in 1766 he rented an additional factory, the Red Works, Burslem, from his cousin, John Wedgwood[14]. The Red Works continued in operation alongside both the new Etruria factory, opened in 1769, and the Brick House works which was relinquished in 1772/3[15]. That Wedgwood found it necessary to take on new premises, first the Brick House and then the Red Works, suggests that his fortunes were improving and that trade was on the increase. The new business arrangement begun with Greatbatch in 1762 must have contributed to Wedgwood's success and suggests an expansion in his operations, the sort of expansion which may have necessitated additional premises.

It has been assumed that Greatbatch left Whieldon in 1759, the year in which the partnership between Whieldon and Wedgwood was dissolved, and then began the production of pottery in order to supply Wedgwood[16]. However, the evidence for this is unclear and, indeed, Greatbatch's own words seem to suggest something to the contrary:

For
Mr. Josiah Wedgewood (sic)
at Burslam

January 31st 1762

Sir,

Having considred what you and I
was talking about, am come to a Resolution
to proceed, and have hired men, taken a place
part of which ready, the rest by promise to
be built by May, which when finish'd will
begin immediately, and am preparing things
in Readeaness. I intend to come over to Burslam
as soon as opportunity offers. In the interim
shou'd be glad to have your proposals, what
you can afford to give per doz. for Round Teapts.
all sizes together. Likewise oval & co. & co.
shou'd be glad to have an answer back the
next week End by the Bearer. So Remain
wth Great Respect Yr. Most Oblg'd Hble St.

Wm. Greatbatch[17]

This letter is invaluable. Here is evidence that Wedgwood and Greatbatch had decided upon a business arrangement by the end of January, 1762. Production at Greatbatch's new factory was well under way by the end of the same year, and its commencement is announced in an undated letter to Wedgwood:

Sir

We have begun as yesterday to make ware and have
most of the moulds in readiness only the large
size ware. I have four men pressing constantly
and will push forwards as fast as possible.
There will be I expect about 60 Doz. in about
a fortnight time ready, and 120 Doz. more in
3 weeks after that, in the mean time shou'd
be glad to have your advice in the form of the
plates if you have opportunity. So remain
Yr. Most Oblg'd
and Hble St.

Wm. Greatbatch[18]

On 13th December, 1762, Greatbatch wrote:

Decr. 13th 1762

Sir,

I recd. Thos. Wedgwoods letter yesterday, and we
shall fire up on Wednesday without fail, we
shou'd have fir'd sooner had it not been
Danls. neglect, shou'd be glad you send Crates

in the mean time. So Remain Yr. Most Oblg'd
and Hble St.

Wm. Greatbatch

Ps.

We can fire again this next week but I think
we cannot make any Coffee pts. nor large Teapts.
We are making cups and saucers, Double coffees and
saucers and jocalates, Basons in short almost all
the sorts but coffee pts. & co. If you think it
convenient to fire shou'd be glad of advice.[19]

The evidence is incontrovertible and conclusive: Greatbatch started to produce pottery, as part of a recent agreement with Wedgwood, at some date during the year 1762. Yet, despite this, later writers still conclude that Greatbatch left Whieldon in 1759 and began to supply Wedgwood with pottery from that time. The simple fact is that we have very little idea of what Greatbatch was doing before 1762. There is, however, just one piece of evidence, to suggest that Greatbatch was supplying potters, other than Wedgwood, by May 1762. In an entry in a cash-account of the potter John Baddeley, of Shelton, dated, 29th May, 1762, is a payment of £2.10s made to *Will Greatbach*[20]. The possibility exists that this payment was not for pottery, but for blocks, as other entries include *pd. Greatbach for Blocks*[21]. However, a further entry, of 21st November, 1761, introduces an element of doubt: *pd. John Greatbach for Blocks £1.11.6*[22].

Greatbatch has been credited by ceramic historians with a variety of wares. However, many of the hypotheses about Greatbatch and his wares have been founded upon the two most confusing and ambiguous documents to survive amongst the correspondence between him and Wedgwood. The first of these reads as follows:

June 26th 1760

Sd. Mr. James Maidmont

4 Large Size fruit Dishes	*at 2/2*	—	*8*	*8*
8 less Do. Do.	*at 20d*	—	*13*	*4*
8 less Do. Do.	*at 14d*	—	*9*	*4*
8 Round Do.	*at 14d*	—	*9*	*4*
2 Doz Large plates	*at 6/-*	—	*12*	*0*
4 Doz less — —	*at 3/9*	—	*15*	*0*
		3	*7*	*8*

July 8th

1 Doz 9 Inch plates	*at 6/-*		*6*	*0*
15 Doz 8 Inch Do.	*at 3/9*	*2*	*16*	*3*
Crate —		*0*	*1*	*0*
		3	*3*	*3*
Total		*6*	*10*	*11*[23]

This is a puzzling document, presumably an invoice for goods sold to Mr. James Maidmont, or Maidment, a well-known and successful dealer in ceramics at this time, who is known to have had premises in St. Pauls, London[24]. The handwriting is probably that of William Greatbatch although the name *Wm. Greatbach,* misspelt, appears on the reverse in a different hand. This latter hand appears on other invoices of Greatbatch's and most probably belongs to a clerk engaged in filing away invoices, presumably in the employ of Josiah Wedgwood at Burslem. This invoice would seem to have been destined for filing under the name of William Greatbatch. The question of what part was Greatbatch playing in the provision of this small order must be asked. Does the occurrence of Greatbatch's name in a different hand suggest that this is part of Greatbatch's account?

A second invoice, equally ambiguous, has been referred to on many occasions by later writers. It reads:

Crate   *July 22d. 1760*
No. 1   *Left at the Cross Keys Wood Street London*

ov. 2d	*18 Large Oblong Dishes*	—	*21d*	—*1/6* —	*£1 — 11 —*	*8*
	24 less Do. Do.	—	*15d*	—*1/3* —	*1 — 10 —*	*0*
	36 less Do. Do.	—	*10d*	— *8d* —	*1 — 10 —*	*0*
	4½ doz 9½ inch plates	—	*5/*	— *4/* —	*1 — 2 —*	*6*
	30 Round 11 Inch dishes	—	*10d*	— *8d* —	*1 — 5 —*	*0*
Over charged 9d 8 9 Inch plates		—	*4½d*	— *4d* —	*0 — 3 —*	*9*
	2 mossaic teapts large size	—	—	—*10d* —	*0 — 2 —*	*0*
	2 fluted Do. Do.	—	—	—*10d* —	*0 — 2 —*	*0*
Wt. 246lb	*3 foxglove teapts*	—	*12s*	— *9d* —	*0 — 2 —*	*3*
	Crate				*0 — 1 —*	*0*
					7 — 10 —	*2*

Crate
No. 2 2d

No. 2 2d	*21 Large Oblong Dishes*	—	*21d*	— —	*£1 — 16 —*	*11*
	20 Less Do. Do.	—	*15d*	— —	*1 — 5 —*	*0*
	34 less Do. Do.	—	*10d*	— —	*1 — 8 —*	*4*
	15 Round Do. Do.	—	*10d*	— —	*0 — 12 —*	*6*
	4 Doz & 5 plates 9½ Inch		*5/*	— —	*1 — 2 —*	*1*
	6 8 Inch Do.	—	*3d*	— —	*0 — 1 —*	*6*
	2 large leaves	—	*8d*	— —	*0 — 1 —*	*4*
	6 less Do.	—	*7d*	— —	*0 — 3 —*	*6*
	2 pr. Baskets & stands	—	*3/6*	— —	*0 — 7 —*	*0*
	6 Large Boats	—	*5d*	— —	*0 — 2 —*	*6*
	11 Do. less	—	*4d*	— —	*0 — 3 —*	*8*
	7 Do. less	—	*3d*	— —	*0 — 1 —*	*9*
	1 Doz jars 24s	—	—	— —	*0 — 4 —*	*0*
Wt. 240lb	*2 Doz large toys*	—	*2/6*	— —	*0 — 5 —*	*0*
	Crate				*0 — 1 —*	*0*
					7 — 16 —	*1*

Crate

No. 3							
7 pr. Cornu Copias	15d	—	—	0 —	8 —	9
3 pr. Large Fluted Candlesticks	2/6	—	—	0 —	7 —	6
3 pr. less Do. Do.	20d	—	—	0 —	5 —	0
25 Candlesticks less Do.	6d	each	—	0 —	12 —	0
2 melon sauce Bts. & stands	16d	each	—	0 —	2 —	8
4 less Do. Do.	12d	—	—	0 —	4 —	0
3 less Do. Do.	8d	—	—	0 —	2 —	0
2 leaf Candlesticks	4d	—	—	0 —	0 —	8
2 fluted teapts.	12s	—	—	0 —	2 —	0
2 mossaic Do.	Do.	—	—	0 —	2 —	0
4 woodbine Do.	Do.	—	—	0 —	4 —	0
4 less Do.	Do.	9d	—	0 —	3 —	0
4 Green Do.	Do.	7d	—	0 —	2 —	4
1 fluted Do.	Do.	—	—	0 —	0 —	7
2 Chinese Do.	Do.	—	—	0 —	1 —	0
4 Green teapots	12s	—	—	0 —	2 —	0
5 Do. Do.	18s	—	—	0 —	1 —	8
3 Doz & 5 mustard pts	—	—	—	0 —	8 —	6
5 Doz large toys	2/6	—	—	0 —	12 —	6
Wt. 150lb 18 Doz small Do.	12d	—	—	0 —	18 —	0
Crate				0 —	1 —	0

5 — 1 — 8

Brot. over — 15 — 6 — 3

20 — 7 — 11

Goods sent   £32 — 7 — 2
less Goods sold to   20 — 7 — 11

11 — 19 — 3
12 — 3   19 — 7 — 4

£11 — 7 — 0   1 — 0 — 7

Wm. Greatbach[25]

Once again this invoice has been subjected to alterations by a clerk — the notes on overcharging, the prices and totals, for example. Otherwise, the handwriting is once again almost certainly that of Greatbatch. However, the name *Wm. Greatbach*, misspelt once more, is not in his hand and is presumably that of the clerk. The role of Greatbatch in the supply of pottery to London must be considered.

All those writers who have discussed Greatbatch and his connection with Josiah Wedgwood have used this invoice as the basis for identifying the products of his factory. Not one has considered the evidence of the letter of 31st January, 1762, quoted above, and not one has admitted any possibility other than that the wares listed have been produced by Greatbatch. If the latter is indeed the case, we must ask where did Greatbatch manufacture this pottery, and why did he then find it necessary to rent a factory in 1762?

It is clear from the two invoices quoted that Greatbatch was involved with Wedgwood from as early as June, 1760. That his name appears on these documents, in the hand of a clerk, suggests that he had an account with Wedgwood. However, the likelihood of Greatbatch having produced the goods supplied on these two occasions is not great, in view of the fact that he quite clearly had no factory of his own at that time. The most plausible interpretation of the evidence is that Greatbatch was, in 1760, acting for Wedgwood in London as an agent or factor, dealing with customers, orders and shipments of pottery, such as that left at the Cross Keys. The Cross Keys was a coaching inn just off Cheapside, at that time a major trading centre, and a most convenient place at which to deposit goods for collection.

Evidence for the early career of William Greatbatch is both scanty and ambiguous and much that has been written in works of ceramic history is, at best, pure speculation. What, then, do we know for certain?

The first piece of conclusive evidence is Greatbatch's resolution of January, 1762, to do business with Josiah Wedgwood. Details of the nature of this arrangement are not given at the time, but may be inferred from the later documents. Thomas Byerley, as we have seen, says of Greatbatch: *when he first set up at Lower Lane for some years he made biscuit ware only — for the new work at Burslem where it was sent to be coloured and glazed* [26].

The factory which Greatbatch refers to in his letter of 31st January, 1762, was that at Lower Lane which Byerley is describing. Lower Lane was an area of settlement which had developed along the main Stoke to Uttoxeter road, turnpiked in 1759, ignoring the boundaries of the two townships of Fenton Vivian and Fenton Culvert (below, page 79). The first item of Greatbatch's correspondence to be headed Lower Lane is an invoice dated 23rd December, 1762[27]. From that time on, letters are regularly headed in this way and no credence can be given to the assertion that in 1764 Greatbatch moved from Lower Lane to Lane Delph[28]. The evidence for this seems to be the appearance of letters from Greatbatch which are headed *Lane Delph* or *Lane Delf*, although the first of these is dated 26th December, 1762[29]. From this time on, Lane Delph or Lane Delf are used with roughly the same frequency as Lower Lane, and this does not mean that Greatbatch had two factories! Rather his factory was in Lower Lane in 1762, upon his commencing in business, just as it was twenty years later upon his bankruptcy[30]. Moreover, the excavation of Greatbatch's factory waste tip, which has given rise to this volume, was also in Lower Lane. We have already seen in Thomas Byerley's letter that Greatbatch owned *two or three houses at Lane Delf*[31], and it may be significant that his wife Sarah's family are described as being of Lane Delph[32]. It is likely that it was at Lane Delph that Greatbatch lived with his family.

The correspondence between Greatbatch and Wedgwood gives us a fairly clear idea of the nature of their business. Greatbatch was engaged in producing a range of wares which he supplied to Wedgwood. These wares are named and their prices are given. What is most apparent, however, is that nothing supplied to Wedgwood from 1762 onwards bears the slightest resemblence to those wares described in that ambiguous invoice of 22nd July, 1760. Green teapots, foxglove teapots, mosaic teapots and others, are conspicuous by their absence in the later invoices, thereby lending credence to the assertion, made above, that the wares of the 1760 invoices are unlikely to have been produced by Greatbatch.

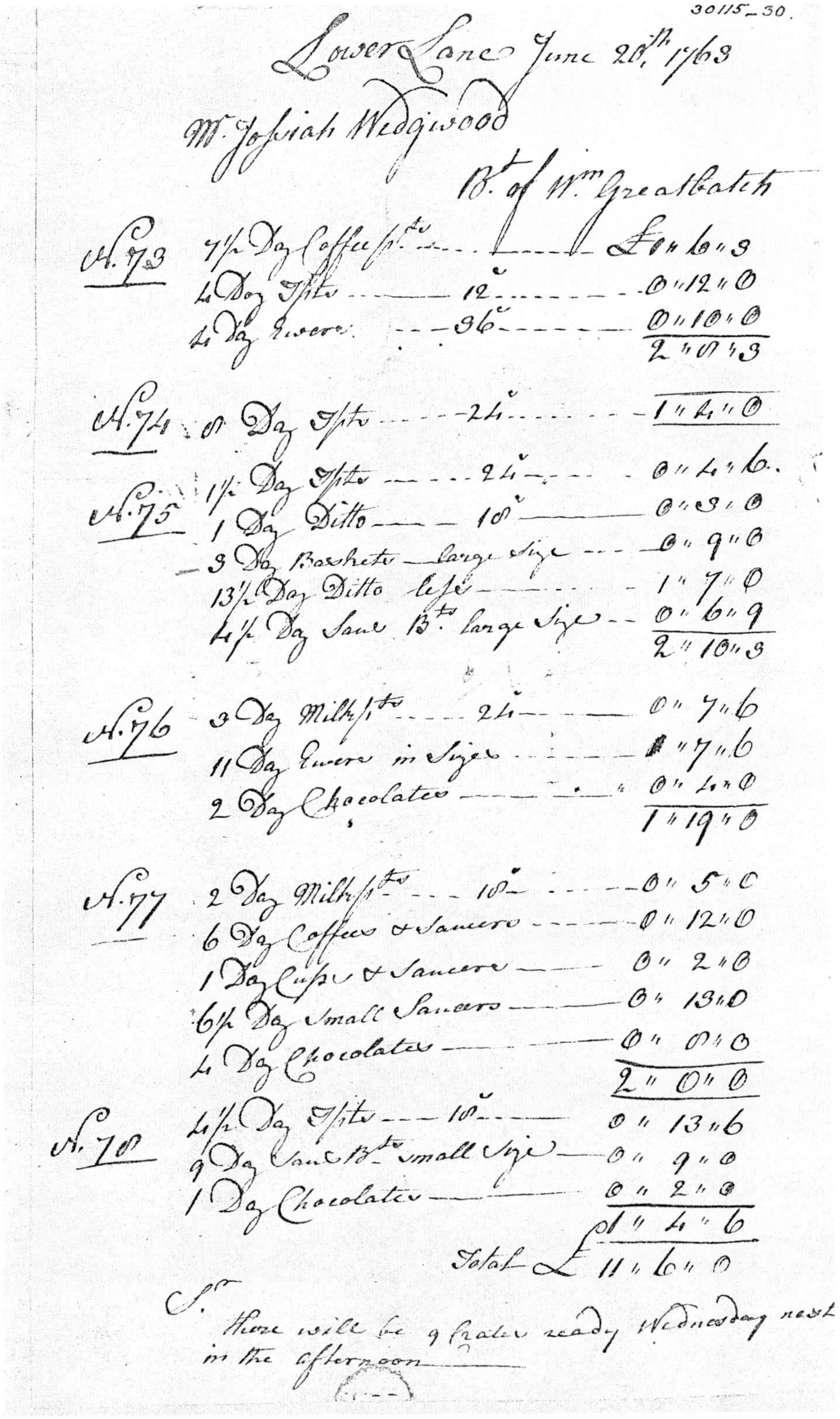

30115_30.

Lower Lane June 20th 1763

Mr Josiah Wedgwood

Bt. of Wm Greatbatch

No. 73
- 7½ Doz Coffee p.ts — £0 " 6 " 3
- 4 Doz Ditto — 12 — 0 " 12 " 0
- 4 Doz Ewers — 36 — 0 " 10 " 0
  - 2 " 0 " 3

No. 74 — 0 Doz Ditto — 24 — 1 " 4 " 0

No. 75
- 1½ Doz Ditto — 24 — 0 " 4 " 6
- 1 Doz Ditto — 10 — 0 " 3 " 0
- 3 Doz Baskets large size — 0 " 9 " 0
- 13½ Doz Ditto less — 1 " 7 " 0
- 4½ Doz Sauce Bt. large size — 0 " 6 " 9
  - 2 " 10 " 3

No. 76
- 3 Doz Milk p.ts — 24 — 0 " 7 " 6
- 11 Doz Ewers in size — 1 " 7 " 6
- 2 Doz Chocolates — 0 " 4 " 0
  - 1 " 19 " 0

No. 77
- 2 Doz Milk p.ts — 10 — 0 " 5 " 0
- 6 Doz Coffees & Saucers — 0 " 12 " 0
- 1 Doz Cups & Saucers — 0 " 2 " 0
- 6½ Doz Small Saucers — 0 " 13 " 0
- 4 Doz Chocolates — 0 " 0 " 0
  - 2 " 0 " 0

No. 78
- 4½ Doz Ditto — 10 — 0 " 13 " 6
- 9 Doz Sauce Bt. small size — 0 " 9 " 0
- 1 Doz Chocolates — 0 " 2 " 0
  - 1 " 4 " 6

Total £ 11 " 6 " 0

Sr.
there will be 9 crates ready Wednesday next in the afternoon

Fig. 4

Invoice of 20th June, 1763, for six crates of ware supplied to Wedgwood by Greatbatch. (Wedgwood MSS: 30115-30. Reproduced by Courtesy of the Trustees of the Wedgwood Museum, Stoke-on-Trent, Staffordshire, England).

An undated, but obviously early note gives a first impression of the type of pottery which Greatbatch was supplying to Wedgwood:

Coffee pts. & Teapts. at — *3/6 pr. Doz*
Milk pts. Sugr Dishes & Bowls *3/-*
Ewers at — — — — — *2/6*
Cups Saucers & Jocalates — *2/-*

Seconds

Coffee pts. & Teapts. at — *2/-*
Milk pts. Sugr. Dishes & Bowls at *1/9*
Ewers at — — — — — *1/6*
Cups Saucers & Jocalates at — *1/3*
Cream boats — 36s — *2/-*
least size Sa. boats — *12s* — } *12d*
next do. do. — *12s* — }
next do. do. *do.* — } *18d*
next do. do. *do.* — }

NB These prices are not agreed upon, the T.Pots & co. are abot. 6d pr. doz too much.[33]

Despite the note to this list, these are the prices which appear in the first surviving invoice, dated 23rd December, 1762[34]. It was not long, however, before the matter was raised by Wedgwood, as on 26th December, 1762, Greatbatch found it necessary to write:

As to the price of the ware pr. Doz. I cannot Possible make for less than 3/6 pr. Dozn. — the large ware. The small Do. at 3/ pr. Doz. to stand by them to be good. Their will also be some seconds which you must take for I cannot keep them to look at. I shall fire again this week and will pack on Monday following.[35]

The surviving invoices in the Wedgwood archive span the period December, 1762, to January, 1765, a little over two years. They detail thirty-six separate deliveries to Wedgwood in 250 crates, out of a total of 563 crates which were supplied during this period. The contents of individual numbered crates are itemised, with the prices of each type of ware, by the dozen in most cases or by the piece for some of the more special types. Some fifty-three individual items are named. Figure 15 illustrates the scale of the supply.

Byerley has told us that Greatbatch *for some years .. made biscuit ware only*, a statement which has subsequently been accepted without question. At no point in the correspondence between Greatbatch and Wedgwood is the state of the ware supplied mentioned, although Greatbatch refers to nothing which might lead one to a different conclusion. One of Greatbatch's letters to Wedgwood does, indeed, appear to refer to an order for biscuit ware: on 1st October, 1763, Greatbatch explains that he is unable to supply part of an order from his next firing because of a shortage of moulds (below, page 55)[36]. If Wedgwood needed the ware direct from the oven, as seems to be implied by the letter, then this order, at least, was for biscuit ware.

Reilly has argued that the prices of the various types of ware listed in the invoices suggest that the goods are in the biscuit state and that, consequently, the bulk of Greatbatch's production was of biscuit ware [37]. However, he compares Greatbatch's prices to Wedgwood with Wedgwood's prices to his customers, a comparison which is invalid on account of the inflated prices which Wedgwood is known to have applied to his wares, charging whatever the market would bear. A detailed examination of contemporary prices being charged for similar wares is necessary before any definitive conclusion can be reached. This has not yet been undertaken, but what little evidence is available suggests that Greatbatch's prices to Wedgwood are not sufficiently different to those charged by his contemporaries for wares which were clearly glazed, for them to be used as evidence for the supply of *biscuit ware only*. For example, in September, 1763, Robert Garner & Co. were supplying Wedgwood with brown china teapots at four shillings per dozen; tortoiseshell teapots at 2/6d per dozen and cream ewers at 1/6d per dozen[38]. The tortoiseshell, at least must have been glazed ware, and yet Greatbatch's price for teapots whose state and type are unspecified, was three shillings per dozen at this same time. Similarly, Greatbatch's price for ewers was 2/6d and brown china teapots, when they appear in 1764, are four shillings per dozen, the same as Garner's.

Other evidence, notably that of the archaeology, appears to contradict Byerley and the later writers. The evidence of the excavation of the Greatbatch site and the chronology of the pottery recovered from it will be discussed in detail below (pages 77-78), but it will suffice to say here that both glazed and biscuit wares, cream-coloured earthenwares and others, are represented at every level of the site. On the basis of this, the conclusion must be that both biscuit and glazed wares were deposited at the same time, from the very beginning of the site's use as a dump.

Three possibilities present themselves: we may not have recovered evidence of the first years of Greatbatch's production; Byerley was mistaken in making this statement; or Greatbatch did, indeed, supply Wedgwood solely with biscuit wares, at least for a short time, but continued himself to produce and market a range of finished wares alongside his commitment to Wedgwood. Much depends upon our interpretation of Byerley's words, and it may be that an arrangement to supply Wedgwood, and Wedgwood alone, with biscuit wares did not preclude independent production by Greatbatch.

There is, in the correspondence, sufficient evidence to contradict Byerley's view of the situation. Firstly, there is the, as yet inconclusive, evidence that Greatbatch's prices were not necessarily those of biscuit wares. Secondly, it is abundantly clear that Greatbatch was supplying Wedgwood with more than pottery: block moulds, too, were an important feature of this business arrangement (below, page 113). Thirdly, there are requests made to Wedgwood by Greatbatch for wares to be sent to him in quantities which suggest that they were resale: in a note on 24th December, 1763, Greatbatch asks Wedgwood to send him twenty-four dozens of teapots, milk pots and ewers, printed or painted in *Landscip* (landscape) patterns, as well *as a crate of white chocolat cups made by some of yr. Neighbours* [39]. Fourthly, on 26th May, 1764, he writes to Wedgwood about a new sprigged *Brown China Tpt.* and informs him that *There will be about a Crate to come out of the next oven of the same...and think will suit you if want any* [40]. The interpretation here can only be that this ware will be ready after the next firing, regardless of whether Wedgwood wishes any. If Greatbatch was able to produce ware without having a definite order from Wedgwood, he must have had the means of disposing of it in the event that Wedgwood was not interested: in other words, Greatbatch had a market other than Wedgwood for his pottery. This is confirmed by Greatbatch's response of 12th October, 1763, to Wedgwood's complaint about prices (below, page 51) in which he refers to his supply to Wedgwood as a *settled Article,* while allowing for the possibility of clearing wares by his own hand.

There is one final piece of evidence to suggest that supplying Wedgwood was not Greatbatch's only business in the early years of his career. The invoices, which itemise the contents of crates sent to Wedgwood, suggest that the scale of the supply was not great. For example, in May, 1763, and November, 1763, two months for which the records are complete, Wedgwood received the largest of the deliveries listed, comprising twenty-two and twenty-seven crates of ware respectively, which contained 534½ and 403½ dozens of ware. Other deliveries for which we have the whole month's invoices varied from 146 to 362 dozens of ware in quantity. Pottery ovens of the 20th century could contain anything up to three thousand dozens of ware and, even allowing for the smaller capacities of 18th century ovens, it is difficult to see that these monthly totals supplied by Greatbatch could amount to even one oven full per month. Greatbatch must, therefore, have had another outlet for his surplus capacity. This simple fact underlines the potential for error in accepting at face value unconfirmed oral reports which is essentially what Byerley's accounts amount to.

The correspondence from Greatbatch to Wedgwood, although one-sided, confirms much of what we already know of Wedgwood. He was clearly a keen businessman and was not averse to complaining about either the quality or the price of wares. Evidence for this may be seen in both the letters and the invoices. A study of the latter shows evidence for the fluctuations in the price of wares and it is significant that these are always adjustments downwards. The first evidence that Wedgwood was seeking a reduction in prices occurs in a note of 27th April, 1763:

Sir,

I have charg'd the sugr. Dishes 3/- pr Doz for
I cannot afford them for less, there is so much loss in
making them, the Milk pts. & Bowls will be charg'd
no more than 2/6, the Charge of the Butter Tubs &
Stands & Cannisters I hope will please. So Remain
Yr. Oblg'd & Hble St.

Wm. Greatbatch[41]

Henceforth, the following decrease in prices may be seen in the invoices:

16th April, 1763   Small sauce boats — from 1/6 to 1/0 per dozen.
27th April, 1763   Milk pots — from 3/- to 2/6 per dozen.
9th May, 1763   Teapots — from 3/6 to 3/- per dozen.
                          Bowls — from 3/- to 2/6 per dozen.

These alterations are limited in number and the complaint from Wedgwood about prices would appear to have been far less critical than that which caused Greatbatch to reply on 12th October, 1763:

Sir,

I have recd. your's and am sorry their shou'd be
such complaint of the goods on account of the prices
& quality. In the first place you mention the great
fall of the Prices pr. Doz which Don't doubt the truth
and will settle the Prices to your satisfaction if
I possible can. In the next place your certain my
proffit is much larger than yours, which you are the
best judge will allow. I am certain in this that my
proffit's very Triffling & Don't doubt but cou'd have
clear'd as much by my own hand only this is a setled
Article & the other is not. The fire has been too
easy I own but think the last oven full was very
well on that account, but will fire harder next.
Their was some few things too easy which I order'd
to be set by wch. I find was neglected. I charged the
men, as I cou'd not look every piece over my
self, not to put one peice of ware in, either easy,
crooked, or any other fault whatsoever as I was
Determin'd their shou'd be no fault found on that
subject for the future. — I am very Glad of your
Resolution in sending a Person as it will free
all complaints. Shall Draw the oven on Monday
morning and will be ready to Pack by ten O'Clock.
Have Recd. your Bill inclos'd & order. Will take
care it is compleated the next oven full. I am yrs & co.
in Haste.

Wm. Greatbatch[42]

As a result of Wedgwood's complaint, Greatbatch apparently made a drastic reduction in the prices of some fifteen different types of wares. This can be seen in, and after the invoice for crates 158 — 166, which were supplied after 12th October, 1763[43]:

— October, 1763	Teapots — from 3/- to 2/6 per dozen.
	Coffee pots — from 3/6 to 3/- per dozen.
	Chocolates — from 2/- to 1/6 per dozen.
	Cups and saucers — from 2/- to 1/6 per dozen.
	Milk pots — from 2/6 to 2/- per dozen.
	Bowls — from 2/6 to 2/- per dozen.
	Sugar dishes — from 3/- to 2/6 per dozen.
	Ewers — from 2/6 to 2/- per dozen.
	Canisters — from 2/6 to 2/- per dozen.

3rd November, 1763	Coffees and saucers — from 2/- to 2/6 per dozen. Saffron pots — from 3/- to 2/6 per dozen. Butter tubs — from 4/- to 3/6 per dozen.
19th December, 1763	Saucers — from 2/- to 1/6 per dozen.
12th January, 1764	Plates — from 2/- to 1/6 per dozen.

Further reductions in price are made in November, 1764:

15th November, 1764	Saffron pots — from 2/6 to 2/3 per dozen. Sugar dishes — from 2/6 to 2/3 per dozen.

These reductions were probably made necessary by the difficulties which Greatbatch refers to in a letter of 11th November, 1764:

Have Recd. yours Dated Novr. 2nd & shall contract
my bussiness in a Nearer compass by parting
with two men this Day. As to Reserve in modeling
it is far from me. It is the want of a proper Design
wch. makes me neglect finishing as I wou'd do. Have sent you
two unwrought Draughts Inclosed to have your
sentiments on, was I to make them I shou'd not
follow them exactly but these by way hint to some
thing in this way. Shou'd be glad you wou'd form
something you think is likely to take as you
understand what will suit trade Better than me.
If you leave it to me will exert my self the Best
in making a Tpt. first before I proceed any farther
for your approbation. It is far from me to having
any thoughts in Dropping our connection as long
as can carry it on with any Tolerable Degree of
advantage, but I know there is an absolute Necessity
to have something new & shal imploy the small
Genius I have in inventing something I hope that
will be of advantage to both.[44]

Business may have been bad for the two men at this time, but Greatbatch had the resolve to continue. This is an important point to bear in mind, in view of the fact that little correspondence between Greatbatch and Wedgwood survives beyond January, 1765. We can only assume that the business arrangement continued beyond this date. Certainly there is no hint of further trouble or uncertainty in the correspondence which post-dates the above letter. There is just one invoice and accompanying note to suggest that business continued into the next decade, long after Wedgwood had moved from Burslem to his new works at Etruria.

Fig. 5
Wedgwood's factory at Etruria (after Meteyard).

Wm. Greatbatch
    1774
To Mr. Thos. Wedgwood
Etruria

Mr. Thomas Wedgwood, to Wm. Greatbatch

1773
April 16th, to goods, as by bill   .   .   .   4 — 16 —   0
May 16th, to Ditto   .   .   .   .   6 —   7 — 10½
                                                                    ─────────────
                                                                    11 —   3 — 10½
                                                        Dist.   — 11 —   0
                                                                    10 — 12 — 10
                                                  two Hogsheads   0 —   6 —   6
                                                                    ─────────────
                                                                    £10 — 19 —   4

Mr. Thos. Wedgwood,

> I should be much obliged to you if you wou'd
> assist me with the above for a very large quantity
> of cash to Disburse before Monday. Your complying
> will exceedingly oblige yr. Obedt, Hble. St.

                    Wm. Greatbatch[45]

Although of little intrinsic value, this item of correspondence at least confirms the continuation of business between Greatbatch and Wedgwood, although the nature of business at this date remains unknown. This is perhaps what one might have expected. In this particular case, Greatbatch is dealing with Thomas Wedgwood who was now the works manager at Etruria after Josiah gave up the Brick House works in 1773[46].

The correspondence between Greatbatch and Wedgwood leaves little doubt as to who is the dominant partner in business. It is Wedgwood who is the initiator of ideas and new types; it is Wedgwood who has his finger on the needs of the market; it is Wedgwood who complains about price and quality. Greatbatch, by contrast, appears to be striving to please with both the quality of his wares and with new designs. Reductions in prices follow the complaints and it is interesting to note that the invoices record only one price rise in the two year period covered: on 21st January, 1765, the price of ewers increases from 2/- to 3/- per dozen[47].

Many letters bear witness to Greatbatch's eagerness to please Wedgwood. These are of special interest for the insight they provide into the daily business of the factory at Lower Lane. For example:

Lower Lane July 21st 1763

Sir,

*I am very sorry that you shou'd
have reason to complain of the goods sent,
but you may depend on having the sugr. Dishes
and covers straight away for the future. I was
not in the way when the sugrs. where pack'd. I
ordred them to set them that were good only.*

*I have no covers but will take care to send
them pr. next. — we shall draw this day (?) Sevin-
night, you may send some body if you please but
I will take care to set it out myself for I am
much averse to any complaints.*

*The baskets I had order'd before you send to be plac'd single - they will be crooked if doubled.
The sugr. dish
nobs Thos. Wedgwood order'd to be set low on acct.
of placing them. You may Depend I will take care
to avoid any more complaints if possible. So Remn.
in Haste Yr. Most Oblg'd & co.*

Wm. Greatbatch[48]

Another letter reads:

To
Mr. Josiah Wedgwood
Burslam

Sir,

Have Recd. yours, and am sorry I cou'd not Oblige you
with the order sent as I only wanted coles to put fire
to the oven to morrow night. I would have staid but
we have only four moulds of that size & wou'd
be four or 5 days before we shou'd have got that quantity
made, had I known as yesterday noon I could have
fitted the order as we finished 30 Doz or more.

If you cannot possible do without 'em this oven please give me a line
tomorrow and will get them ready with
Possible speed. So Remain yr. Hble. St. & co.

Wm. Greatbatch

Lower Lane Saturday Afternoon[49]

Greatbatch refers to particular trouble with his staff which had clearly caused him great embarassment and Wedgwood a great inconvenience:

Its no wonder as I found this morning that
so many chocolates shou'd be Broken. The cart
Laden unloosed & the crate fell off which was
conceal'd from me till now. I cou'd not Possible
look the choc'lates out which you Desired me to do on
acct. of the Tpt model which had under my hands
at that time but Desired the man that did
to be particular in sending good ones which I
always Do to prevent as much as possible any
Dispute that may happen afterwards. Its as
much against my Inclination to send wasters as
it is yours to Receive them but I own that these
choc'lates were nothing else when sent that is the most
part of them, but setting them aside the ware is not
amiss I expect but the most curious eye may
happen to send some few amongst quantities so.

Lower Lane
Friday noon

N.B. The Packers I order'd to pack the same as if they
were to be carried ever so far, as the carters can
Testify when they have staid, but will guard
as much as possible against inconveniences & shou'd
be glad you wou'd always let me know when you see any.[50]

This letter not only points to the dangers of transporting consignments of pottery by road, but also refers to Greatbatch as modeller, a designer and maker of block moulds for those more elaborate types of ware which needed to be press-moulded or slip-cast. Simeon Shaw writes of Greatbatch being an *excellent modeller and a general workman of first rate abilities*[51], and much more may be learned of this from Greatbatch himself.

The letter of 11th November, 1764, quoted above (page 52), shows that Greatbatch was having problems in finding a suitable design and required Wedgwood's opinion of his ideas. Rather more enthusiasm is displayed in Greatbatch's other correspondence:

> *There is Breakfast plates to go in the oven and am*
> *Going on with the modelling as fast as possible.*[52]

On 8th May, 1764, Greatbatch writes:

> *Shou'd be glad to have your advice in the shape*
> *of the Squirrel & Bird Tpt Block, & whether*
> *you wou'd have a ground upon it or not,*
> *the work will be compleated to Day or to morrow*
> *to lay on.*[53]

Then on 26th May, 1764, he writes:

> *Have made a Tpt. model on fancy & will make*
> *a few out of the mould for the next oven.*[54]

In an undated letter, which probably dates to some time in the spring of 1764, Greatbatch requests advice from Wedgwood:

> *I expected your advice in the shape*
> *of the Tpts. agreed on — the work*
> *is compleated for the shell & other*
> *Tpt. — Shou'd be glad you wou'd cut*
> *the shape upon paper you wou'd have*
> *them to be, & whether you wou'd*
> *have a ground upon them or not.*[55]

The idea of Wedgwood cutting out the shape of a teapot for Greatbatch to work from is interesting but illustrates very much the way in which potters must have worked at that time.

Finally, on 2nd November, 1764, Greatbatch announces:

> *The candlestick you order'd*
> *me to make is in great forwardness & think*
> *it will be exceeding neat.*[56]

Evidence, too, may be found in the correspondence of Greatbatch as the general workman. On 16th September, 1763, Greatbatch wrote to Wedgwood:

Lane Delf Sepr. 16th 1763

Sir,

I intended to have come over to Burslam
as this day, but Bussiness falls out
that I cannot Possible come. But
will the first Opportunity that offers.
The Turner as I mention'd has not
been at work as yet which Obliges
me to be at the Lathe constantly. [57]

A lathe is the subject of another short note to Wedgwood which is undated:

Sir,

Desire you'l send some cash by the
Bearer hereof and you'l greatly Oblge
Sr. yr. Hble St. & co.

Wm. Greatbatch

I hope you'l not fail as I want to buy a
Lathe and some other work house utensils wch.
are selling this Day at James Kents.
I intend to come over myself on Friday. [58]

James Kent was a fellow potter whose factory was nearby in Lane Delph. His factory, on the site of the later Minerva Works, was owned by the Broade family and occupied by Kent until 1764, at which time a new tenant was being sought[59].

It may have been this trip to James Kent's which necessitated the folowing request for money:

Sir,

Desire you will send by the Bearer hereof the Bill
you promised me for Mr. Kent, & seven Guineas. by
Complying wth. the Above you will Greatly Oblge
Yr. Hble St. & Co.
Wm. Greatbatch

Lower Lane

Wednesday Evening

Reced. 7 Guineas in pursuance of the above
October 18th 1764 by me Jno. Eaton
his X mark [60]

Greatbatch refers to more equipment, or rather the lack of it in a note of 1st July, 1763:

> *There be eight crates pack'd ready I have*
> *only pack'd 18 Chelsea Baskets but have about*
> *3 Doz more. I do not pack them on account they would not*
> *stand quite steady for they be very Difficult to made*
> *steady without grinding. I have never a stone at present*
> *but have spoke for one which I expect every Day.*[61]

The correspondence between Greatbatch and Wedgwood is a great source of interest and information. However, as we have already seen, there are severe limitations to this evidence which make it impossible for us to form a clear picture of Greatbatch's career as a potter and his relationship with Wedgwood. The absence of Wedgwood's letters has certainly deprived us of some most useful references, but the survival of so few of Greatbatch's own letters and notes beyond January, 1765, is an even greater loss. Consequently, a complete picture from the documentary evidence alone is impossible.

Other contemporary sources do little to add to the evidence of Greatbatch's letters. Less than three years of Greatbatch's career are adequately documented and the remaining seventeen years are a mystery. After this, the one piece of evidence to which we can refer relates to the end of Greatbatch's career. This came in 1782 and Shaw's statement that *heavy losses at length ruined him*[62] appears to be not far from the truth, for the London Gazette of 12th — 16th February, 1782, carries the following notice of bankruptcy:

Whereas a Commission of Bankrupt is awarded and issued forth against William Greatbach, of the Parish of Stoke upon Trent in the County of Stafford, Potter, and he being declared a Bankrupt, is hereby required to surrender himself to the Commissioners in the said Commission named, or the major Part of them, on the 8th, 9th, and 30th Days of March next, at Three o'Clock in the Afternoon on each of the said Days at the Crown Inn, in Newcastle under Lyme, in the said County of Stafford and make a full Discovery and Disclosure of his Estate and Effects, when and where the Creditors are to come prepared to prove their Debts, and at the second Sitting to chuse Assignees, and at the last Sitting the said Bankrupt is required to finish his Examination, and the Creditors are to assent or to dissent from the Allowance of his Certificate. All Persons indebted to the said Bankrupt, or that have any of his Effects, are not to pay or deliver the same but to whom the Commissioners shall appoint, but give Notice to Mr. Thomas Sparrow, Attorney, in Newcastle under Lyme afforesaid.

Unfortunately the papers of Mr. Sparrow, the Attorney, do not survive and, hence, the details of Greatbatch's bankruptcy are not known. However, the impact of this bankruptcy may be seen in the Land Tax Returns for Fenton Culvert. The Returns for 1781 show Greatbatch paying tax to the value of £1.1.2 on property, clearly a factory, of which the owner was William Baker, whilst also paying 3/9d tax on a house of which he was both the owner and the occupier[63]. No Land Tax Returns survive for 1782, but by 1783 Greatbatch had vacated the factory which was then occupied by William Baker[64].

What became of Greatbatch following his bankruptcy and his ceasing work at Lower Lane is something of a mystery, not aided by several conflicting pieces of information.

Thomas Byerley, as we have seen, stated that Greatbatch came to Etruria in 1788. He also stated that prior to this Greatbatch was employed by Turner — John Turner of Lane End — and was followed to Etruria by the rest of his family. Shaw tells us of Greatbatch's involvement in the building of the New Field Manufactory, at Tunstall, and of an agreement to manage the factory for its proprietor, Admiral Smith Child[65]. Elsewhere, Shaw states that *during the peace of 1763 Child established here* (at New Field) *a large manufactory, and a very spacious and elegant Mansion*[66]. Sadly, there is no evidence to corroborate either of these two references, but Shaw's date of 1763 for the construction of the New Field Manufactory does, at least, appear to be incorrect. Admiral Child did not inherit New Field Hall until 1770 and the date of the factory's subsequent erection is not known[67], although by the end of the 18th century it was being worked by the potters John and Caleb Cole[68].

Other surviving documentary evidence only serves to confuse the matter of Greatbatch's activities after his bankruptcy. There are in the Wedgwood archive four letters written at Etruria by Greatbatch, during the years 1786 and 1787, which appear to cast doubt on Byerley's date of 1788 for Greatbatch's arrival there. The first of these reads:

Mr. Thos. Byerly at
No. 12, Greek Street, Soho,
London.

Mr. Byerly,

Sir,

I have receiv'd your of the 10th Augst. in
which you mention your want of Brown only
and that you cannot send a better specimen of
(brown only) than some grape pattern plates, lately
sent down, one plate I have recd. but its so much
different a color from brown only that you must
have alter'd the color very much for its darker
than I ever saw your dark brown, or their
must be some mistake in the plate I have
got, to prevent mistakes shou'd be glad
you send by first opportunity a specimen
of the color, or colors wanted. Your complying
will very much oblige yours who am
with great Respect your most obedt
& Hble. St.

Wm. Greatbatch

Etruria August 26th 1786 [69]

The address to which Greatbatch was writing was that of Portland House, Wedgwood's London showroom at that time, which he had acquired in 1774.

Towards the end of the same year, another letter to Thomas Byerley:

Mr. Thos. Byerly at No. 12
Greek Street, Soho,
London.

Etruria, Decr. 10th 1786

Sir,

I have sent you in a crate from the
Black work[70] which Expect you will receive
safe and hope will please.

13 ll Brown only	*1 ll Ditto by Coach*
3 ll Grass Green	*NB, if soft harden with flint*
6 ll Light Brown	

I intend to send pr. next waggon a
quantity more of the same Brown only
Common yellow, green and Dark Brown,
then you may make the Color by mixing
either lighter or darker as may best suit.

I am Respectfully your most obt

Hble St.

Wm. Greatbatch

The next letter is to Josiah Wedgwood, also at Greek Street:

Josiah Wedgwood Esqre,
Greek Street,
Soho,
London.

Sir,

This morning I received your order with
regard to Lady Enniskillin's Service of
ware, but it came too late to prevent
the Dishes being fired, they being drawn
out of the kiln before yours came to hand
and are Exceeding good. I am at a loss how to
proceed until I receive your directions.
In the mean time have stopped the Center
Peice and Competeirs from being fired
waiting your answer. I am with Regard
your Most Obedt. Hble. St.

Wm. Greatbatch

Etruria July 17th 1787[72]

A final letter to Thomas Byerley:

To Mr. Thos. Byerly
No. 12, Greek Street, Soho,
London.

pr. Mr. Howarth

Etruria Octr. 8th, 1787

Mr. Byerly,

Sir,

Sent by Saturdays Waggon for
your use in London as vide

10 ll Brown only
6 ll Green
6 ll Blue   *In Crate No. 126 with*
1 ll Rose   *a Box of Clay*
1 ll Dark Purple — which I hope will answer
its Intention and merits your approbation
which is the constant wish of Yr. Obedt
             Hble. St.

        Wm. Greatbatch

P.S.

I intend to send more Cr. by the next waggon
on Saturday. I wou'd advise you to
use these Crs. by themselves as I believe they
are softer than those you have and they will
fire with less Charcoal & will be better for the
ware, shou'd you find them softer than usual
by giving a line send flux to soften the Old Colors.[73]

There can be no doubt about Greatbatch's employment at Etruria during 1786 and 1787. These letters clearly show that he was dealing with both Byerley and Wedgwood at their London showroom in Greek Street, and that he was engaged in the manufacture of colours for enamel decorating to be done at Wedgwood's London decorating shop. Greatbatch's experience of working with colours is quite apparent and his position at Etruria was clearly one of responsibility and authority. His involvement in the decorating shop at Etruria is confirmed in a letter written to Wedgwood by his son, Josiah II, on 5th April, 1788:

I read the passage in your letter to Belfield & to Fox for a good deal of the very bad ware comes out of his room. I talked to them besides & assured them that they could not continue long, if they were so inclined, to let such bad workmanship go through their hands for that you would give up the enamelling here (Etruria) *if it was not better carried on.*

…In our enamelling room every man does to many kinds of work & while that is the case our edging & lining will never be equal to what is done in London — there I believe it is the business of one man to do nothing but line & the same of edging. In order to come near the London work we must make a similar arrangement & keep as constantly to it as we can & this I have desired W. Greatbatch & Belfield to settle between them…[74].

One last letter survives which sheds further light both on Greatbatch's relationship with Wedgwood and Byerley and on his bankruptcy:

Mr. Thos. Byerley at Mr. Wedgwoods
Greek Street, Soho Square,
London

Bros'ly May 12th, 1788

Dr. Sr.

I take this opportunity to inform
you that I am now at Brosely giving orders
and directing a new kind of kiln to fire enamel
with coals which is expected to answer the purpose
and Partly to be out of the way to prevent being
arrested as some people may possible be spitefull
as the certificate is advertised to be granted the 17th
Inst. May, which am in hopes it will be then
finally finish'd and free me from all apprehensions
in future. Mr. Wedgwood advise me to give you a
line to desire you wou'd learn by some means
whether it was granted the above date or not and
advise me of it at Brosely. I apprehend you must
get information from the Bankrupt office or from Mr.
Peak, Mr. Sparrow's solicitor — I shou'd think the
latter. I purpose instead of staying at Brosely to be
at Etruria the latter end of this week — cou'd you by
any means have learn'd on the Saturday afternoon
next and gave me a line by Post directed to
me at Etruria. What is done will be acknowledged as a great
favour. Mr. Sparrow is desired to get the Certificate down
with all speed but Mr. Wd., advises to this lest
he, Mr. Spw., shou'd neglect. I am exceeding sorry
in giving you such a dissagreable trouble but hope
you will do this needfull which will always
be esteem'd a great favour by Yr. Obedt. Hble. St.

Wm. Greatbatch

P.S. My Complyts to Mrs. Byerly & self
and family.[75]

Greatbatch has explained quite clearly his reasons for being in Broseley, Shropshire. He wished to be safely out of the way of any of his creditors who might cause trouble since the advertisement announcing the impending granting of the certificate discharging him from bankruptcy had been made in the London Gazette of 22nd — 26th April, 1788:

Whereas the acting Commissioners in the Commission of Bankrupt awarded and issued forth against William Greatbatch, late of the Parish of Stoke upon Trent, in the County of Stafford, Potter, have certified to the Rt. Hon. Edward Lord Thurlow, Lord High Chancellor of Great Britain, that the said William Greatbatch hath in all Things conformed himself according to the Directions of the several Acts of Parliament made concerning Bankrupts; This is to give Notice, that, by virtue of an Act passed in the Fifth Year of His late Majesty's

Reign, his Certificate will be allowed and confirmed as the said Act directs, unless Cause be shewn to the contrary on or before the 17th Day of May next.

Greatbatch's presence in Broseley is interesting. The involvement of North Staffordshire potters in the pottery producing area around the Severn Valley is well-documented in the 18th century with many individuals moving there to settle and, presumably, to continue in the manufacture of pottery. Greatbatch's visit to the area is apparently of short duration and might be explained by the interest of Broseley potter Edward Blakeway in the development of new manufacturing techniques. This culminated in a partnership in 1793 with John Rose. From about 1783 until 1795, Blakeway appears to have been operating the pottery at Jackfield, on the River Severn, formerly worked by the Thursfield family. After this time, he and Rose moved across the river to Coalport[76]. The outcome of Greatbatch's involvement at Broseley is not known.

We may assume that Greatbatch returned to Etruria, as was his intention, immediately after the allowance of his certificate. After this time, the documentation which relates to his employment at Etruria commences on 28th May, 1790, and continues until 20th February, 1807. His position at Etruria was, without doubt, one of considerable responsibility, perhaps that of general manager. Amongst his many concerns was the ordering of deliveries of fritt from nearby Cheddleton mill, coal, flint, stone, marl, fire bricks, ashes and *Biskt pitchers*, or unglazed waste pottery, the latter of which was to be ground for use in the manufacture of fire bricks. In addition, he was overseeing payments for work done — Ralph Parr, for example, received 1/6d for *drawing Hot glaz'd ovens* on 19th February, 1791[77], and a further 3 shillings on 31st December, 1791, for *drawing hot glaze kilns and firing a Number of crusibles*[78]. The disposal of the factory's waste was another of his concerns: *Please to pay Joseph Boulton, Peter Hassall & Co, for carrying, loading & unloading all the ridled Burnt shraff into Mr. Wedgwood's Meadow — 14s 0d*[79], and also *Please to pay the bearer Thos. Brooff for taking a Boat load of shords — 2/6*[80]. Greatbatch was also attending to the provision, or repair of items of factory equipment: blungers, paddle stails for the same, *a slop pot for Wm. Breeze wheel, 2 Benches fix'd up in the mill chambers*[81], and *3 hoops upon a lead cask and such other repairs as are wanting for Mr. Wedgwood Sons & Co*[82].

At the time that he was working at Etruria, it appears that Greatbatch became a member of the Freemasons, a movement whose popularity was growing rapidly at this time. *Wm. Greatbatch* is listed as *Potter of Etruria* in the membership list of the Etruria lodge, an entry dated 15th February, 1803[83]. Attention has been drawn to the masonic elements of some of the prints[84] which appear on some of the pottery produced by Greatbatch before his bankruptcy, but there can be no significance to these beyond the widespread popularity of masonic subjects during the third quarter of the 18th century, subjects which were frequently used by the manufacturers of printed pottery.

It is probable that Greatbatch retired from work at the Etruria factory at some stage during, or shortly after the year 1807, when his notes cease. He would have been seventy-two years old at that time. Byerley's letter of 25th May, 1807, (above, pages 28-29) suggests that the central issue is the payment of a pension to Greatbatch which was equal to his salary: *I never heard that any engagement or promise was made him to continue the whole or part of his salary during his life*[85]. There is some evidence to suggest what the outcome of this letter was.

Simeon Shaw writes of the high regard in which Greatbatch was held by Wedgwood, a regard which manifested itself in the very high salary paid to him during his subsequent employment at Etruria, as well as *a house rent free*[86]. The Etruria Rent Book for 1797 — 1810 shows that Greatbatch was occupying House

No. 53, whose rent in 1798 was £16.14.0 *per annum*, a very great sum[87]. This had increased to eighteen guineas *per annum* by 1805, twenty pounds in 1809 and twenty-five pounds in 1810. Shaw appears to have been well-informed, for in 1798 Greatbatch's rent is noted as having been paid by JW and TB, while between 1799 and 1807 it was paid *by Manufactory*[88]. By 1809, Greatbatch is noted as paying the whole of his rent himself, perhaps as a consequence of Byerley's overtures to Josiah II.

Both the Etruria Rent Book and the Stoke Rate Book of 1807 — 1808 bear witness to Greatbatch's continued presence at Etruria, as well as to the fact that he occupied one of the larger houses in the village. In the Rate Book, Greatbatch is listed under *J. Wedgwood Esq.* as occupying a house valued at 5/4d *per annum*[89].

Wedgwood must have thought very highly of Greatbatch. His employment at Etruria, and more particularly the high salary he received, cannot have been simply an act of charity on Wedgwood's part, but must have reflected his potential worth to the company.

One possible reason for Greatbatch's position at Etruria presents itself. In 1788, almost certainly at Michaelmass (29th September), Thomas Wedgwood terminated his partnership for the production of useful wares with his cousin Josiah and left Etruria[90]. He thereupon began an independent potting career, having taken premises at the Hill Works, Burslem, but this was cut short by his death on 10th October, 1788[91]. Thomas's move from Etruria deprived Josiah Wedgwood of an invaluable and most reliable partner who had been responsible for the production of his most prestigious commission, the service for Catherine the Great of Russia, and upon whom he had depended for the day-to-day running of the factory. Did Wedgwood intend Greatbatch to be the replacement, as works manager, for Thomas Wedgwood? Byerley's words suggest that this might indeed be so: *William G. came to Etruria in 1788 — when Thomas Wedgwood declared his intention of settling at Hill House with his family*[92]. Wedgwood certainly had need of a replacement for 'useful' Thomas: despite assistance from his nephew, Thomas Byerley, he had little support from his sons who had no interest in potting. Greatbatch was an experienced and practical potter who Wedgwood valued highly, as his salary shows, and who was capable of taking on the day to day running of the factory. Greatbatch must indeed have earned his position at Etruria and fully deserved Shaw's praise for being *a general workman of first rate abilities*[93].

1. Shaw 1829, 190.
2. W/M: 1131.
3. *ibid.*
4. Shaw 1829, 189.
5. Words of Enoch Wood, Aaron Wood's son. See above, page 24, footnote 36.
6. W/M: 1131.
7. Luxmore 1924, 47 — 50.
8. Mankowitz 1953.
9. Towner 1957, Towner 1963, Towner 1978.
10. Wedgwood MSS: 121-23528.
11. First referred to as the Ivy House in Meteyard 1865.
12. John Wedgwood Rent Account Book, p. 30. City Museum & Art Gallery, Stoke-on-Trent.
13. For example Niblett 1984, 3.
14. John Wedgwood: *op. cit.*, note 20, p. 30.
15. Niblett 1984, 5.
16. Towner 1957, 26; Towner 1978, 34.
17. Wedgwood MSS: 30105-30.
18. *ibid.*: 22325-30.
19. *ibid.*: 22323-30.
20. Aqualate Papers, D-1788, V.96 (SCRO), referred to in Mallet 1967, 210 — 211.
21. *ibid.*
22. *ibid.*
23. Wedgwood MSS: 22322-30.
24. Mountford 1972a, 91.
25. Wedgwood MSS: 30104-30.

26. *ibid.*: 121-23528.
27. *ibid.*: 30106-30.
28. Towner 1957, 26.
29. Wedgwood MSS: 22324-30.
30. Land Tax Returns for Fenton Culvert (SCRO).
31. Wedgwood MSS: 121-23528.
32. Stoke upon Trent Parish Register III.
33. Wedgwood MSS: 22401-30.
34. *ibid.*: 30106-30.
35. *ibid.*: 22324-30.
36. *ibid.*: 22348-30.
37. Reilly 1989 I, 188.
38. Wedgwood MSS: 4954-6.
39. *ibid.*: 30133-30.
40. *ibid.*: 22376-30.
41. *ibid.*: 22332-30.
42. *ibid.*: 30126-30.
43. *ibid.*: 30127-30.
44. *ibid.*: 22390-30.
45. *ibid.*: 22403-30.
46. Niblett 1984, 5.
47. Wedgwood MSS: 30137-30.
48. *ibid.*: 22341-30.
49. *ibid.*: 22348-30.
50. *ibid.*: 22402-30.
51. Shaw 1829, 190.
52. Wedgwood MSS: 22398-30.
53. *ibid.*: 22374-30.
54. *ibid.*: 22376-30.
55. *ibid.*: 22337-30.
56. *ibid.*: 22389-30.
57. *ibid.*: 30123-30.
58. *ibid.*: 27397-30.
59. Haggar 1951, 22 note 1.
60. Wedgwood MSS: 22387-30.
61. *ibid.*: 22340-30.
62. Shaw 1829, 190.
63. Land Tax Returns for Fenton Culvert (SCRO).
64. *ibid.*
65. Shaw 1829, 190.
66. *ibid.*, 20.
67. Victoria County History 1963, 92.
68. *ibid.*, 101.
69. Wedgwood MSS: 14276-81.
70. The crate of ware which Greatbatch has sent from the Black work is presumably of black basalt intended for the decorating shop. The Black work was that part of Wedgwood's Etruria factory which was set aside solely for the manufacture of black basalt which would otherwise have resulted in the contamination of other wares made at the factory.
71. Wedgwood MSS: 14277-81.
72. *ibid.*: 14278-81.
73. *ibid.*: 14279-81.
74. W/M: 1460; Farrar 1906, 62 — 63.
75. Wedgwood MSS: 14280-81.
76. I am indebted to Dr. Barrie Trinder for this information.
77. Wedgwood MSS: 22409-30.
78. *ibid.*: 22410-30.
79. *ibid.*: 14298-81, dated 17th August, 1793.
80. *ibid.*: 14318-81, dated 20th March, 1803.
81. *ibid.*: 14281-81.
82. *ibid.*: 14289-81.
83. Entry No. 320, referred to and illustrated in Greenwald 1979, 241.
84. For example Plate XIX.
85. Wedgwood MSS: 121-23528.
86. Shaw 1829, 190.
87. Etruria Rent Book 1797 — 1810, p. 55. Wedgwood MSS: 28683-43.
88. *ibid.*
89. Stoke Rate Book, 1807 — 1808, p. 69 (Hanley Reference Library: o/s S.850.352).
90. An early reference to this occurs in a letter from Josiah Wedgwood II to his father, dated 3rd March, 1788. W/M: 1460.
91. Wedgwood MSS: E50-29975. Also tombstone in Burslem Churchyard.
92. *ibid.*: 121-23528.
93. Shaw 1829, 190.

CHAPTER 3

THE GREATBATCH SITE, FENTON AND ITS POTTERS

The discovery, early in 1978, of a small quantity of 18th century factory wasters in Fenton, Stoke-on-Trent, unexpectedly brought the name of William Greatbatch to the attention of ceramics students. These wasters came to light on ground which had been used briefly as a campsite by gypsies who left behind them a deep hole in which fires had been lit. Immediately after the gypsies' departure, the area was visited by Mr. J. Linden Evans who recognised the pottery amongst the spoil from this hole for what it was and notified Donald Towner of the discovery. Towner's identification of these wasters as products of Greatbatch's factory[1] ultimately led to the involvement of the Archaeology Section of the City Museum & Art Gallery, Stoke-on-Trent, and a small-scale trial excavation was begun by volunteers of the Stoke-on-Trent Museum Archaeological Society under the direction of the author. This excavation was to last for more than two years, from October 1979 to November 1981, and was to result in the recovery of several tons of pottery wasters, saggars, kiln furniture and other material associated with the production of pottery during the second half of the 18th century. The attribution of the wasters to Greatbatch was confirmed in the most striking manner possible. Hundreds of pieces were found to be marked with a previously unidentified monogram consisting of Greatbatch's initials *WG*, while several pieces marked with his name in full removed any doubt about this link.

The discovery was made on a small triangular plot of waste land immediately to the south of the main Stoke to Longton road, City Road, and immediately to the west of its junction with Glebedale Road, formerly Station Road, on the outskirts of the present town centre of Fenton[2] (Fig. 6). The plot of land occupies an elevated position above both roads, falling away steeply to the north. The plot itself has been levelled by the construction of a tennis court earlier this century. To the west of the plot there is now a car park where once stood the 19th century Sutherland Pottery, demolished in 1962. Now completely overgrown, the land is used merely as a site for the advertising hoardings which mark its northern and eastern limits.

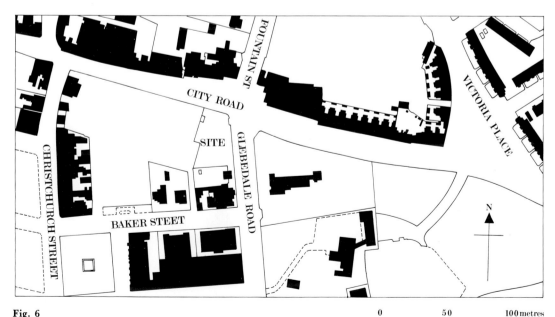

Fig. 6
Location of the Greatbatch site in present day Fenton.

0   50   100 metres

A study of the early maps of the area has revealed no evidence that this land was ever developed in any way. The earliest of the useful maps of the area, Yates' *Map of the Countie of Stafford*, published in 1775[3], printed at one inch to the mile, is an extremely valuable guide to the extent of settlement and industrial development in the area at this time (Fig. 7). The course of the main Stoke to Longton road, which had been turnpiked in 1759, is clearly shown: leaving Stoke to the south of the churchyard, it runs in a generally south-easterly direction, passing through the named settlements of Lower Lane and Lane Delph, before arriving, after one and a half miles, at the settlement of Lane End, now absorbed within the town of Longton. Lower Lane is roughly the area occupied by the present day centre of Fenton, while Lane Delph to the south-east has lost its early name and has been swallowed up by the modern development which extends, unbroken, between Fenton and Longton. It can be seen from Yates' map that settlement has grown up as a ribbon development along the turnpike road, with the largest concentration of buildings being that at Lane Delph. The Greatbatch site is located roughly to the east of the easternmost of the buildings shown on the south side of the road at Lower Lane, the road having adhered to its course in this area since the time of Yates' map.

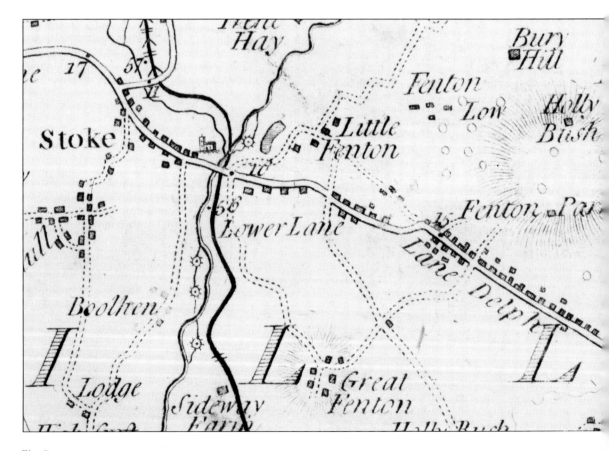

Fig. 7
Fenton in 1775: detail from Yates' Map.

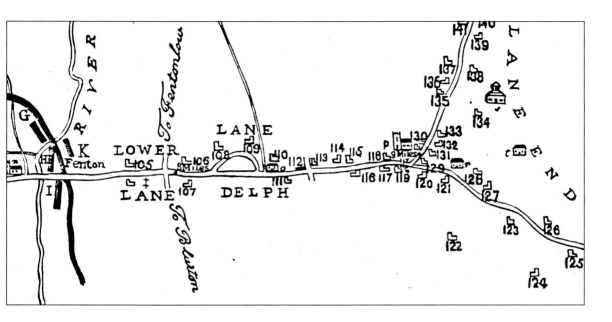

Fig. 8
Detail from Allbut's *Map of the Potteries, Staffordshire,* published in 1802, showing Stoke upon Trent, Lower Lane, Lane Delph and Lane End. This version reproduced for P. W. L. Adams, *A History of the Adams Family* (1941).

The factories indicated in the Fenton area are:

105	Harrison and Hyatt	Lower-lane
+ +	Robert Clulow and Co.	Lower-lane
106	Bourne and Baker	Fenton
107	Chelenor and Adams	Fenton
108	Bagnall and Hull	Lane-delf
109	John Lucock	Lane-delf
110	William Pratt	Lane-delf
111	Mason and Co.	Lane-delf
112	Thomas Forester	Lane-delf
113	— — Shelley	Lower-lane
114 115	Samuel Baker (Barker)	Lower-lane
116	Samuel Spode	Folley
117	Joseph Myatt	Folley
118	Robert Garner	Lane-end
119	Charles Harvey	Lane-end

The site cannot be pinpointed more exactly on Allbut's map of 1802, which was printed at two inches to the mile[4]. This most useful map illustrates and numbers individual factories, with a list of their occupants given separately. The factories in Lower Lane are clearly shown and our site must lie to the east of the factory numbered 107, which is listed as then being occupied by Chelenor and Adams (Fig. 8).

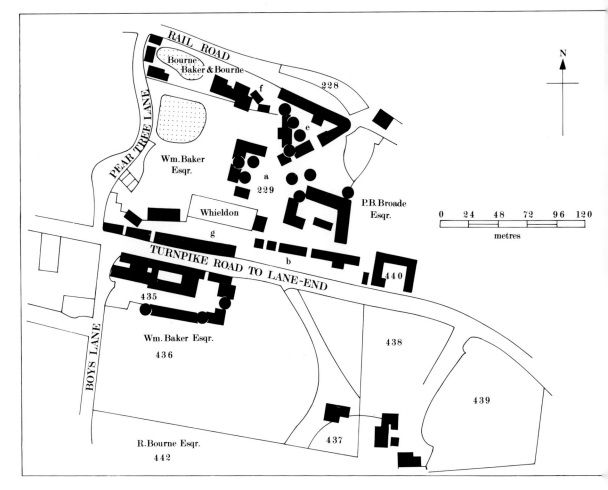

Fig. 9
The area of the Greatbatch site in 1828: detail brought together from the Tithe Redemption Certificates (Lichfield Joint Record Offic

Details from Schedule

228 One other messuage and a stack yard.
     Occupiers: John Bentley, Messrs. Bourne, Baker and Bourne.
229a Potworks and site thereof.
     Occupiers: Messrs. Bourne, Baker and Bourne.
229b Four messuages and garden adjoining Pear Tree Lane.
     Occupiers: Various.
229e Potworks and site thereof.
     In hand.
229f Steam engine, mills and other buildings and the sites thereof.
     In hand.
229g Twenty four messuages and gardens.
     Occupiers: various.
435 A messuage and potworks with the sites thereof, and twenty four other messuages
     with the sites thereof and gardens.
     Occupiers: In hand and various.
436 Also lands called the Ruck Hole and plantations.
     Occupiers: Messrs. Bourne, Baker and Bourne.
437 A messuage with offices and outbuildings and the sites thereof, garden, pleasure
     ground and plantations.
     In hand.
438 A messuage with offices and outbuildings and the sites thereof, garden, pleasure
     ground and plantations.
     In hand.
439 A piece of land called Lane End Ryton.
     Occupiers: Messrs. Bourne, Baker and Bourne.
440 Two other messuages with the sites thereof.
     Occupiers: Joseph Woolley, James Clews.
442 A piece of land called Church Ryton.
     Occupiers: Messrs. Bourne, Baker and Bourne.

The site first becomes clearly recognisable in the Tithe Redemption Certificates of 1828[5], where it can be identified immediately to the east of a large potworks (No. 435), later the Sutherland Pottery, forming part of a larger plot of land belonging to the potters, Messrs. Bourne, Baker and Bourne (Fig. 9). In the accompanying Schedule, this plot (No. 436) is described thus: *Also Lands called the Ruck Hole and Plantations.*

The name Ruck Hole is significant. The term is derived from the local term for a pottery factory waste tip *shord* (i.e. sherd or shard) *ruck*. Clearly, in the late 1820s the land was recognisable, or remembered as a place where pottery waste from a nearby factory had been, or was still being dumped.

The cartographic detail of the 1828 Tithe Redemption Certificates is reproduced almost exactly by Hargreaves' *Map of the Staffordshire Potteries*, which was published in 1832 and printed at six inches to the mile (Fig. 10). The most striking difference between the two is that Hargreaves' map shows the large plot of land, *the Ruck Hole and Plantations*, divided in such a way as to create a small triangular plot immediately to the east of the potworks, which is the area occupied by the Greatbatch site.

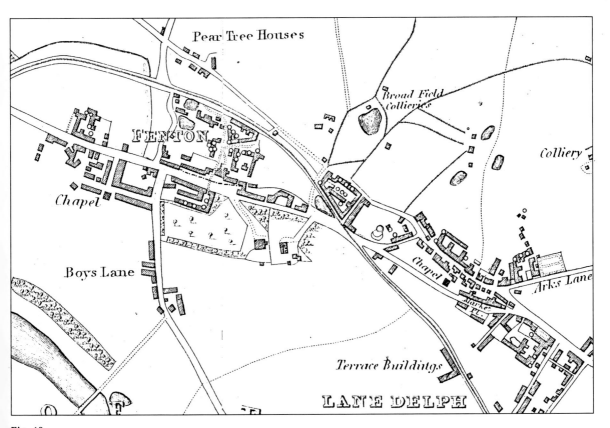

Fig. 10
The area of the Greatbatch site in 1832: detail from Hargreaves' *Map of the Staffordshire Potteries, & Newcastle.*

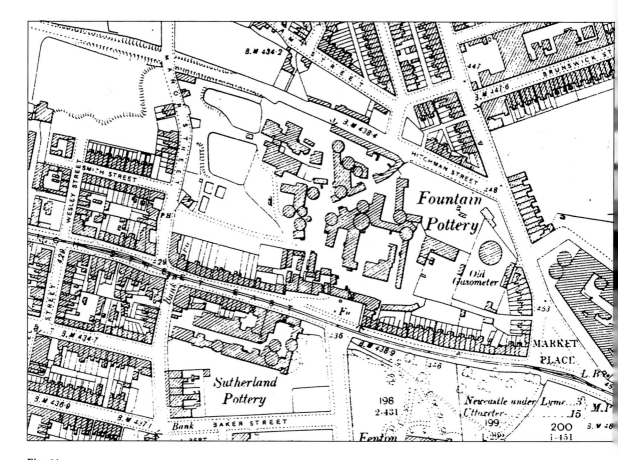

Fig. 11
The area of the Greatbatch site in 1900.

Later maps of the area add nothing to this picture, although by 1900 the plot had been divided by the construction of Station Road, now Glebedale Road (Fig. 11). There is no sign whatsoever of the site having been developed in any way since the early 19th century, at the latest. The excavation of 1979 — 1981 confirmed this.

Contrary to the earliest report of the discovery of the Greatbatch wasters[6], there had been no factory on this site. Archaeological excavation here confirmed the accuracy of the Schedule accompanying the Tithe Redemption Certificates. The plot of land had indeed been a *Ruck Hole*, a pottery waste tip used by a nearby factory during the second half of the 18th century. An enormous quantity of pottery wasters, saggars, kiln furniture, ash, bricks and other factory refuse had been deposited into an existing hole of some considerable size which was almost certainly a marl hole, or clay winning pit of the sort which were ubiquitous in the Potteries.

The practice of disposing of factory waste in this way is quite normal in the area, even to the present day. The Potteries towns are littered with the waste of centuries of pottery production which has been tipped into every available clay pit, marl hole or mine shaft, as well as being used as hard core in construction or as an aid to drainage. There is no pattern to this practice of tipping, other than the logic of economising on transport wherever possible and making use of sites in the neighbourhood of the producing factories. Such tips may be large or small, shared communal dumps, or areas used by single factories. It is because of the proven association of this one, relatively small waste tip in Fenton with a single known potter, William Greatbatch, that it is of such great importance to the field of ceramic research.

The excavation uncovered an area of approximately twelve metres square within the marl hole, which was cut to a depth of three metres into the natural clay. The southern and western edges of the hole were defined, the latter sloping downwards from the west at an angle of between forty-five and sixty degrees. The manner in which the greater part of the hole was filled is immediately apparent upon looking at the clearly defined tipping lines. A vast quantity of waste had been tipped into the marl hole from the west: narrow layers of grey, brown, red, black and white ash from the factory's ovens contained fragments of saggars, firebricks, kiln furniture and waste pottery, all completely intermixed. Within several of the layers individual depositions could be identified: stacks of saucers or teabowls, for example, which appeared to have been carried to the spot and dropped, to be recovered in the place where they fell.

These layers of waste represent a chronological sequence of deposition within which there were three major phases recognisable. Each of these phases was physically quite separate. The earliest of the phases, Phase I, comprised a series of horizontal layers, some 0.5 metres deep, across the very bottom of the marl hole. The topmost layers of this phase had been compacted as if by trampling. Phase I underlay both Phase II and Phase III. Phase II comprised numerous individual layers which had been tipped from the western edge of the marl hole, but was separated from the latest phase, Phase III, by a brown humic layer, suggesting that the tip had been in a state of disuse for a period of time. Phase III had been deposited in the same manner as Phase II, by tipping from the west, with the layers trailing off to the east.

A period of disuse would explain the many differences which exist between the pottery recovered from these two later phases. These differences are apparent in both the style and the quantities of the various types present. A development of production is clearly represented by the pottery from the two phases, with a move towards lighter wares in the Neo-Classical taste and away from the coloured glazes and elaborate moulded forms of the rococo style. Similar difference exists, too, between the wares of Phase I and the succeeding Phase II, most notably

Plate 2
The Greatbatch site: section through Phase III.

Plate 3
The Greatbatch site: section through Phase II.

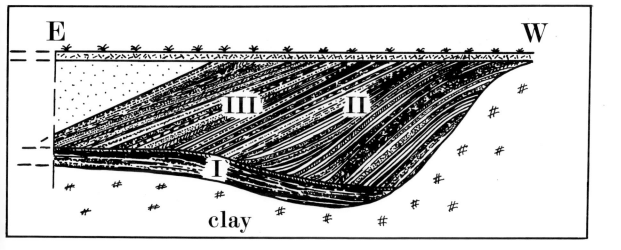

Fig. 12
Schematic section through the Greatbatch factory waste tip to illustrate the relation of the three phases of tipping.

Plate 4
Detail of waste and layers of tipping (Phase III).

Plate 5
Wasters *in situ* during excavation (Phase III).

Fig. 13
WG monogram used by Greatbatch on flatwares of Phase III.

in the quantities of blackware and white salt-glazed stoneware which were found in Phase I; the former is almost totally absent from the later phases, while salt-glazed stoneware occurs in much smaller quantities in Phase II. Alongside the many differences in the pottery from the three phases, there is also considerable uniformity which argues persuasively in favour of a process of continual development. Many of the pottery types were common to all three phases, particularly moulded fruit wares — cauliflower, pineapple, etc. — and the details of their moulding suggests that they were produced from the same range of block moulds. The same applied relief decoration, too, appears on vessels throughout, as do handles, handle terminals and other features.

It was the pottery from Phase III of the site which was initially attributed to Greatbatch[7]. The excavation produced large quantities of sherds which bore the impressed initials *WG*, either as a monogram (Fig. 13), or as an element of a pseudo-Chinese seal mark (Fig. 43). In addition to these potentially ambiguous marks, there were a number of signatures which formed part of printed inscriptions (Plate 149). Many printed designs which had previously been attributed to Greatbatch on the grounds of stylistic similarities to signed pieces were also recognised amongst the excavated pottery. There are no problems whatsoever in assigning the Phase III wares to Greatbatch.

Neither Phase I nor Phase II produced any signed pieces apart from workmen's tools; indeed, marks of any sort were few. However, the evidence for linking the pottery of these phases to each other, and to the wares of Phase III, is very good indeed. The continued use of the same moulded reliefs, moulded bodies, handles and terminals, argues more strongly for a continuation in production than changes in glaze colour or varying quantities of the different types produced can argue against. The only real problem is the dating of these earlier phases.

For Greatbatch, we have both a start and a terminal date: his correspondence shows quite clearly he commenced business during the second half of 1762, while by February 1782 he was bankrupt. He had vacated his factory by the following year at the latest, although we may assume that he ceased production immediately upon being declared bankrupt. The question is how much of this twenty year period is represented by the wasters recovered from the Greatbatch site.

There is strong evidence to suggest that Phase III extends more or less until the time of his bankruptcy. One workman's profile found on the site was dated 1777 (Fig. 16), while numerous sherds of the well-known transfer print *The XII Houses of Heaven* have been recovered, together with its inscription *Published as the Act directs Jany. 4 1778 by W. Greatbatch Lane Delft Staffordshire* (Plate 148). Other vessels found on the site match exactly pieces in collections which bear dated inscriptions which range from 1774 to 1777. In the light of this, it is suggested that the date range for the wares of Phase III is *c.* 1770 — 1782.

Phase II is much more difficult to date with certainty as there is little concrete evidence. The only dated piece from this phase is another workman's profile, broken into two, which bears the fragmentary inscription *(1)761*[or *7*]. The final digit appears to be a '1', with the hooked top stroke which is typical of the period, and yet this is almost identical to the '7'. A more accurate date is suggested by a creamware teapot in the Central Museum and Art Gallery, Northampton, which bears the painted inscription *Spencer Howe And Liberty*, a reference to the 1768 parliamentary election in Northamptonshire (Plate 91). This is an example of the most common type of teapot recovered from both Phases II and I of the Greatbatch site, one which, it is suggested, was in production for some time before 1768. Finally, there are elements of the decoration used on Greatbatch's earlier wares which can be shown to post-date the published source of their inspiration. These are a pair of oriental figures, which appear as applied decorative reliefs (Fig. 37, Type 38), and clusters of sea shells, which are worked into moulded wares (Plate 10), both taken from *The Ladies Amusement*, a collection of copper plate engravings published by Robert Sayer. This volume appeared in two editions, the first in 1759/ 60 and the second in 1762. *Shell teapots* first appear in Greatbatch's invoices to Wedgwood in 1764 (below, page 98). The limited evidence, together with the general style of the Phase II wares and the darker colour of creamwares of this phase, suggests a date range of *c.* 1765 — 1770.

There is no additional dated material for Phase I, but the conclusion must be that it pre-dates Phase II, at least slightly. Consequently a date range of 1762 — 1765 cannot be far wrong. In short, we have represented on the Greatbatch site, virtually the whole of the twenty year period during which he was in production, with the possible exception of a short period — of two or three years at most — which appears to separate Phases II and III.

* * *

Having identified Greatbatch's factory waste tip, we must turn to the question of where the factory itself was located. Given the problems of transporting large quantities of waste in the 18th century, it is unlikely that the tip was far removed from the factory site from which the waste originated. There is, in fact, some evidence to support this view. However, before looking at the evidence for Greatbatch's factory, it is necessary, first of all, to explain something of the area in which Greatbatch was working.

Fenton has always been something of a neglected corner of the Potteries. Contemporary descriptions of the area are few and date, almost entirely, to the 19th century. Writers seem to have found little which merited their attention and, consequently, their comments tend to rapidly dismiss the area. In 1817, for example, Pitt described it thus: *Lower Lane and Lane Delph present nothing remarkable, and indeed they may be properly incorporated with Lane End, of which they form a kind of suburbs*[8]. This attitude has prevailed even to the present day and, not surprisingly, Fenton is the one Potteries town to have been ignored by that great local writer Arnold Bennett, whose Five Towns should, in fact, have been Six.

The complex nature of the area now known simply as Fenton confuses even the local inhabitants. From the 13th century the area comprised two separate manorial townships, Fenton Vivian and Fenton Culvert[9], known alternatively as Little Fenton and Great Fenton, whose boundaries are first shown on Hargreaves' map of 1832 (Endpaper). The original centres of population within these townships were at Little Fenton and Great Fenton; by the third quarter of the 18th century, however, the growth of the pottery industry saw additional spreads of settlement along the newly turnpiked road at Lower Lane, at Lane Delph, and at the Foley, the area midway between Lane Delph and Lane End which is not named on Yates' map.

In 1843, Ward wrote of Fenton:

The population and trading establishments of the two Fentons are so intermixed, that it is impossible to treat them singly throughout, nor is it necessary to do so. The houses, manufactories, and buildings, principally stand upon or near the boundary line of the Townships (i.e. Fenton Vivian and Fenton Culvert), *being dispersed along the main road, between Stoke and Longton, a distance of about two miles. They hardly assume the character of a town, but rather present the appearance of three separate villages...*[10]

These settlements may well have been quite separate in origin, but even in the 18th century the distinctions between them were blurred and our documentary sources bear witness to the confusion. As a result of this it is often difficult to locate the homes or factories of known individuals within the general area.

Shaw has told us that Greatbatch *commenced business on his own account at the manufactory at Fenton, now a small part of the extensive establishment of Messrs. Bourne, Baker and Bourne*[11], and reference has already been made to evidence which serves to corroborate this (above, page 58). The Land Tax Returns for 1781, the earliest surviving for the area, show that William Greatbatch was the tenant of a large factory in the township of Fenton Culvert whose owner was William Baker; the tax payable was £1.1.2[12]. Following Greatbatch's bankruptcy in 1782, the factory appears to have been vacated by its tenant and to have been occupied by its owner, William Baker[13].

William Baker, a master potter, was the father of the William Baker of the Bourne, Baker and Bourne partnership. He died in 1785[14], and in 1793 his widow, Sarah, married another potter, Ralph Bourne[15]. By 1794 Ralph Bourne had entered into partnership with his stepson William Baker, operating from a factory in Fenton Vivian: in 1794, *Bourne & Co.* are tenants of a factory owned by *Mrs. Baker*, whose Land Tax is 13/6d, while by 1796 they are listed as *Bourne, Baker & Co.*[16] The partnership seems to have operated under, or at least been recognised by various names: also in 1796 we find both *Bourne, Baker & Bourne*[17] and *Ralph Bourne & Co.*[18], while in 1799 and 1800 we have *Mrs. Bourne & Sons*, and in 1801 *Mrs. Bourne & others*[19]. *Bourne, Baker & Bourne* reappear in the Land Tax Returns for 1817[20]. The third member of the partnership was John Bourne, the brother of Ralph.

The Fenton Vivian factory from which the partnership operated in its various guises is listed in the ownership of William Baker from 1797. The factory itself is shown on Allbut's map of 1802 and listed as being occupied by *Bourne and Baker, Fenton*[21]. It is situated on the north side of the Stoke to Longton road, in the area between present day Fountain Street, William Street and Manor Road, and within a fifty to one hundred metres of the site of Greatbatch's waste tip. In the 18th and early 19th centuries this was Lower Lane. The Schedule of the Tithe Redemption Certificates indicates that, in 1828, the factory was owned by Messrs. Bourne, Baker and Bourne[22]. The factory can be seen to have been a large complex with various tenants in different parts (Fig. 9).

We know, however, that Bourne, Baker and Bourne operated *two extensive manufactories* in Fenton[23], the second of which was on the south side of the Stoke to Longton road almost directly opposite their factory on the northern side of the road[24].

In 1798, we find *Bourne & Baker* both owning and occupying a factory in Fenton Culvert[25] as well as their factory in Fenton Vivian. The Land Tax payable on this works — £1.1.2 — indicates that this was the same factory vacated by Greatbatch between 1781 and 1783 and occupied by William Baker by 1783. This factory is in Fenton Culvert rather than Fenton Vivian because, at this point, the boundary between the two townships runs directly along the main road; however, the area is still that known as Lower Lane, as the settlement which grew up along the road did not respect the township boundaries. The Land Tax Returns indicate that in 1791 Greatbatch's former factory passed from the Baker family into the ownership of the potter Sampson Bagnall, who worked there until 1797[26]. From 1798, *Bourne and Baker* are listed as owners and occupiers, although in 1800 the partnership appears in its extended form of *Bourne, Baker & Bourne*[27]. In 1803, the factory is divided into two apparently equal parts, each with a Land Tax of 10/7d payable, between William Baker and Ralph Bourne; this is still the case in 1827[28].

Shaw's evidence for the location of Greatbatch's factory is supported admirably by the Land Tax Returns. The factory shown in the Tithe Redemption Certificates in 1828, and again on Hargeaves' map of 1832, is the very site where Greatbatch was in production between 1762 and 1782. The factory can be identified on later maps of the area: in 1878 it is shown as an encaustic tile works[29], while in 1900 it is named as the Sutherland Pottery (Fig. 11); the factory was demolished in 1962.

There can be no doubt about the location of Greatbatch's factory, but questions must be asked about the accuracy of Allbut's 1802 map. As we have shown, at this time the factory was most definitely in the ownership of William Baker and Ralph Bourne, both of whom were also working there. Allbut, however, identifies manufacturers Chelenor and Adams on this site (Fig. 8, no. 107), but this cannot be substantiated. *Challener, John & Adams* are listed as *Manufacturers of Staffordshire ware* in 1796[30], and they also appear in the Land Tax Returns for Fenton Culvert between 1795 and 1800 occupying small premises whose tax was only 3/9d, compared with £1.1.2 payable by Greatbatch on his factory; in 1801, *John Chalinor* appears alone, and in 1803 the factory is in the ownership and occupancy of *Bourne, Baker and Bourne*[31]. The Land Tax Returns do not allow us to identify the site of this factory.

That Greatbatch's factory should be on the south side of the Stoke to Longton road, adjacent to his waste tip, would appear logical. Moreover, the way in which the wasters had been tipped — from the western edge of the marl hole — does itself suggest such a location for the factory. It is reassuring that documentary evidence can confirm this, underlining the importance of looking to original sources for evidence. This is particularly important in the present case, where we lack authoritative accounts of the area by contemporary writers, and where those few who did set pen to paper in the 19th century displayed an almost total disregard for one of the largest areas of settlement in the Potteries.

It is surprising that Fenton should have been neglected by writers when we consider how many pottery manufacturers were established in the area by the second half of the 18th century. The names of many of these manufacturers are known to us, partly through surviving documents of the period, and partly through the information contained in Shaw's *History*, although specific reliable detail about their businesses and their products is slight. The years after 1780 are considerably better documented than those which precede, with the advent of the trades directories, but the majority of Greatbatch's contemporaries are little more than names to us, supplemented here and there by a little factual evidence and a great deal of tradition.

THOMAS WHIELDON

Greatbatch's best known contemporary in Fenton was Thomas Whieldon with whom he had almost certainly served his apprenticeship. Limited documentary evidence and references in Shaw's *History* have been supplemented by the results of archaeological excavations on the site of Whieldon's factory to give us a reasonably clear picture of the nature, if not the scale of Whieldon's production.

In 1747 Whieldon is recorded as the tenant of a newly-built potworks in Fenton Vivian. His landlord was the potter John Peat, bankrupt soon after, whose property included: *all those Pot ovens, houses, Buildings, Ware houses, Work houses, Throwing houses with Appurtenances in the holding of Thomas Whieldon, Lately built & standing Upon one of the said closes in ffenton Vivian aforesaid Called Stokeley Leasows & Adjoyining to the Great Road leading from Newcastle to Uttoxeter*[32]. In 1748 Whieldon purchased the factory[33].

By 1750 Whieldon owned an additional potworks at Fenton Low, an area half a mile to the north-east, for on 25th March of this year, he let this to the potter William Meir[34]. Subsequent tenants included the potter Edward Warburton, his widow Alice and son Edward, who paid rent until at least 1762 when the records cease[35]. Edward Warburton the younger died in 1767[36], but as the potworks at Fenton Low were amongst the possessions left by Whieldon in his will in 1795[37], long after he himself had ceased in business, it would be reasonable to assume that there were other tenants.

Past writers, confused by the multiplicity of Fentons, have concluded that Whieldon first worked at the potworks at Fenton Low, later to move to the factory at Fenton Vivian or Little Fenton. Additional support for this view was found in the large quantity of wasters of mid-18th century date which have been recovered periodically from the area of Fenton Low[38]; these were of types commonly associated with Whieldon and the temptation to assign their production to Whieldon was, therefore, understandable. There is, however, no evidence whatsoever that Whieldon ever potted at Fenton Low. This idea seems to have arisen out of a misunderstanding of the Fenton referred to by Shaw in a passage which states that: *In 1740, Mr. Thomas Whieldon's manufactory at Little Fenton, consisted of a small range of low buildings, all thatched*[39]. Shaw refers to Little Fenton (i.e. Fenton Vivian), which is most definitely not Fenton Low, and in view of Shaw's tendency to generalise over dates, it is probable that it is the date, and not the location of Whieldon's factory which is given incorrectly. Consequently, the large quantity of ceramic wasters recovered from the ground at Fenton Low are perhaps best attributed to one or other of Whieldon's tenants[40].

Whieldon is first recorded as a potter of *Stoke upon Trent* in 1744 when, at the age of twenty-five he married Anne Shaw[41], but apart from this little is known of his early career. His Account Book provides much information for his business during the period 1749 — 1762 and, of course, his partnership with Josiah Wedgwood from 1754 — 1759 is well-known. Beyond this, there is a marked shortage of documentary evidence. It is not even known at what date Whieldon ceased potting, which he certainly had done by the time of his appointment as High Sheriff of Staffordshire in 1786. It is curious, however, that even as early as 1758 Whieldon is referred to, not as a potter, but as *Gentleman*, upon the occasion of his second marriage[42]. One suspects a rather more relaxed attitude towards business by this date.

This emphasis upon Whieldon is considered appropriate here for a number of reasons. Firstly, Whieldon is a central figure in any discussion of the pottery of the mid-18th century. Secondly, there is the probable link with Greatbatch, and, thirdly, he is, apart from Greatbatch, the best documented Fenton potter of the period. Finally, so much rubbish has been written about Whieldon and his wares that every opportunity must be taken to counter this, particularly when there are direct implications for the ceramics under discussion in this volume. Many of the wares manufactured by Whieldon are of types now known to have been made by Greatbatch and have been found on the Greatbatch site. *Whieldon ware,* or *Whieldon-type ware* are terms which are widely accepted in describing a variety of ceramics, particularly the tortoiseshell wares, but which lead to problems in any objective research into the pottery of the period. The limitations of such generic terms are well-known, but they continue to be used, preventing us from seeing local ceramic developments in a wider perspective. As we come to realise that more and more potters were producing wares which were, if not identical, at least very similar, the need for such generic terms disappears. What is quite clear is that there was a great deal of overlap between the North Staffordshire potters, in the types of ware they produced, in specific styles, and in types of decoration used. The potters all influenced, and were influenced by, each other. We cannot accept Whieldon's wares as the source of inspiration for all others.

Shaw tells us that Whieldon manufactured knife hafts, snuff boxes, *toys and chimney ornaments, coloured in either the clay state, or bisquet, by zaffre, manganese, copper, &c. and glazed with black, red, or white lead. He also made black glazed tea and coffee pots, Tortoiseshell and melon table plates...and other useful articles*[43]. He goes on to refer to those moulded forms for which Aaron Wood had modelled the blocks: *pickle leaves, crabstock handles and cabbage leaf spouts, for tea and coffee pots*[44]. Wedgwood writes of the white salt-glazed stoneware, tortoiseshell and agate ware produced during his partnership with Whieldon[45], while Whieldon's Account Book makes reference to a variety of tortoiseshell ware, creamware, white salt-glazed stoneware, toys, and *Images* (presumably figures), both glazed and unglazed[46].

The evidence quoted is supported by the archaeological finds from the Whieldon site which included all of the above, as well as red stoneware, glazed red earthenware, a range of coloured glazed wares, and a small quantity of plain creamware. Stylistically, the majority of the pottery could be dated to the period 1740 — 1760. A small quantity of creamwares and pearlwares of the period 1760 — 1790 were the result of the later dumping of wasters on the site. There is no evidence to suggest that these later wares were produced by Whieldon, and the presence of the marks of other makers, including Greatbatch, amongst this material, points to the accumulation of waste from a wide area.

THOMAS BARKER

Thomas Whieldon is a manufacturer who has received much attention, largely on account of his association with Josiah Wedgwood. Pottery has been regularly attributed to him, even before the excavation of his factory site provided a sound basis for such attributions. Another Fenton potter, Thomas Barker, has received rather less attention. Not referred to in Shaw, no pots have been attributed to Barker, and his existence as a major manufacturer has been overlooked. Our sights finally came to focus on Barker during the research which followed a small excavation of a factory waste tip, which had been in use during the years around 1765 — 1770[47], in the area known as the Foley. The quantity of pottery recovered was not great but the range of material was impressive. White salt-glazed stoneware, creamware and red stoneware made up the bulk of the pottery. The red stoneware was of particular interest because of its distinctive relief decoration and pseudo-Chinese seal mark which had already been identified on pieces in collections. The subsequent matching of decoration, handles, spouts, and the seal mark with extant pieces has seen them positively attributed to this source.

Amongst the several potters who were working in Lane Delph, the Foley and Lane End during the second half of the 18th century, it has been possible to identify one, and only one who owned and was working a factory in the immediate vicinity of the Foley excavation[48]. This was Thomas Barker, who is first recorded in the Foley in 1780[49], by which time he had been in business for many years. The evidence for attributing the Foley wasters, and hence those extant pieces identified subsequently, to Barker is good and provides an insight into the products of a typical factory of the period. The range of wares from this site is relevant to any study of the ceramics from the Greatbatch site, with which there are many similarities, while, at the same time, there are direct parallels with the pottery from the Whieldon site.

Whieldon, Greatbatch and Barker were all manufacturers working within little more than a mile of each other. Greatbatch was probably apprenticed to Whieldon, and Barker's brother, John Barker, is listed by Shaw as one of the four apprentices of Whieldon[50]. The potential for similarities in production is obvious; we should not be surprised that these potters and their many other contemporaries should share ideas, drawing upon common sources of inspiration for their response to the current demands of the consumer.

WILLIAM BACCHUS

About the majority of the other potters working in Fenton at the time of Greatbatch we know little. Listed in the first of the local trades directories in 1781, along with Thomas Barker, is William Bacchus, potter of Fenton[51]. William Bacchus appears later, in 1787, as a manufacturer of *Queens ware in all its various branches*[52], but was mistakenly referred to by Shaw as T. Bacchus whose factory, he claims, was on the site of the *two extensive Manufactories* of Messrs. Bourne, Baker and Bourne[53]. Bacchus can be located more precisely in the Fenton Vivian factory of William Baker, already referred to, which was on the northern side of the Stoke to Longton road opposite Greatbatch's factory. In 1781 Bacchus

Fig. 14
WB monogram identified on creamwares tentatively attributed to William Bacchus.

is listed as the tenant of a large factory in Fenton Vivian owned by William Baker — father of the William Baker of Bourne, Baker and Bourne partnership — whose Land Tax value is £1.3.10[54], compared with the £1.1.2. paid by Greatbatch in the same year[55]. By 1784, however, the property has been divided, with Baker taking on part himself and Bacchus left with a part whose tax is 13/6d[56]. He is listed here until 1794, with the exception of a two year interval, during which time the tenants are Hyatt and Bourne. Bacchus also turns up in London as a dealer in china, glass and earthenware, first in 1777, but then throughout the 1780s[57]. In 1783 the stock in his potworks at Fenton Vivian was insured for £170[58].

A small number of creamware sherds have been attributed to Bacchus on the strength of a *WB* monogram identified on wasters recovered on the northern side of the Stoke to Longton road, in Fenton Vivian, during the search for the Whieldon site[59]. Such an attribution, on the strength of initialled pieces alone, must be considered tentative in the extreme. The marked sherds are all of plates with 'royal' rims and appear to be of the period 1780 — 1790. These pieces are of great interest, however, because of the style of the initialled monogram *WB*, in cursive script (Fig. 14), which copies almost exactly the *WG* monogram used by Greatbatch.

Beyond this, our evidence for the Fenton potters is slight. Only the Land Tax Returns for 1781 provide positive evidence for contemporaries of Greatbatch. Thomas Barker and William Bacchus we have already referred to, but chief amongst the rest are Richard Myatt with factories in Fenton Culvert and Lane End, and William Pratt in Fenton Vivian. Also listed in the 1781 trade directory is William Edwards, potter of Lane Delph[60], who is listed under Lane End in 1787[61]; Edwards is mentioned by Shaw as the manufacturer of *very good coloured earthenware* in 1750[62].

*   *   *

The earliest of the detailed lists of potters in the Fenton area, compiled in 1783, lists some of those potters already mentioned, and many others[63]. However, it is impossible to identify the areas in which they operated as they are listed under a general heading *Lane End & Lane Delph & Co*. Although Shaw gives us more information about some of the potters, this is as yet largely unsubstantiated by other evidence; until archaeology can be brought to bear on their factory sites or waste tips, these manufacturers will remain as much in the background as Greatbatch was before his factory waste tip was uncovered in 1979.

1. Identification made by Donald Towner in 1978. See Towner 1980 for a description of the discovery.
2. At NGR SJ8916 4463.
3. Yates 1775.
4. Allbut 1802.
5. Lichfield Joint Record Office.
6. Towner 1980, 266.
7. *ibid.*
8. Pitt 1817, 410.
9. Victoria County History 8, 208.
10. Ward 1843, 551.
11. Shaw 1829, 156.
12. Land Tax Returns for Fenton Culvert (SCRO).
13. *ibid.* Returns for the year 1783.
14. Buried 29th November, 1785. Stoke upon Trent Parish Register III.
15. 21st December, 1793. Norton-in-the-Moors Parish Register II.
16. Land Tax Returns for Fenton Vivian (SCRO).
17. *Report of the meeting of the Committee of Manufacturers...* Item 17 in Enoch Wood's Scrapbook, City Museum & Art Gallery, Stoke-on-Trent.
18. Chester & Mort 1796.
19. *ibid.*
20. Land Tax Returns for Fenton Vivian (SCRO).
21. Allbut 1802.
22. Lichfield Joint Record Office.
23. Shaw 1829, 69.
24. Victoria County History 8, 219.
25. Land Tax Returns for Fenton Culvert (SCRO).
26. *ibid.*
27. *ibid.*
28. *ibid.*
29. 1878 survey at 1:5,000, Sheet XVIII 6.6.
30. Chester & Mort 1796.
31. Land Tax Returns for Fenton Culvert (SCRO).
32. City Museum & Art Gallery, Stoke-on-Trent. Reproduced in Mountford 1972b, 175 — 181.
33. On 16th October, from John Sympson, potter of Hanley Green, and Alice Allen, widow of Newcastle-under-Lyme. The indenture recording the sale (SCRO Cat. No. D/239/M/2401a) is reproduced in Mountford 1972b, 181 — 182.
34. Thomas Whieldon's Account and Memorandum Book. City Museum & Art Gallery, Stoke-on-Trent (unpub.).
35. *ibid.*
36. Stoke upon Trent Parish Register III.
37. Lichfield Joint Record Office.
38. Morley-Hewitt 1954.
39. Shaw 1829, 155.
40. Halfpenny 1986, 16.
41. Barlaston Parish Register.
42. Marriage Bond of Thomas Whieldon and Alice Parrott (Lichfield Joint Record Office).
43. Shaw 1829, 155 — 156.
44. *ibid.*, 156.
45. Wedgwood's Experiment Book, page 71. Wedgwood MSS: E.26-19115.
46. Thomas Whieldon's Account & Memorandum Book. City Museum & Art Gallery, Stoke-on-Trent (unpub.).
47. Barker 1984.
48. Barker forthcoming.
49. Land Tax Returns for Fenton Culvert and Lane End (SCRO).
50. Shaw 1829, 156.
51. Bailey 1781.
52. *ibid.*
53. Shaw 1829, 69.
54. Land Tax Returns for Fenton Vivian (SCRO).
55. Land Tax Returns for Fenton Culvert (SCRO).
56. *ibid.*
57. Sun Insurance Company policies, referred to in Blakey 1981, 17 & 25, and Blakey 1990, 23 — 24.
58. Policy no. 480263, Vol 314, in Blakey 1990, 24.
59. Mountford 1972b, 168. Finds in the City Museum & Art Gallery, Stoke-on-Trent, Cat. No.: K27.1978.
60. Bailey 1781.
61. Tunnicliff 1787.
62. Shaw 1829, 170.
63. Josiah Wedgwood's Commonplace Book Vol I, page 151. Wedgwood MSS: 28408.

CHAPTER 4

GREATBATCH'S POTTERY: THE DOCUMENTARY EVIDENCE

Although in recent years many pieces of pottery have been attributed to Greatbatch, the ceramic historians of the 19th and early 20th centuries largely ignored him and made no attempt to identify wares which might have been made by him at his factory in Lower Lane. The reason for this may simply have been that no pieces were known with a manufacturer's mark which could be linked with Greatbatch and almost the sole evidence for his products was the correspondence and invoices between Greatbatch and Wedgwood which survive in the Wedgwood archive of manuscripts. Luxmore was the first writer to draw attention to this documentary source with regard to Greatbatch and to point to the evidence which it contained for Greatbatch's products[1]; this evidence has subsequently been subjected to various individuals' scrutiny and interpretation.

This documentary evidence is both interesting and extremely valuable, but in terms of attributing surviving pieces to Greatbatch, its usefulness is limited. It is a sad fact that documentary sources of this period rarely supply sufficient detail to allow the wares referred to to be identified. Writers were not concerned with the requirements of present day ceramic historians, and when looking at contemporary source material we must be prepared for generalisations, brevity and confused terminology. This is not to say that attributions are not made on such evidence — indeed many writers have delighted in this practice — but they must be considered suspect. Greatbatch has fared much the same as many of his contemporaries in attracting a whole host of dubious attributions and these must be re-examined in the light of the new evidence available for his wares.

The invoices for the wares supplied to Wedgwood by Greatbatch have been referred to in Chapter 2. Between January, 1763, and January, 1765, the period covered by invoices listing numbered crates, Wedgwood received from Greatbatch 563 crates of ware. The itemised invoices survive for 250 of those crates, representing thirty-six separate deliveries. Sadly, this documentary evidence leaves seventeen years of Greatbatch's later manufacturing career unrepresented and it would be pointless to speculate whether business between the two manufacturers continued in the same manner. However, we can, at least, chart the scale of supply over this two year period with some degree of accuracy and the figures obtained are impressive. An average supply of 23.5 crates per month is suggested, although the totals for the months which are documented in their entirety vary from just seven crates in February, 1763, to twenty-eight crates in November, 1763 (Fig. 15).

Fig. 15 (pages 88-89)
Wares shipped by William Greatbatch to Josiah Wedgwood, 23rd December, 1762, to 21st January, 1765, based upon the surviving invoices. Crates are numbered 1 to 563, and the numbers of dozens of each type of ware per delivery are indicated. Where single items, rather than dozens, are referred to, the number of pieces is followed by S; Pr indicates pairs; s indicates small size; and × indicates stands only.
★ Three invoices are combined here into two, problems clearly having arisen with the shipping of crates. On 11th May, 1763, the delivery of Crates 40 — 51 was short of Nos. 42, 46 and 48; Crates 42 and 46 formed a small delivery which followed on 15th May, while No. 48 was included in the delivery of 24th May which, otherwise, comprised Crates 52 — 59.

CRATE NOS.	23 Dec 1762	10 Jan 1763 1–10	25 Feb 1763 11–18	14 Mar 1763 19–31	16 Apr 1763 32–39	27 Apr 1763	9 May 1763	11 May 1763 40–51*	24 May 1763 52–59*	30 May 1763 60–61	15 Jun 1763 69–72	20 Jun 1763 73–78	29 Jun 1763 79–86	18 Jul 1763 87–88	19 Jul 1763 89–95	28 Jul 1763 95–103
TEAPOTS	23	66	55½	74	46½		34½	59½	37½		8	19	37	18	33	42
TEAPOT STANDS								4	14							
SHELL TEAPOTS																
CHINA TEAPOTS																
CHINA TEAPOTS CROOKED SPOUTS																
CAULIFLOWER TEAPOTS																
COFFEE POTS			6	11	8	11	8	10½		2		7½	9		5½	11
COFFEE POT STANDS						4		3								
COFFEE CUPS		2														
COFFEES & SAUCERS				2					11			6				3
CHOCOLATES		7½	4	11									7		9½	
CHOCOLATES & SAUCERS							4						13			2
CUPS	2	14		4			7	3								
CUPS & SAUCERS				16					32			1				4
SAUCERS	1½	12	9	9								6½s				
MILK POTS	5½	18	19	18½		6	3½	8	9½		2	5	6		11½	2
SAFFRON POTS				7½			1½	15	3							
CHINA SAFFRON POTS																
MUSTARD POTS																
BOWLS	1	20	34½	21			11		51						7	
SUGAR DISHES	8½	12	11	10½	6½	6		7	1	11½	14½		8½	5	9	13
SAUCEBOATS — LARGE	2	7		1	9		1½	9	2	4		4½	6		4½	2
SAUCEBOATS — SMALL	5	4½		5½	15		3	25	7	9		9	10		8½	9
SAUCEBOATS, COVERS & STANDS — LARGE																
SAUCEBOATS, COVERS & STANDS — SMALL																
CREAM BOATS					4½		2½		10				3			
SPOON TRAYS	6	3				6		6	8							2½
STANDS & SPOON TRAYS					12											
EWERS	12	4½	4	18½	26		10	5	13	1		15	9		15	17
CANISTERS						3	1	6½		2			7		2	7
BASKETS — LARGE							21½	6			8½	3				1
BASKETS — SMALL								9			4		16½			10
BUTTER TUBS						2+4S	4	6½			6½		5½			5
BUTTER TUB STANDS						2+4S	4	6			10		9			4
CHELSEA BASKETS													1½	2	1	3
CHELSEA STANDS																
TUREENS																
TUREEN STANDS																
PLATES		5												4	14	
BUTTER PLATES																
TABLE PLATES																
BREAKFAST PLATES																
SOUP PLATES																
BASINS																
TWIFFLERS																
FLOWER POTS																
FLOWER POT STANDS																
CANDLESTICKS																
LEAVES — LARGE																
LEAVES — SMALL																
SAVINE POTS			3													
CAULIFLOWER TUREENS & STANDS																
TOTAL (DOZENS)	66½	175½	146	209½	127½	40+	117	189	199	29½	53½	83½	141	29	120½	137½

12 Sep 1763 132-139	24 Sep 1763 140-147	6 Oct 1763 148-157	Oct 1763 158-166	3 Nov 1763 167-176	12&16 Nov 1763 177-182	17 Nov 1763 183-191	25 Nov 1763 192-194	5 Dec 1763 195-202	19 Dec 1763 203-213	27 Dec 1763 214-218	12 Jan 1764 219-224	7 Feb 1764 237-243	2 Nov 1764 483-491	15 Nov 1764 492-501	4 Jan 1765 542-550	9 Jan 1765 551-561	21 Jan 1765 562-563	TOTAL NO. DOZENS
44	36	40	29	30½	7½	32½	2½	42½	28½	28½	6	40	38	39½	47½	39		1,133½
																		18
													6					6
																58		58
															9			9
																9		9
8	11	8	10			8	1	10½	6	5								172
																		7
										6½								8½
		2		9	6				6		8		3					76
		3½					5		16½	2		12						66
		25	30	9	14		6	8	4		12							127
										2½								32½
			40	30½	24	8		18		7	18		20	12				246½
									20	10s								68
5½	7	4	1		6½		6	5	12					15	6½			191
2½	3			6	1½	9	2½				9	8	9				16	94½
																	22	22
					1½					2								3½
			10	7	7	8½			3½		6		11	14	18			238½
14	11½	12½	11	6½	2	7	2	9½	11		18	15	22	5½	5			287½
		1				3			2									61½
		3½				3			5									140½
				1+21S					2x									3+
				3½					5x									8½
																		20
																		31½
																		12
16	28	7	4			4				2		5	23	3	8	2	3	285½
		2	11½	5½	4	10	4		14½				4	8	7			111½
	11	3			8	7												75
	9				10	7												71½
	11	2		2	9	8				2					2½			70½ +
	12	7		2	9	4				2								74+
	1	3	2+10S		20S						3		2					21½ +
2+10S	3		2+10S		20S						3		2					12+
		12S	8S	10S	12S		16S				11S				6S			+
		12S	8S	3S	7S		16S											+
8											12½			13½				79
10																		15
				19	2	11½			12½									45
				10	1			6½	4½		1½							23½
				10	3													13
	11½																	11½
														5½				5½
														10			3	13
														10			3	13
					1					1						14Pr		2+
					3													3
					3													3
																		3
	5S																	+
110 +	137½ +	177½ +	144½ +	145 +	94½ +	117 +	47	100 +	153	70½	85	80	131	154	94½ +	108 +	47	4102

The 250 crates for which there are invoices contained in excess of 4,600 dozens of ware, an average of about 18.5 dozens per crate. Consequently, the 563 crates supplied over the two year period may be expected to have contained in the region of 10,400 dozens of ware. The potter's dozen varies according to the size of the ware, from six to the dozen for large ware such as coffee pots, to thirty-six to the dozen for smaller ware such as chocolate cups or cream boats. Dozens of nine, twelve, eighteen, twenty-four, thirty and thirty-six are all found in Greatbatch's invoices, providing an average per dozen of 19.3 pieces of ware. Using this, we can estimate that over this two year period Wedgwood received from Greatbatch in excess of 200,000 pieces of ware, a not insignificant quantity.

As regards the types of ware supplied, the invoices are rather less helpful. For the most part, the simple names of the vessels are used without any further elaboration and, unless otherwise stated, we must assume that the pieces are of undecorated creamware. The lists of *teapots, sugar dishes, tureens* and *plates* tell us nothing whatsoever about the type of ware, or type of vessel being supplied. Even the most basic detail is omitted. Other names are rather more intriguing, for example *Chelsea Baskets*, but even here we have no means of knowing what is referred to. We may think of the shapes produced by the Chelsea porcelain factory at this time, of moulded or pierced basketwork, but no identification is possible.

Very few of the types listed in the invoices can be usefully discussed and these are the ones which are supported by references in Greatbatch's correspondence. A discussion of the more distinctive types mentioned in the letters will follow and the possible interpretations of the evidence will be examined. However, before proceeding further, it should be stressed that no account will be taken of the two invoices of June 26th, 1760, and July 22nd, 1760, which are reproduced in full above (pages 43-45). It is considered that these do not refer to wares *produced* by Greatbatch and that, therefore, they have no relevance in this chapter. This negates many of the attributions of wares to Greatbatch made by previous writers.

Apple Teapot. In an undated letter to Wedgwood, Greatbatch wrote: *have sent you an apple tpt. Should be glad to know if you wou'd have leaves on the side the same as use to be*[2]. On 21st January, 1765, it was two apple teapots that Greatbatch sent to Wedgwood; no further detail is given[3].

Apple teapots are well-known in collections. They are essentially tortoiseshell wares, coloured with under-glaze oxides in the same manner, which regularly have crabstock handles, spouts and knops, and which are sometimes additionally adorned with leaves applied to the body, as Greatbatch's note suggests. The globular, or squat globular form of these wares is often enhanced by indentations to the body which are intended to suggest the irregular shape of an apple. A fine example of the type, although not a Greatbatch piece, is illustrated in Towner 1978[4].

Sherds of this type have been recovered from the Greatbatch site. The absence of leaves on the bodies of these pieces suggests what answer Greatbatch may have received from Wedgwood to his undated letter.

Basket work'd Teapot. On 21st January, 1765, Greatbatch sent Wedgwood *1 Basket work'd Tpt*[5]. It is tempting to make the connection between this single reference and one of the largest types of moulded ware to have been made by Greatbatch, the fruit basket ware (Plate 6), although there is another type which could equally be termed basket worked. This latter is the basket and pineapple ware (Fig. 39) which, although very different to the fruit basket ware, is just as dependent upon its moulded basketwork body.

Plate 6
Basket work'd teapot by Greatbatch, *c.* 1765. (City Museum & Art Gallery, Stoke-on-Trent)

Cauliflower. Cauliflower wares were amongst the most numerous of the moulded wares recovered from the excavation of the Greatbatch site and yet, surprisingly, few are referred to in the surviving documents. Another reference is to a delivery made on 21st September, 1763, which included:

> *12 setts Colly flower ware viz.*
> *1 Coffee pot, 1 stand to it,*
> *1 Teapot and stand, 1 M. pot,*
> *1 Sugar Dish, 1 slop Bason,*
> *1 Spoon Boat, 6 Cho. and 6 saucers,*
> *6 Teacups and 6 Sau, 6 Coffees and*
> *6 saucers. 1 Tea cannister.*[6]

On 24th September, 1763, five *couliflower* tureens and stands were supplied to Wedgwood, although no price is given[7], and on 9th January, 1765, nine dozen cauliflower teapots — 18s — were sold at 2/3d per dozen[8].

Chelsea Baskets. These are listed, along with their stands in many of the invoices, but no identification is possible. Baskets are priced at six shillings per dozen, while with their stands they are nine shillings per dozen. One letter, dated 1st July, 1763, refers to problems with the Chelsea baskets:

> *There be eight crates pack'd ready I have*
> *only pack'd 18 Chelsea Baskets but have about*
> *3 Doz more. I do not pack them on account they would not*
> *stand quite steady for they be very Difficult to made (sic)*
> *steady without grinding.*[9]

China. There are several references to china in the documents, but from the context it is clear that it is red stoneware which is referred to. *Red china* or *brown china* were the common terms for this type of ware during the 18th century, with Greatbatch showing a preference for the latter. On 16th September, 1763, Greatbatch writes to Wedgwood that he has *sent the two China Baskets & Breakfast cup & saucer*[10], but no identification is possible here. On 2nd December, 1763, he writes: *I have sent you some brown China tryals*[11], and on 9th December:

> *I have sent you a square China teapot as*
> *a specimen. Shou'd be glad to have your*
> *judgement on it. The couler is light I own*
> *but dare ingage to make any quantity of*
> *a Darker couler if required.*[12]

December, 1763, was clearly a time of experimentation with red stoneware, for on 12th December Greatbatch wrote:

> *I have rec'd yours wrote by Mr. Byerley*
> *and have made a new handle & spout*
> *to the China Teapot but it is impossible*
> *to send you a Teapot by the Bearer hereof.*
> *Had you conveniency to fire one or two*
> *you might have them in the morning.*[13]

The meaning of this is clear. Greatbatch is perhaps between firings and is, therefore, unable to fire the newly modified teapot; he is proposing to send unfired teapots for Wedgwood to add to his next firing. Red stonewares were numerous amongst the finds from the Greatbatch site but nothing has been identified which fits the description of a *square China teapot*.

On 8th May, 1764, Greatbatch had ready for delivery *a good quantity of China Tpts the same as Mr. Wheildons & other sorts*[14]. Something of Thomas Whieldon's red stonewares, produced at his Fenton Vivian manufactory, is known as a result of the archaeological excavations carried out there[15] but no close comparison between these and Greatbatch's red stonewares is immediately apparent. The meaning of this reference is unclear.

However, later in the same month, on 26th May, Greatbatch wrote to Wedgwood:

> *Have sent you a sprig'd Brown China Tpt &*
> *There will be about a Crate to come out of the*
> *next oven of the same, I won't say all sprig'd*
> *so well, because it would be Impossible, but will*
> *I think be as good as any made in the common way*
> *and think will suit you if want any.*[16]

Sprigged decoration — the use of applied moulded reliefs — was commonly used on red stonewares of the mid-18th century. This method was used particularly in connection with applied leaves, flowers, berries and vine stems, which tend to be of a high relief and rather clumsy in their execution. Greatbatch's red stonewares are notable for the quality of their sprigged decoration and for the emphasis placed upon finely modelled reliefs depicting human figures (Plate 7), rather than the traditional vine stem designs used by many of his contemporaries.

Plate 7
Sprig'd Brown China teapot by Greatbatch, *c.* 1765. (The Henry Weldon Collection. ©1990 Henry H. Weldon. Photography by Gavin Ashworth FBIPP, FRPS)

China teapots also appear in the invoices. On 15th November, 1764, nine dozen *China Tpts Crooked spouts* were supplied in three sizes — 12s, 18s and 24s — at four shillings per dozen, and a note on the same invoice adds that *the China Order'd by Mr. Byerly will be ready this day*[17]. Elsewhere, Greatbatch used the term *crooked* with reference to damage caused through the incorrect placing of ware in the oven[18], but in this context it would appear to be deliberate and the crooked spouts are possibly crabstocks; the fact that ordinary china teapots are also priced at four shillings per dozen would seem to further support this interpretation. More of the same type were clearly required by Wedgwood, for on 23rd November, 1764, Greatbatch wrote: *Have pack'd ready eight crates, and the Remaining part of the China Tpts. wth. crooked spouts are fired*[19]. On 9th January, 1765, fifty-eight dozen china teapots were supplied in three sizes — 12s, 18s and 24s; the price was four shillings per dozen[20]. A final reference to china is found in the invoice of 21st January, 1765, when twenty-two dozen *saffron pots, China,* are supplied at 3/6d per dozen[21].

Chinese Teapot. On 11th January, 1764, Greatbatch received payment of 10/6d from Wedgwood for *1 Chinese Teapot*[22]. This is clearly a block mould, as are the other items listed in the same invoice. Towner was of the opinion that Greatbatch 'seems to use the words "China" and "Chinese" indiscriminately'[23] and consequently discusses the two together. This is not the case and, as we have seen, Greatbatch was quite specific in his use of the term *China*, referring, as did his contemporaries, to red stoneware.

The identification of the *Chinese teapot* was interpreted by Towner to mean the well-known hexagonal moulded teapots which depict Chinese figures in their decorative panels, and he illustrates two quite different examples which, it seems more likely, are by different manufacturers[24]. While this identification may be correct, it must be remembered that there are many other wares of the period which could be described as *Chinese* on account of their depictions of Oriental scenes or figures. Certainly no credence can be given to the suggestion that Greatbatch made all the known examples of the moulded hexagonal type: these not only vary considerably in their styles, colouring, finish and features, but also have been recognised amongst groups of wasters from several different sites within the Potteries. Although sherds of this type have been found on the Greatbatch site (below, page 261), making the connection between them and the documentary reference to a block mould is perhaps stretching the evidence a little too far. A salt-glazed block mould of this type may be seen in the Victoria and Albert Museum[25] but again there is no evidence to suggest any connection between this and Greatbatch.

Corinthian candlesticks. These make their only appearance in Wedgwood's account of *sundries overcharged* by Greatbatch, under the date 2nd November, 1764[26], when fourteen Corinthian candlesticks are overcharged by one shilling each. Although an invoice does survive for a delivery made on this date, there is no mention of Corinthian candlesticks and we must presume that another invoice is missing. No identification of this type of candlestick is possible.

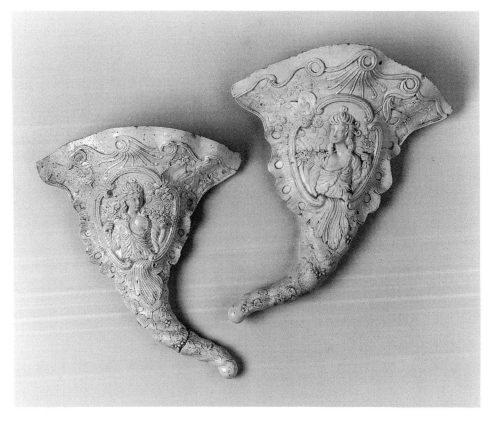

Plate 8
Salt-glazed cornucopia block moulds depicting Flora in central panel. (The Wedgwood Museum. Reproduced by Courtesy of the Trustees of the Wedgwood Museum, Stoke-on-Trent, Staffordshire, England. Photographer: Brent Burgess)

Cornu Copias. An invoice of 11th January, 1764, lists block moulds supplied by Greatbatch to Wedgwood and includes *1 pr. Cornu Copias*[27], priced at twelve shillings. A collection of thirty-eight block moulds discovered early this century in the Wedgwood factory at Etruria includes block moulds for a pair of cornucopiae with twisted stems, scrolled upper edges and a female figure, possibly Flora, framed within a scrolled cartouche (Plate 8). The link between these blocks at Etruria and Greatbatch, using the invoice of 11th January, 1764, as evidence, was made by Luxmore[28]; he may well be correct in this assumption, but it cannot be proven. This type of cornucopia is well known in collections, occurring in white salt-glazed stoneware and green glazed creamware. If there is no conclusive proof that Greatbatch modelled the block moulds, there is at least clear evidence that he manufactured cornucopiae of this type: sherds of green glazed and biscuit pieces were recovered from the Greatbatch site (below, page 182). However, it would seem unlikely that all surviving cornucopiae of this type are to be attributed to Greatbatch, in view of the large number known, and it is likely that they were produced by other manufacturers.

Earl Bute. In an undated letter, Greatbatch asks Wedgwood to *send a piece printed tpt. with Earl Bute on it, have sent cash to pay for it*[29]. Whether this was for resale, or for Greatbatch's personal use is not known. John Stuart, Earl of Bute (1713 — 1792) headed the government from May, 1762, to 8th April, 1763. He introduced a tax on cider to pay for the war with France over Canada, but was forced to resign because of the unpopularity of this move.

Faces. The invoice for block moulds, dated 11th January, 1764, lists three *faces* at fifteen shillings for the three[30]. Towner was of the opinion that this 'almost certainly refers to the well-known wall vases in the form of a face'[31], such as those in the City Museum & Art Gallery, Stoke-on-Trent[32], but this cannot be proven. There are other wall vases which might equally be described as *faces*, such as those ornamented with a satyr's head which are found in both white salt-glazed stoneware and lead-glazed earthenware[33].

Landskip pattern. Two references in the documents have resulted in numerous attributions to Greatbatch which now need to be re-examined. First, a note dated 24th December, 1763, lists the following:

4 Doz 12s ⎫		*Pencil'd or printed ware*
10 Doz 18 ⎬ *Teapots*		*but must be all Landscip*
4 Doz 24 ⎭		*pattern, not one wth. a head*
2 Doz 18 Milk pots & covers		*amongst them — none in*
2 Doz 18 ⎫ *Ewers*		*Colours but all black*
2 Doz 24 ⎭		*wth. a Cream Ground.*
24 Doz in all[34]		

It is quite clear that the type of ware referred to is printed or black enamel-painted creamware depicting landscape subjects. What is less clear is in which direction the wares are moving. The note is in Greatbatch's hand and, apparently, states his requirements. As the note has been sent to Wedgwood, it would appear, therefore, to be a request by Greatbatch for a consignment of wares to be supplied by Wedgwood. There is, however, no link between this note and the other reference to *landskip* pieces.

Amongst the block moulds listed in the invoice of 11th January, 1764, are *Landskip Tpt, Saus Bt., Cream Bt. & Sugr. Box* for which Greatbatch received payment of £1.7.0[35]. The collection of block moulds discovered early this century in the Wedgwood factory at Etruria included pieces which depict landscape subjects. These are two teapot blocks of different sizes with the same subject (Plate 9): this comprises a three-storeyed house, placed centrally, flanked by trees, with cows, sheep, swans and a small boat in the foreground; front and back are slightly different in their layout and are separated by basketwork panels and rococo scrolls. The block for a teapot cover of this type also survives[36]. There is another block in this Etruria group which might also be seen as a landscape: this is a cream boat depicting sheep and cows, but without the house of the teapot blocks[37]. Luxmore made the connection between these block moulds and the *landskip* block moulds of the invoice[38], and it has subsequently been widely accepted that Greatbatch was the modeller of these pieces. There is, however, no independent evidence to support this view.

The vessels produced from these block moulds are well known: they occur in plain or enamelled white salt-glazed stoneware, creamware coloured under-glaze with metallic oxides, and in red stoneware. Some writers have gone even further than Luxmore in suggesting that these pieces were actually made by Greatbatch, but there is no evidence for this whatsoever. None of the numerous examples of this type of teapot which survive have any feature which suggests manufacture by Greatbatch: the handles and spouts used are of types not recovered from the Greatbatch site and, equally important, not one sherd of this type was found at the site. By contrast, sherds of teapots, sauce boats and cream boats of this pattern have been found on other factory and factory waste sites in the area. These include the site of Thomas Whieldon's factory at Fenton Vivian, where biscuit creamware and white salt-glazed stoneware sherds were found, the site of Humphrey Palmer's Church Works, in Hanley, and a nearby group of wasters from Union Street, Hanley, which cannot yet be associated with any manufacturer. These latter two sites produced sherds of white salt-glazed stoneware and under-glaze coloured creamwares[39]. Clearly this type was popular and was produced by a number of local manufacturers of whom Greatbatch was not one. Indeed, there were no moulded wares from the Greatbatch site which even vaguely resembled a landscape of any sort.

The term *landskip* is not confined to these documents; it is found in other contemporary references in connection with other manufacturers. For example, an invoice of 29th May, 1762, records the delivery to Josiah Wedgwood of, amongst others, five dozen *landskips* (*sic*) *teapots* made by Robert Garner and Co.; the price was six shillings per dozen[40]. It would also appear that Wedgwood was producing his own *landskip* teapots at Burslem at this time. A list of payments made by Wedgwood to his workmen at Burslem during the year 1762 shows that these were being made by Edward Bourne and Nathan Heath, for which they were receiving from Wedgwood the sum of ten pence per dozen[41].

The so-called *landskip* wares are an interesting group, given the potential link with surviving block moulds. However, whether or not Greatbatch was responsible for the modelling of these block moulds, or even some of them, cannot be known. The dangers of linking a contemporary term — especially one so widely used as *landskip* — with extant pieces is obvious, although the temptation to do so is great. Despite the traditional link with Greatbatch, there is no evidence that he produced *landskip* wares at his factory, or that he was responsible for the production of the block moulds now in the Wedgwood Museum.

Plate 9
Salt-glazed teapot block moulds, of the so-called *landskip* type. (The Wedgwood Museum. Reproduced by Courtesy of the Trustees of the Wedgwood Museum, Stoke-on-Trent, Staffordshire, England. Photographer: Brent Burgess)

Leaf candlestick. One leaf candlestick is listed among the blocks in the invoice of 11th January, 1764, price four shillings[42]. This cannot be identified.

Pineapple ware. This type, at the height of its popularity during the early 1760s, is referred to on three separate occasions in the documents. Firstly, on 11th January, 1764, Greatbatch receives payment of eight shillings from Wedgwood for *1 pine Apple Teapot*, which is without doubt a block mould[43]. On 8th May, 1764, he writes to Wedgwood:

Sir,

There are now ready two or (sic) the crates of
the Pine apple ware, and a Large quantity
of Plates....

The order of the Pine Apple ware wch. Thomas (Wedgwood)
gave me will be compleated the next ovenfull
— his order consist of about 80 Doz.[44]

Ten days later Greatbatch was able to write: *We are drawing the oven to day and Expect there will be near Pine ware enough to compleat Thomas's order first sent*[45]. There are no references in the surviving invoices to pineapple ware.

There is now abundant evidence from the excavated material for Greatbatch's production of pineapple wares. This was a popular moulded type in Greatbatch's repertoire, although less so than cauliflower and fruit basket ware (below, pages 259-260).

Queen print. In a letter of 16th September, 1763, Greatbatch asks Wedgwood: *Please to send by Bearer a 2 Dish Tpt. with the queen print upon*[46]. A two dish teapot is one which will hold two dishes or cups; the print is presumably of George III's Queen, Charlotte. The young Queen was a popular subject with the pottery manufacturers following her marriage and coronation on 22nd September, 1761. Several prints of Charlotte are known to exist on creamware. To what use Greatbatch intended to put this teapot is not known, although this is yet another illustration that the trade between Greatbatch and Wedgwood was not wholly one-sided.

Saffron pots. These are fairly common items in the invoices, appearing first in that of 14th March, 1763, when they are overcharged at 3/6d, instead of at 2/6d. By 2nd September, 1763, their price has increased to 3/- per dozen, only to drop to 2/6d by 3rd November, 1763; one year later, on 15th November, 1764, their price stood at 2/3d per dozen when, it is stated, the number per dozen is twenty-four.

Saffron pots are often referred to in contemporary invoices and appear to be 'teapots' of a small size. Saffron was used in the 18th century as a non-alcoholic cordial to elevate the spirits, being infused with water in the manner of tea. References in John Wedgwood's Crate Book list saffron pots in both one and two dish sizes under the year 1770[47], while in 1763 *Red Saffron* pots, presumably red china or red stoneware, are mentioned in John Wedgwood's Sales Account Book[48]. Greatbatch, too, was producing red stoneware saffron pots, as the delivery of 21st January, 1765, indicates; their price at this time was 3/6d.

Savine pots. A single reference to *savine pots* occurs in the invoice of 25th February, 1763, when just three dozen were supplied to Wedgwood at 2/6d per dozen. The term is otherwise unknown in a ceramic context. The Oxford English Dictionary tells us that the shrub savine (*Juniperus sabina*) was used as a drug in the 18th century, and that an ointment made from the new shoots, powdered and mixed with butter, provided common relief for asthma. It is reasonable to assume, therefore, that *savine pots* were small ointment pots.

Shell teapots. In an undated letter, Greatbatch wrote to Wedgwood: *I expected your advice on the shape of the Tpts. agreed on — the work is compleated for the shell & other Tpt*[49]. The context here shows beyond doubt that Greatbatch is referring to the completion of modelling the blocks of these particular teapots. It would seem reasonable, therefore, to assign this letter to the early part of 1764 as *shell teapots* make their first appearance in Wedgwood's account of *sundries overcharged* by Greatbatch under 14th July, 1764, when ten and a half dozen *Shell Tpots* have been charged at 3/6d, an overcharge of one shilling per dozen[50]. On 28th July, 1764, five and a half dozen of the same were charged at three shillings, this time an overcharge of sixpence per dozen; the same overcharge was made on seven dozen on 29th September, 1764, and on six dozen on 2nd November, 1764. There are no invoices for the first three of these deliveries of shell teapots, although that of 2nd November, 1764, does survive[51]. On this date, Wedgwood received six dozen teapots in three sizes — 12s, 18s and 24s — at a cost of three shillings per dozen, subsequently corrected to 2/6d.

Plate 10
Creamware teapot with moulded shell decoration, coloured with under-glaze oxides. Greatbatch, *c.* 1765. (Delhom Collection, Mint Museum of Art, Charlotte, North Carolina. Photographer: Bill. J. Moretz)

Reilly suggests that the shell teapots may be those shell-moulded wares which are well-known in creamware as Wedgwood's wares, and which are often marked with the Wedgwood name, and makes a tentative association with Greatbatch[52]. However, nothing of this type was recovered from the Greatbatch site, although there were quantities of a type of ware — teapots, coffee pots, jugs, bowls, sugar bowls, canisters and other forms — which was moulded with shell groups and seaweed sprays (Plate 10). This type is the most likely candidate to be associated with the *shell teapots* of the invoice — indeed, it is the only candidate from the excavated material. This type alone of all Greatbatch's wares reflects the influence of the contemporary passion for collecting shells, which is so apparent on the ceramics of the period.

Squirrel and Bird Teapot. On 8th May, 1764, Greatbatch wrote to Wedgwood: *Shou'd be glad to have your advice in the shape of the Squirrel & Bird Tpt. block, & whether you wou'd have a ground work on it or not*[53]. Nothing is known which might correspond with this type, either amongst the excavated material or in collections. Teapots moulded in the form of a squirrel are well-known in white salt-glazed stoneware[54] but, although they have a bird worked into the pattern on the body of the squirrel, they are generally considered to be earlier than the Greatbatch reference, dating perhaps to the years around 1755.

White chocolate cups. A note dated 24th December, 1763, provides clear evidence of in-trading between the Staffordshire potters, a practice which is well-documented elsewhere. Greatbatch writes: *Pray do us the favr. to get a crate of white chocolat cups made by some of yr. Neighbours as soon as possible*[55]. We can be confident in the evidence here that Greatbatch did indeed have an independent trade going on at this time alongside his business dealings with Wedgwood. A crate of chocolate cups is certainly not for his own use. The *white* ware referred to here is, of course, salt-glazed stoneware which was still, at this time, a staple commodity within the Staffordshire pottery industry. It was clearly still produced by Wedgwood's neighbours in Burslem, most notably by his cousins John and Thomas Wedgwood of the Big House, who are well-known as manufacturers of white salt-glazed stoneware.

Printed wares. These few references to Greatbatch's wares are the only useful contemporary references to survive. Byerley's account of Greatbatch's early career has already been discussed and the probable inaccuracies in this have been pointed out in Chapter 2. The only other valuable source in this line of research is Shaw, whose History was published forty-seven years after Greatbatch's bankruptcy. On the basis of his statement that Greatbatch *for some time had a most rapid sale of teapots, on which was printed, in black, by Thomas Radford, the history of the Prodigal Son*[56], these well-known printed wares have for many years been associated with Greatbatch.

The series of Prodigal Son prints comprises the following subjects:

The Prodigal Son Receives his Patrimony,
The Prodigal Son Taking Leave,
The Prodigal Son in Excess,
The Prodigal Son in Misery,
The Prodigal Son returns Reclaim'd,
The Prodigal Son Feasted on his Return.

The prints display a uniformity of style and are clearly all engraved by the same hand. The vessels, normally teapots, upon which the prints appear are likewise uniform in their forms and features, with handles, spouts and knops being shared by the vessels.

The clearly defined nature of the Prodigal Son printed wares encouraged Towner to identify other prints which, he felt, were associated with this group[57]. The following prints from Towner's list are found on vessels, again normally teapots, which are identical to those decorated with the Prodigal Son series:

The Fortune Teller,
The XII Houses of Heaven,
Juno,
Aurora,
Cybele,
Captain Cook being directed by Britannia,
The Hon'ble. Aug'tus Keppel, known today as Admiral Keppel,
A Man of War,
Harlequin and Columbine,
A Lady and Gentlemen in a Garden,
The World with Sun, Moon and Stars.

Towner considered, however, that Greatbatch himself, and not Thomas Radford, was the engraver of the prints under discussion. He was also of the opinion that the majority of these wares were produced at Leeds and the possibility that Greatbatch might have been the manufacturer was dismissed by him. Perhaps he felt it sufficient that Greatbatch should have engraved the plates for the prints, and he suggests either that Greatbatch bought in wares from Leeds to decorate, or that his copper plates were sold, perhaps after his bankruptcy[58].

There is no evidence whatsoever that Greatbatch engraved these or any other prints. Indeed it is most unlikely that an established manufacturer whose principle skill lay in modelling would turn his hand to another very specialised area of production when there was a business to run. Other evidence supports this view.

Towner was unable to accept Radford as the engraver of the prints listed above for three reasons. Firstly, there was his connection with the Derby Potworks at Cockpit Hill, where he was presumed to have worked until its closure in 1779; secondly, there are the great stylistic differences between Radford's signed prints on Derby creamwares and the Prodigal Son and other prints; and, thirdly, there is the occurrence of Greatbatch's name in some of the prints.

Thomas Radford is well-known as an engraver. He worked at the Derby Pot Works from the mid-1760s and his name appears in prints on creamwares of this period which were made at that factory[59]. There is, in fact, no evidence for the date of Radford's departure from Derby, but if we accept Shaw's statement — and there is no evidence to contradict this — he must have been in North Staffordshire by late 1777. The reason for this is that one of the prints listed above, *The XII Houses of Heaven*, bears the inscription *Published as the Act directs Jany. 4. 1778 by W. Greatbatch Lane Delf Staffordshire*; if Radford was the engraver of this, the work must have been commissioned during the previous year. The meaning of the inscription is quite clear: Greatbatch was the *publisher* of the the print and not the engraver, as Towner asserted. Williams-Wood corrects this mistaken idea[60]. The Act of Parliament referred to in *The XII Houses of Heaven print* was that promoted by William Hogarth, which became law on 24th June, 1735. Hogarth, as an engraver and seller of prints, had suffered greatly from the plagiarising of his work by other, disreputable artists. Hogarth's Act, in consequence, was introduced to secure for engravers and designers the exclusive rights to their work for a period of fourteen years.

The other print which sometimes bears Greatbatch's name, although not in the same form, is Harlequin and Columbine. This often has the name *Greatbatch* worked into the print. Again, there is no hint here that Greatbatch was anything but the manufacturer of the piece and not the engraver.

It cannot be shown conclusively, on the evidence available, that Thomas Radford engraved any of these prints, but the argument of stylistic differences between these and his Derby prints carries no weight. Not only are the two groups of prints some ten to fifteen years apart in their production, but those used by Greatbatch were intended for over-painting in enamel colours, unlike the Derby prints, and would consequently have required a different approach by the engraver.

It is clear, however, that by the 1780s Radford was working in North Staffordshire. Shaw tells us that:

Mr. John Baddeley, of Shelton (John Baddeley II), *some time employed Mr. Thomas Radford to print Tea Services by an improved method of transferring the impression to bisquet ware; which was attempted to be kept secret, but was soon developed; and the glaze prevented the beautiful appearance which attached to the Black printed.*[61]

John Baddeley II had commenced work in Shelton in 1784 and Radford may have found work there immediately. The nature of Radford's employment, whether with Greatbatch or with Baddeley, is uncertain; he may simply have operated as a freelance engraver and transfer printer, rather than as an employee at either of these factories. He appears to have been successful and by 1796 he is listed as an engraver at Shelton, along with Thomas Radford junior[62].

The evidence for Greatbatch's pottery, from the documentary sources alone, is minimal. His early wares, from the years 1762 to 1765, cannot positively be identified solely on the basis of the written evidence. His transfer-printed wares are more closely associated with him as a result of Shaw's statement and the good survival of Prodigal Son printed teapots. The range of prints which occur upon identical vessels allows these, too, to be associated with Greatbatch with some degree of confidence, but without the evidence of archaeology we could still have been talking in terms of wares being bought in from outside to be decorated at Greatbatch's factory. Although a most unlikely scenario, it is one which could not easily be disproved with the available evidence until the excavation brought to light the pottery itself which was needed to clarify matters.

The excavation of the Greatbatch site cut across the limitations imposed by the documentary evidence and has provided us with an enormous sample of Greatbatch's wares, quite literally straight from the factory. Such evidence enables us to confirm the list of prints which Towner associates with Greatbatch and to expand it significantly. It enables us to view wares at the different stages of their production, providing positive evidence against any importation of pieces from elsewhere, and to identify many of the problems encountered in their manufacture. Finally, this evidence has removed any shadow of doubt from individual pieces about their place of manufacture and the identity of their manufacturer. In short, despite the paucity of the documentary evidence, Greatbatch's products have now become the best documented of all the wares of the period.

1. Luxmore 1924, 47 — 50.
2. Wedgwood MSS: 30139-30.
3. *ibid.*: 30137-30.
4. Towner 1978, 37 plate 7A.
5. Wedgwood MSS: 30137-30.
6. Quoted in Towner 1963, 186: no reference given. Apparently in the Wedgwood archive, but not located by the author.
7. Wedgwood MSS: 30124-30.
8. *ibid.*: 30136-30.
9. *ibid.*: 22340-30.
10. *ibid.*: 30123-30.
11. *ibid.*: 22352-30.
12. *ibid.*: 22353-30.
13. *ibid.*: 22354-30.
14. *ibid.*: 22374-30.
15. Mountford 1972b.
16. Wedgwood MSS: 22376-30.
17. *ibid.*: 22391-30.
18. *ibid.*: 22341-30. See below, page 123.
19. *ibid.*: 22392-30.
20. *ibid.*: 30136-30.
21. *ibid.*: 30137-30.
22. *ibid.*: 22359-30.
23. Towner 1978, 34.
24. *ibid.*, 41, plates 9A and 9B.
25. Schreiber Collection, Cat. No.: 326-1889.
26. Wedgwood MSS: 22353-30.
27. *ibid.*: 22359-30.
28. Luxmore 1924, 49.
29. Wedgwood MSS: 30139-30.
30. *ibid.*: 22359-30.
31. Towner 1963, 191.
32. Cat. No.: 3660 (salt-glazed stoneware block) & 2951 (tortoiseshell); illustrated in Barker & Halfpenny 1990, 64.
33. See, for example, Mountford 1971, plates 153 & 154.
34. Wedgwood MSS: 30133-30.
35. *ibid.*: 22359-30.
36. Luxmore 1924, plate 65 no. 13.
37. *ibid.*, plate 67 no. 16.
38. *ibid.*, 49.
39. These sites are unpublished at the time of writing, although reports are in preparation. Material in City Museum & Art Gallery, Stoke-on-Trent.
40. Wedgwood MSS: 6-30925. For a full discussion of Robert Garner, see Barker forthcoming.
41. *ibid.*: E.31-24107. Payments made on 20th February and 16th August, 1762.
42. *ibid.*: 22359-30.
43. *ibid.*
44. *ibid.*: 22374-30.
45. *ibid.*: 22375-30.
46. *ibid.*: 30123-30.
47. John Wedgwood's Crate Book, pages 20 — 21. City Museum & Art Gallery, Stoke-on-Trent (unpub.). I would like to thank Leslie Grigsby for help in identifying saffron pots.
48. John Wedgwood's Sales Account Book, page 73. City Museum & Art Gallery, Stoke-on-Trent (unpub.).
49. Wedgwood MSS: 22337-30.
50. *ibid.*: 22358-30.
51. *ibid.*: 22388-30.
52. Reilly 1989 I, 191.
53. Wedgwood MSS: 22374-30.
54. See, for example, Luxmore 1924, plate 78, and The Mint Museum 1982, 97 no. 163.
55. Wedgwood MSS: 30133-30.
56. Shaw 1829, 190.
57. Towner 1957, 31 — 32.
58. *ibid.*, 31.
59. Williams-Wood 1981, 95 — 97.
60. *ibid.*, 172.
61. Shaw 1829, 213.
62. Chester & Mort 1796, 33.

CHAPTER 5

THE TECHNOLOGY OF 18TH CENTURY POTTERY PRODUCTION

Having identified the site of Greatbatch's factory, we would hope to learn something more about the way in which it operated. Greatbatch's correspondence with Wegwood provides a few tantalising insights into the practical, day to day business of his factory, together with a little information on the processes employed, but few details about the size and layout of Greatbatch's factory, the number of workers employed, their individual responsibilities, or the overall scale of production. It might appear, therefore, that we have little chance of recovering the type of information necessary for a detailed understanding of the working of this particular 18th century potworks.

Fortunately a considerable amount of information may be gleaned from a study of the waste from the Greatbatch site. Here we are in a unique position to pursue answers to questions of technology. The excavated waste material, together with hints from Greatbatch's correspondence and an element of inference based upon what we know of other contemporary factories, offers a technological framework within which to view Greatbatch's production.

The archaeological evidence suggests that Greatbatch's wares are unlikely to represent any significant innovations, either in the types of ware or in the technical processes employed in their manufacture. Rather Greatbatch was operating in exactly the same way as his contemporaries, and was producing a similar range of wares. He may well have had his strengths as a manufacturer — his skills as a modeller have already been commented upon (above, page 56) — and both surviving and excavated pieces bear witness to the high quality achieved in his products. In this, at least, he stands considerably above many of his fellows, and Shaw's statement that his ultimate bankruptcy was the result of a bad debt, rather than of production problems, may well be believed. Essentially, however, Greatbatch's wares were typical of their period and were the result of those same innovations and technical improvements, made over a period of a half century or more, which had determined the nature of production methods and the range of wares available in the 1760s and beyond.

Greatbatch's correspondence with Wedgwood provides virtually no useful references to his factory. Although a few letters refer to the setting or drawing of an oven, it would not be stretching the evidence too far to suggest that Greatbatch's factory had upwards of two ovens, with possible changes in their number occurring during the course of its operation. At no point in the letters does Greatbatch make any clear reference to whether glost or biscuit wares are being produced, although it has always been assumed, in the light of Byerley's remarks, that it was biscuit ware which Wedgwood received. This matter is discussed above (page 49) and the preferred interpretation of the available evidence is that Greatbatch was producing both biscuit and glost wares from an early stage, and probably even supplying the same to Wedgwood.

Whether or not those wares supplied to Wedgwood and listed in the invoices between December, 1762, and January, 1765, were all biscuit, the presence of glazed wares in the earliest phase of Greatbatch's waste tip does suggest, however, that it was not long before a glost oven had become available. Indeed, the existence of a factory at this date with just one oven is most unlikely. After 1720 all references to ovens occurring in potters' wills are in the plural[1] and this expansion in the size of factories is clearly the general trend as the century progressed. The existence of a further, third oven at the factory may be inferred from the presence of significant quantities of salt-glazed stoneware in Phases I and II of the tip, although the almost total absence of this type in Phase III suggests that such an oven was out of use by, if not before, 1770. A separate oven reserved solely for the high temperature single firing of salt-glazed stoneware was essential as any attempt to fire earthenwares in an oven used for salt-glazing would lead to contamination of the ware from the residual salt glaze which coats the interior of the oven. The dry-bodied stonewares — red stoneware, black basalt, buff stoneware and caneware — would not have required a separate oven, for these could simply be placed in the hottest parts of the biscuit oven.

It is certain that Greatbatch had, or came to have at least one more decorating oven, known since the middle of the 18th century as a muffle[2], for the low temperature firings necessary to harden-on enamel colours which were used over-glaze to decorate the ware. The decoration of Greatbatch's wares, first by outside specialist decorators and subsequently by decorators employed in-house at his factory, will be discussed below (pages 204-206). The employment of in-house decorators, from about 1770 onwards, would have been of a smaller size than the biscuit or glost ovens. The under-glaze colours, particularly the oil-based under-glaze blue, also required hardening-on before the glost firing at a temperature of 680 — 750 degrees centigrade, rather lower than the temperature required for the over-glaze enamel colours.

Apart from the ovens, the only other building on the factory which is referred to in the letters is the warehouse:

> *Shou'd be glad you wou'd send cart for ware,*
> *the ware house is so full of ware that we can't*
> *Possible put any more in it and have got*
> *the Oven full....*[3]

It is sad that there is so little information available about Greatbatch's factory for there must have been many other rooms and workshops whose existence we can only guess at. Various workhouses would have been essential, most with a clearly defined function. Other documentary sources emphasise the way in which labour within the pottery industry was becoming more specialised, a fact which is reflected in the variety of different houses referred to. Such specialised areas might include a slip house, a throwing house, a turning house, a handling room, a dipping house and a decorating shop[4]. Moreover, contemporary references clearly show that some of the different types of ware were produced in quite separate workshops, to avoid the risk of contamination from different types of clay.

Workers. How many workers may have been employed at Greatbatch's factory cannot be known, despite several references to individuals in the correspondence. What little contemporary evidence there is suggests that in the region of two dozen men, women and children would have worked in a typical factory. For example, for the years 1750 — 1753 documented in Thomas Whieldon's Memorandum Book, between sixteen and twenty-five workers are recorded, including children[5]. Amongst those listed were a slip-maker from Lane End, *little Bet Blour* (Bloor) *to learn to flower* (i.e. to decorate the scratch blue wares), *John Austin*

The Staffordshire Pottery.

Plate 11
The Pottery Factory. The prints used in this Chapter to illustrate the various aspects of pottery production are taken from the volume *A Representation of the Manufacturing of Earthenware (with twenty one highly finished Copper Plate Engravings, and a short explanation of each, shewing the whole process of the POTTERY), published in 1827.*

for placeing white (salt-glazed stoneware), *Thomas Dutton for vineing* (i.e. sprigging), *William Keeling for handling, William Cope for handleing & vineing & caste ware, John Barker for the huvel* (hovel), *George Bagnall for fireing for this year, Elijah Simpson for turning, Samuel Jackson for throwing Sagers & fireing,* and a boy of Ann Blour *for treading the lathe.* It is quite clear that Whieldon's workmen had their own specific duties.

In the factory of John Baddeley of Shelton, a major local manufacturer with an extensive business who was involved briefly in the production of soft-paste porcelain as well as the more usual earthenwares and stonewares, a weekly figure of between twenty-five and forty-five workers has been recorded for the period June, 1761 — June, 1762[6]. A number of these were employed on a part-time or casual basis; there were some women and children amongst these.

Something of the employment at John and Thomas Wedgwood's Big House works in Burslem is known as a result of the partial survival of John Wedgwood's hiring records for the period 1756 — 1778[7]. The maximum number of workers hired, as far as it is possible to tell from the incomplete records, appears to have been twelve, comprising six men, one woman, two boys, two girls and one apprentice.

A further reference of the same period is provided by Arthur Young who visted North Staffordshire in 1769 and wrote: *I viewed the Staffordshire Potteries at Burslem and the neighbouring villages, which have of late been carried on with such amazing success. There are 300 houses* (i.e. potworks) *which are calculated to employ on an average 20 hands each or 6,000 on the whole, but if all the variety of people that work in what may be called the preparation for the employment of the immediate manufactories, the total number cannot be much short of 10,000 and it is increasing every day*[8].

The references in Greatbatch's correspondence are not so helpful. In December, 1762, he writes that, having just begun to produce ware, he has *four men pressing constantly*[9]. These were skilled workmen, as was the turner, the absence of whom forces Greatbatch to work at the lathe himself (above, page 57). The employment on a pottery factory of a turner, who finished newly-thrown wares on a lathe by removing excess clay, as well as shaping and decorating the vessels, had been essential throughout most of the 18th century, for the fine, thin-walled and carefully finished wares demanded by the customer could not easily and consistently be produced by throwing alone. The final workmen referred to by Greatbatch are the packers and the carters (above, page 55) who may possibly have been self-employed and not, therefore, part of the factory's workforce. The presence of throwers, various decorators, placers and firemen may be presumed and, it must be remembered, Greatbatch himself attended to the modelling of blocks for the moulded wares. There was sufficient flexibility in Greatbatch's workforce for him to be able to part with two workmen when business was bad in November, 1764 (above, page 52).

Some of Greatbatch's employees are known by name. Four men are regularly named as the bearers of letters to, and receivers of money from Wedgwood: Ralph Edge, Ralph Wolfe, John Eaton and John Allerton, of whom the last two, at least, were illiterate, making their mark *X* upon the receipt of money. It is possible that one of Greatbatch's pressers was a William Sutton, at least in the later years of production. One of several potter's tools recovered from the excavation was a creamware plate profile which is inscribed *Wm Sutton .....1777* in conjoined script (Fig. 16). Other profile fragments are inscribed with the initials *WD*: this person cannot be identified.

Plate 12
Clay preparation: making a slip.

Preparation of the Clay. The full range of contemporary technology is represented by the wasters and associated material from the Greatbatch site, from the unfired clay to the finished product. At no point do Greatbatch's letters refer to the clay used. Although local red-firing clay would have been used for some of the wares, such as the red stonewares or the blackwares, in the main this would have been imported white-firing ball clay from the south-west, which was then being used by all the local potters for their salt-glazed stonewares and for the various types of creamware. The need to temper the clay with flint to strengthen and whiten the ware, and the use of flint in the glaze recipes has already been discussed (above, page 14).

Excellent contemporary accounts of pottery production in both Newcastle-upon-Tyne and Newcastle-under-Lyme have been provided by a French visitor to this country, Gabriel Jars, who witnessed the manufacture of both earthenwares and stonewares in about 1765[10]. His description of the preparation of the clay in the production of white salt-glazed stoneware is equally relevant to the lead-glazed earthenwares whose clay bodies were prepared in exactly the same way:

"Boiling the Slip" to evaporate the water, leaving a clay about the consistence of dough.

Plate 13
Clay preparation: evaporating the water from the slip.

The main feature of this ware consists in the preparation of the clay and in its mingling with flint so that it is made thoroughly white and free from blemishes. Clay is put into a tank with water to make it sloppy. Water is well mixed with it by stirring it with a piece of board. The water holding this clay is put through a large sieve to separate what has not been dissolved in the water and is caught in the sieve, being returned to the original tank. As to the clay which passes through, one waits until there is a sufficient amount of it and then it is agitated vigorously in the water it is in, being passed through a finer sieve. To mingle it with the flint, preparations are made as in the Northumberland Newcastle. The flint is calcined in the same way in a lime kiln, being then pulverised and ground in a mill generally driven by water. Flint in that state is taken to the factory. To make a good mixture it has to be watered to the same consistency as the clay.

The proportions used are to add one part of flint to six parts of one of the clays; and one part of flint to five parts of the other sort of clay. When the clay has been sieved twice as referred to above, an even finer sieve is used for it to pass through a third time. It is then that the proportions are measured out.

A small tub is filled six times with clay that has passed through the sieve. Then one of these small vessels is filled with flint that has gone through the sieve of the same mesh. This is continued until one has the amount of slip required. To make the mixture more exact the two slips must have a similar consistency. These are well stirred together and then one finishes by passing them a fourth and then a fifth time through the sieve. They are then poured into a brick tank under which is a fire (i.e. to drive off the water)[11].

Such processes can only be identified archaeologically by the fortuitous excavation of the slip house on a factory site. The only evidence for the preparation of the bodies at Greatbatch's factory is contained in a letter of 4th November, 1763, when Greatbatch had a bill to pay:

Lane Delph Novr. 4th, 1763

Sir,

Desire you'l favour me wth. some cash
by the bearer hereof and you will greatly
Oblge yr. Hble. St. & Co.

Wm. Greatbatch

I have Recd. a flint Bill to the amount
of £30 which is to be paid at Martinmass.
A bill or cash if convenient would Oblge yrs. & co.

as above[12]

There is no indication of who had supplied the flint, or whether it had been supplied in its natural state or calcined and crushed from one of the many flint mills which were operating locally at that time.

Throwing, Press moulding, Slip casting. After the clay has been beaten and wedged, *all the vessels which are not to be moulded are made on a wheel with a vertical shaft kept in motion by a little boy turning a wheel*[13]. This is a reference to the great wheel which appears to have been in general use in North Staffordshire by about 1720[14]. The development of the great wheel was probably closely connected with the increased production of fine earthenwares and stonewares in the early 18th century. The thrower was now able to achieve much greater control over his wheel, for the power was supplied by another person, usually a child, turning a handle of a large flywheel which was connected to the potter's wheel by a rope (Plate 14).

First process of potting is "Throwing," forming round pieces of ware with the Hands and Machine.

Plate 14
The thrower. Note the use of child labour to turn the great wheel and to prepare clay for the thrower.

The majority of Greatbatch's wares were thrown or press-moulded, although slip-casting was used as a means of producing a small number of elaborate wares. The quality of the throwing exhibited by the pottery is very high and this, coupled with the turning, has invariably produced fine, thin-walled pieces. We have already mentioned the pressers employed in the factory and with the evidence of the excavated pottery we can now form some idea of the volume of work undertaken by these. All of the flat wares — the plates, platters, stands, trays, etc. — were press-moulded, a considerable part of the factory's output. Also press-moulded were the popular fruit wares, pineapple and cauliflower, fruit basket wares, shell wares and other ornate types, together with less elaborate forms such as sauce boats, canisters, candlesticks and tureens.

For all of these forms, the factory would have required both block moulds and a large supply of working moulds of plaster of Paris. These latter would be replaced regularly as use resulted in a wearing of the detail, something which is apparent in many of the wasters. On average a plaster mould would suffice for between sixty and seventy pressings before replacement became necessary. Despite Greatbatch's well-known skill as a modeller, is it possible that he could have provided, single-handed, all the blocks for the factory? This would have involved several hundreds of blocks for the wares produced, often with several variations in size for a particular type. There were also handles, spouts, knops and terminals which required block moulds. We must at least consider the possibility that some of the block moulds were supplied from outside by specialist modellers, or else that Greatbatch employed one or more of these at his factory. Minor variations in modelling noticed on the excavated cauliflower wasters does suggest that several blocks were available for the same size of vessel, and the hand of more than one modeller is apparent.

The manufacture and supply of block moulds is an area of the ceramics industry which is poorly understood. Reference has been made to the problem[15], but it seems likely for the present that every possibility must be considered, from modellers working for a single factory for their whole career, to individuals who supplied any customer. The potential for the loan, purchase or exchange of block moulds is great and must be born in mind when looking at a manufacturer's moulded wares.

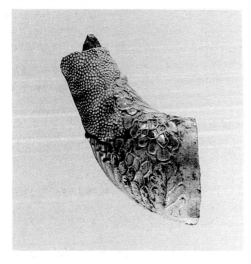

Plate 15
Salt-glazed block mould for a cauliflower spout.
Phase II.

Plate 16
Lead-glazed block mould for a Type 6 handle.
Phase II.

Whole or fragmentary block moulds are rare finds on excavations of factory or factory waste sites. Such items were extremely valuable, time-consuming to make and expensive to purchase, and were rarely discarded, even if no longer required: there would always be a neighbour who could make use of a redundant block mould. It is surprising, therefore, that four blocks, two complete and two damaged, were found among the excavated pottery. Two damaged salt-glazed blocks are of a cauliflower spout (Plate 15) and a cauliflower cover; a third is a lead-glazed handle of Type 6 (Plate 16), possibly discarded because of the slight twist it displays; while the fourth is of unglazed red stoneware, the model for a pair of sprigged reliefs of Type 28 — this is undamaged (Plate 17).

Plate 17
Block mould in unglazed red stoneware for Type 28 sprigged reliefs. Phase II.

We have noted Greatbatch's references to his endeavours in modelling. The evidence of some of the invoices underlines the extremely high cost of some of the block moulds. On 11th January, 1764, payment for the following consignment was received:

1 Leaf Candlestick — — —	£0 — 4 — 0	
1 Oval Fruit Basket & stand —	0 — 12 — 0	
1 pr. Cornu Copias — — —	0 — 12 — 0	
3 Oblong Fruit Dishes — —	3 — 3 — 0	
1 Round Ditto — — — —	1 — 1 — 0	
2 plates Do. — — — —	2 — 2 — 0	
1 pine Apple Teapot — — —	0 — 8 — 0	
Landskip Tpt. Saus Bt. }	1 — 7 — 0	
Cream Bt. & Sugr. Box }		
3 Faces — — — — —	0 — 15 — 0	
1 Chinese Teapot — — —	0 — 10 — 0	
	10 — 14 — 6	
Recd. on Acct. of the above	3 — 3 — 0	
Balance	7 — 11 — 6	

To Bill
Recd. the contents of the above Bill
being pr. me

Wm. Greatbatch[16]

These pieces are all blocks, as their high prices clearly show. While a pineapple teapot block mould, one of the cheaper items listed, cost 8 shillings, comparable moulded wares, cauliflower teapots, were being bought from Greatbatch by Wedgwood for just 2/3d per dozen[17]. Against this, the presser's wage in 1784 was 12 shillings per week for a very good workman[18].

Working moulds of plaster of Paris were taken from the blocks and were used by the presser or the slip caster until the detail was too worn. It was important for the factory to have a good supply of these as freshly pressed wares had to stand until dry enough to be removed from the mould without being damaged. It was a shortage of moulds which caused Greatbatch problems with one particular order (above, page 55). Plaster moulds rarely survive: once too worn to use, they were discarded along with the wasters, and consequently very few examples of the 18th century are known in collections. By good fortune, a surprising number of moulds were recovered from the Greatbatch site; many more were lost, having become excessively damp and crushed by the weight of waste material tipped upon them. The surviving moulds came from Phases II and III of the site: they are not intact, and many are extremely worn, either through use or as a result of their time in the ground. However, a good number bear recognisable details, with many decorative plate edges clearly identifiable. Cauliflower wares, fruit basket wares and pieces with barleycorn moulding are numerous. There are also parts of two-piece handle and spout moulds (Plate 19), as well as moulds from

which decorative flower terminals would have been taken (Plate 18). The moulds correspond exactly to the wares recovered from the excavation.

Plate 18
Plaster of Paris mould for a pair of Type 20 flower and leaf handle terminals. Phase II.

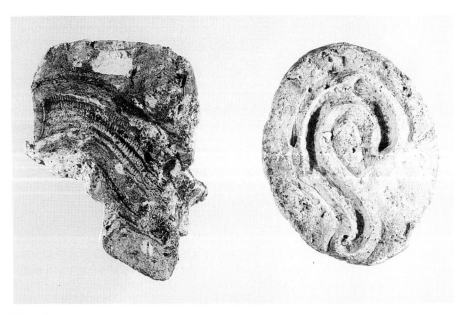

Plate 19
Plaster of Paris moulds for a Type 12 basketwork spout and a Type 4 handle. Phase III.

Plate 20
Plaster of Paris hollow ware moulds for fruit basket teabowls. Phase III.

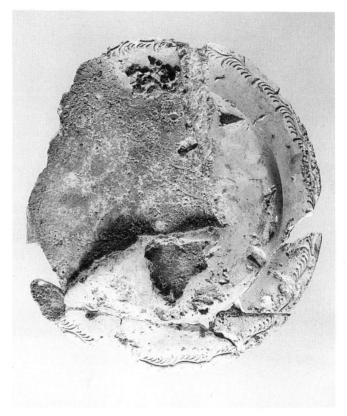

Plate 21
Plaster of Paris mould for a feather edged plate. Phase III.

The press-moulding of wares, whether flat wares pressed over a one-piece flat mould or hollow wares pressed into two-piece moulds, was the work of a skilled craftsman. Tools were required for this and it was normal for the workman to make and retain his own. These included handled profiles used to shape the underside of flatwares. These were of ceramic and were shaped to the exact profile required for a particular vessel, following the underside of the rim, the shoulder and part of the base. Some of the profiles used in the production of circular flat wares have a groove in them which forms the vessel's footring. There are several

116

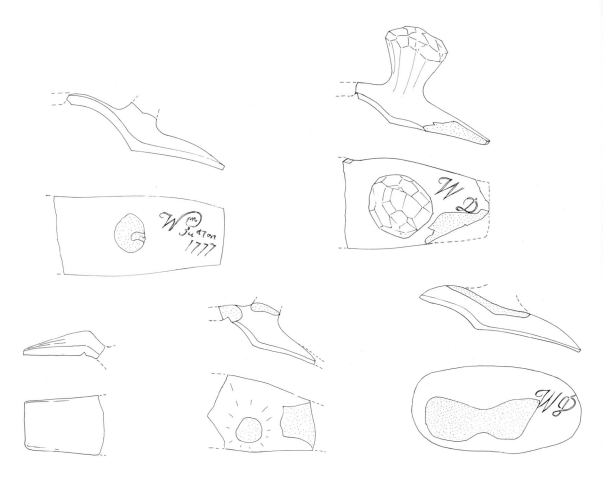

Fig. 16
Fragments of ceramic profiles, tools used to shape the undersides of flatwares while still on the mould. All profiles are in glazed creamware. Phase III. (Scale 1:2)

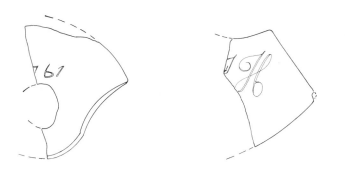

Fig. 17
Fragments of workmen's tools in salt-glazed stoneware, used to finish wares. Left: with date (*1*) *767* (or *1*). Phase II. Right: with incomplete inscription (*?J*)*H*. Phase II. (Scale 1:2)

Making of the clay, dishes, plates, &c. upon moulds or casts of various forms and patterns.

Plate 22
The presser.

examples of ceramic profiles from the Greatbatch site, both with and without grooves for footrings. These are all of glazed creamware (Fig. 16). Some bear initials or inscriptions, such as the *WD* and *William Sutton* inscriptions already noted (above, page 108), and it is interesting to note that the practice of the workman marking his tools has continued to the present century. Another tool was used for shaping or smoothing the inside of pressed hollow wares. This was a thin, flat piece of pottery, often with a hole in the middle to aid the workman's grip, with at least one side shaped to the internal profile of the ware. Fragments of these have been found on the Greatbatch site, but in salt-glazed stoneware (Fig. 17). These, too, were often initialled or inscribed with the owner's name. One other item required by the presser was a cow's lip, resembling a thick chamois leather, which was used to smooth the plain surfaces of the ware.

Less common as a method of manufacture than either throwing or press-moulding, slip-casting was not practised extensively until the 19th century. The method is simple: *The manner in which casts were taken from the moulds, was by pouring a very thin slip into the plaster mould, and letting it stand a short time before it was poured out, by which a perfect impression was received by the coat of thin slip or clay, which closely adhered to the mould. Then another and thicker coat was added, which, after remaining a few minutes in the mould, was returned, and this second casting more than doubled the thickness of the first casting or pouring-in of slip; and these castings were repeated until the required strength of thickness was obtained*[19].

Slip-cast wares are well-known from the mid-18th century onwards, but the technique was reserved only for those pieces which could not have been produced by any other method. The reason for this was that slip-casting was a time-

118

consuming, and hence expensive method. In the absence of deflocculents, not introduced until the 19th century, the plaster moulds needed to absorb large quantities of water and, consequently, became very quickly saturated, requiring prolongued drying out before the moulds could be re-used. Consequently slip-casting was not appropriate for the mass-production of wares in the 18th century.

The newly pressed and cast wares needed to be dried in order to part them from their plaster moulds: *The moulds were then placed before a fire to dry, which done, the pieces of ware were easily separated from the moulds, and the seams or marks where the moulds parted* (in the case of slip-cast wares), *were smoothed or taken off* [20].

All newly produced wares, thrown and moulded, were dried prior to the biscuit firing. This was most important in order to remove all moisture which might otherwise result in firecracking in the oven. Drying took place in a heated room which may have been reserved for this purpose. Such a room could have been heated by a small fire or stove, or have been located immediately adjacent to one of the factory's large ovens in order to take advantage of the heat during firing. Drying houses are often mentioned in documentary sources, being referred to by such names as *oven-house, hot-house* or *stove*[21]. An example of a drying house has been excavated on the Longton Hall porcelain factory: this was a rectangular brick-built structure, measuring 5.1 metres long by 2.8 metres wide, with an internal raised square hearth also of brick[22]. The dried ware was much stronger and easier to handle, allowing additional work to be carried out upon it.

The Turner turning in a lathe and regulating the clay ware which the "thrower" has formed .

Plate 23
The turner. His female assistant is treading the lathe.

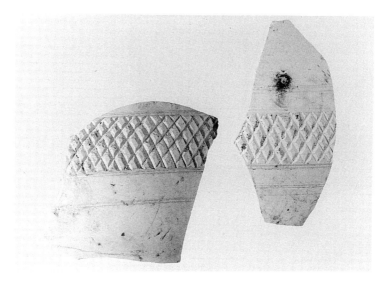

Plate 24
Turned decoration: band in relief after the body of the pot has been removed by 2mm on the lathe. The raised band has then been cross-hatched while still on the lathe with an incising tool. Phase II.

Lathe- and Engine-Turning. The turner was a key workman in the 18th century pottery factory, finishing dried hollow wares upon his lathe, an important tool. Lathes had been used in pottery manufacture since the late 17th century when they were used by the Elers brothers in the manufacture of their red stonewares at Bradwell[23]. By the time of Greatbatch, the lathes used in the shaping of pottery were driven by a treadle, usually operated by a woman lathe-treader (Plate 23). The pot was first fixed to the chuck of the lathe and rotated: with sharp incising or cutting tools, the turner could now remove excess clay from the body of the pot, form footrings, shape bases, incise lines or bands of varying widths, or else add rouletted decoration. Rouletted decoration may consist of rows of dots, zigzags, beading or any of the many varieties which occur. Quite simply, the design was cut into a small wheel which was pressed on to the body of the pot and rotated over it, producing an impressed band of a single repeated pattern. Many different types of rouletted decoration are found on Greatbatch's wares and simple turned banded or linear designs are commonplace. Most types of turned decoration involve the removal of clay from the body of the pot for the pattern itself, although at least one variation of this requires a band of clay to be left upstanding above the body of the pot which has been cut back on the lathe; this raised band is itself decorated with an incised design (Plate 24).

A variation on lathe-turned decoration is that referred to today as engine-turning. Whereas with simple lathe-turned decoration, a piece was rotated upon the chuck of the lathe for the turner to finish, the engine lathe had additional movements. A lateral, or sideways motion which brought the pot, revolving slowly, first into contact with the cutting tool and then removed it from the tool, enabled the turner to produce incised fluted bands running vertically up the height of the pot. A longitudinal motion moved the piece, still revolving, up and down, enabling the turner to produce a variety of reeded designs, of which those most commonly found on Greatbatch's wares are wavy reeds, diagonal reeds and curved reeds[24] (Plate 25). These reeds are produced by an incising tool with a number of separate teeth which produce the mutliple lines.

Plate 25
The main types of engine-turned decoration used by Greatbatch. Left: wavy reed; centre: diagonal reed; right: curved reed.

The introduction of engine-turning into the North Staffordshire pottery industry has been much discussed in relation to Josiah Wedgwood, who provides us with invaluable contemporary evidence, including the statement: *Engine lathe-turning — first introduced into the potteries by Mr. Wedgwood in 1763*[25]. Wedgwood's correspondence, particularly that with Thomas Bentley, charts his interest in and attempts to perfect decoration with the engine lathe. By 1765 Wedgwood had sufficient confidence in his engine-turned wares for him to send, as a gift to Queen Charlotte, *two setts of Vases, cream colour, engine turn'd & printed*[26], while by February, 1767, he was able to write: *We make constant use of the Rose* (i.e. lateral) *and Crown* (i.e. longitudinal) *motion separately, but have tryed very little what effects may be produced by combining them*[27]. By this time, engine-turning was coming to be widely employed by the North Staffordshire potters.

Handles and Spouts. After turning, the wares had handles and spouts applied where necessary. The Frenchman, Gabriel Jars, described this stage in the manufacturing process in the potteries of Newcastle-upon-Tyne in 1765:

When one wishes to make the handle of an ordinary teapot one takes a mould in two fitting pieces which are hollowed in the shape of the handle desired. A roll of clay is laid out in the mould to fill it completely and the other half of the mould is placed over it. The whole is placed in front of the fire for a short while and then the piece is removed from the mould and fitted to the body of the teapot with slip.

As to spouts, these are formed a little differently. There are moulds similar to those mentioned above, thoroughly dried and fitting into each other. At one of the ends which communicates with the hollow interior there is a hole through which one pours a very thin slip, in a way that there remains a hollow inside the formed piece which is the resulting teapot spout. What favours the formation of the hollow is the thorough dryness of the plaster which by its porousness takes up the water as it touches the walls. The mould is placed in front of the fire a short while, as before, to remove the complete piece which is fixed to the teapot as the handle[28].

The Handler fixing handles &c. to what has been turned &c. ready for being baked or fired

Plate 26 The handler.

All of Greatbatch's spouts, and a large number of his handles were produced from plaster of Paris moulds; there is evidence of both slip-casting and press-moulding for their production. Other handles, most notably the ribbed and fluted strap and rope handles which were usually used as intertwined pairs, were extruded from a shaped wooden box, known in the 19th and 20th centuries as a dod box. Handles, spouts and any applied decoration, such as the sprigged or mould-applied reliefs, were luted to the body of the pot by the application of a little slip. Inadequate luting of applied features could result in their separation during one or other of the firings. This is particularly noticeable with Greatbatch's flower and leaf handle terminals which were applied over the junctions between the handle and the body of the pot; the handle junctions did not always provide a good surface for the terminals to adhere to and there is a potential for terminals to lift off.

Applied Decoration. At this same stage, any applied decoration could be added to the ware. Decoration by the application of moulded reliefs was widespread on fine earthenwares and stonewares of the 18th century. Although generally referred to as sprigged decoration, two quite different methods of applying reliefs can be identified: these may be referred to as sprigged and mould-applied. Sprigging involves the forming of the decorative relief in a mould of plaster of Paris, which itself has been manufactured from a block mould of fired pottery, such as that shown in Plate 17. Clay is pressed into the plaster mould, which carries the design in intaglio, picking up the detail; the decorative relief is then peeled from the mould and is applied by hand to the surface of the unfired pot, with a little slip used to fix it in place. The mould-applied reliefs are formed in a mould or die of metal, probably brass. They are applied directly to the pot by pressing the die, with the clay still in place, on to the pot's surface, again using slip to fix the relief.

Plate 27a & b
Applied relief decoration. Left: mould-applied on to a rouletted vessel, with traces of scarring caused by contact with the metal die; right: sprigged, in high relief.

Both types of relief decoration were in use at the same time during much of the 18th century although it appears that mould-applied decoration from metal dies is the earlier method. The relief decoration used by the Elers brothers on their red stonewares in the late 17th century is consistently mould-applied, as is the decoration of the earliest white salt-glazed stonewares and glazed red earthenwares. By the middle of the 18th century, however, individual manufacturers were using both methods: Greatbatch was no exception. The two methods of relief decoration are easily distinguishable. The sprigged designs tend to be of a higher relief, standing fairly proud of the vessel's surface, whereas the mould-applied designs are of quite a low relief, but exhibiting much finer detail (Plate 27). The latter also invariably display a slight scarring around the design, the result of contact between the mould and the pot.

Biscuit firing and placing. The next stage in the production process was the biscuit firing. Placers set the ware in saggars, containers of a coarse, heavily grogged body of local marl, which were usually cylindrical in shape during the 18th century. The use of saggars dates back, in this country, to the introduction of fine lead-glazed hollow wares in the second half of the 15th century. In North Staffordshire, their use in connection with the firing of fine hollow wares was documented by Plot in 1686[29]. At the same time, the introduction of salt-glazed stonewares necessitated some modification to the type of saggar used, with large holes cut into the sides to allow the penetration of the volatilised salt-vapour which formed the glaze.

Saggars served a number of purposes. They acted as a form of baffle, to protect wares from direct heat or from sudden surges of temperature; they served to exclude undesirable fumes or smoke, which might contaminate the ware; they provided shelves upon which the ware could stand, and which themselves could be stacked to a considerable height within the oven, to make the most efficient use of the available space; and, last but by no means least, they prevented the free flow of glaze within the oven which could seriously damage all those wares with which it came into contact. From the 15th century, saggars were essential for the firing of the smaller hollow wares, although flat wares were rarely placed in saggars before the 18th century[30]. These were more easily stacked together in a manner which would avoid excessive contact between glazed surfaces, or else they were placed vertically, leaning against the inner wall of the oven[31]. The only exceptions to this rule were the flat wares of tin-glazed earthenware, the first fine earthenwares of this type to be produced in this country, which required protection within saggars in the same way as the fine hollow wares.

With the introduction of biscuit and glost firings in the manufacture of fine earthenwares, in about 1720, the use of saggars became ubiquitous within the Staffordshire potteries. Henceforth, both biscuit and glazed wares, hollow wares and flat wares, were placed and fired in saggars, with subsequent developments to the types of saggar used and in the means of placing and separating the vessels.

It is likely that saggars were made at most, if not all of the larger pottery factories, necessitating other specialist workers and workshops. In the 19th and 20th centuries, saggars were effectively moulded — built up around a wooden box mould, and with the flat base added separately. In the 18th century, however, this practice was less common, and it was quite normal for saggars to be thrown. The employment by Thomas Whieldon of Samuel Jackson *for throwing Sagers* has already been mentioned[32], while entries for the years 1766 and 1767 in John Wedgwood's Wage and Hiring Book mention the hiring of a Thomas Simpson at 6/6d per week to throw saggars[33].

There is little contemporary documentary evidence for the placing of wares, either during the biscuit firing or during the glost firing, and in the main we must rely upon later accounts and practices. The only reference to placing in Greatbatch's correspondence with Wedgwood, is to the placing of baskets and sugar dishes: *The baskets I had order'd...to be plac'd single — they will be crooked if doubled. The sugr. dish nobs Thos. Wedgwood order'd to be set low on acct. of placing them* [34]. Clearly there were problems with placing double certain types of ware, but whether biscuit or glost placing is referred to is uncertain.

The absence of documentary evidence makes an understanding of biscuit placing in the 18th century difficult. Indeed, it is not even known whether or not specialist kiln furniture was required to stack the wares and no evidence is forthcoming from a study of the wasters from the Greatbatch site. Damage at this stage of the production process was more likely to be from fire-cracking, discolouration, or warping than from vessels adhering to saggars or other kiln furniture. Consequently, it was important that the ware should be properly supported during the biscuit firing as it would not possess the strength to support itself at high temperatures and would be certain to warp or to sag. An interesting example of the problems faced by wares placed double is in the Wedgwood Museum, Barlaston. Here are two biscuit blackware teapot wasters which have been placed one on top of the other for the biscuit firing, with the tripod feet of the uppermost teapot resting upon the shoulder of the teapot below. The strain of placing in this way has proved too much for the pair and the shoulders of the lower teapot have sagged inwards under the weight; the two have also become fused together at the points of contact.

The placing practices of the 20th century would suggest that very little kiln furniture was necessary during the biscuit firing, as great reliance was made upon bedding the wares, especially flat ware, into sand to provide the necessary support. Smaller items of hollow ware may have been double or in 'bungs', with pieces of kiln furniture used both to separate and to support the ware. The presence amongst the excavated wasters of items of kiln furniture which are not glazed themselves does not necessarily indicate that these items were used during the biscuit firing: they may never have been used at all; they may have been used during the glost firing (below, page 136) but not have picked up any glaze; or they may have been used during the enamel firing after decoration. It seems that much more evidence will be needed before a clear picture of placing for the biscuit firing in the 18th century can be formed.

Plate 28
Clay bobs used as setter supports, with the impression of plate edge decoration. Phase III.

One item of kiln furniture alone has been found which can be positively associated with this stage of production. A number of small, roughly cylindrical pieces of clay have been found in Phase III which bear the impressions, on one side, of moulded plate edges (Plate 28). The height of these pieces varies from 4 mm to 21 mm and the face which has no impression is coarse and rather gritty, suggesting that these items were not used to separate the rims of plates stacked inside the saggars. A much more likely suggestion[35] is that they were placed on the saggar bottom, which could be somewhat irregular, particularly after frequent use, and were used to support and to level a biscuit plate or platter which was serving as a setter for further plates (Fig. 18). The use of setters for flat ware biscuit placing is well-known in the 19th and 20th centuries. These are effectively supports made to the profile of the wares to be placed upon them. The wares are placed face downwards, the bottom one upon the setter and separated from it by a layer of sand; each of the pieces above is separated from its neighbours by a layer of sand, and the whole 'bung' of ware is then placed into the saggar and surrounded by yet more sand which stabilises it. In the absence of a purpose-made setter, it would be feasible to use an already fired vessel of the same dimensions and profile to provide the necessary support. This is possibly what is represented by these small pieces of clay and their variable height would attend to the need to level individual bungs of vessels within the saggars. It is also interesting to note that the profile of these pieces slopes inwards, away from the impression, in a manner which reflects the angle of the rim of a plate used in this way.

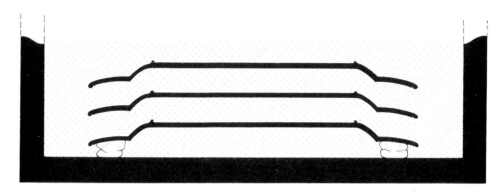

Fig. 18
The use of a setter in the placing of flatwares for the biscuit firing. In this example the setter is an already fired plate which is itself raised off the saggar bottom by clay bobs. The setter, being of the same shape as the wares to be biscuit fired, provides the necessary support. The pieces are separated from the setter, and from each other by layers of sand. (Not to scale)

For those hollow wares which did not require the added support of a setter, 'bedding' was the normal method of placing for the biscuit firing. This involved bedding the ware in a saggar full of sand which both separated the pieces and supported them. Placing in this manner would leave no trace to be recognised.

The saggars used in the biscuit firing can be identified, as they are the ones which have no trace of glaze inside. Their sizes vary, both in height (from about 13.5 — 21 cm.) and diameter (from about 32 — 58 cm.), according to the types of ware to be held, but all appear to be of cylindrical form: the oval saggars typical of the 19th and 20th centuries have not been identified on the Greatbatch site. What appear to be low walled saggars, of between 7 — 10 cm. in height and 33 — 48 cm. in diameter, have been found, but never with glazed interiors. The common tendency for these vessels to have glazed undersides suggests that they were not saggars at all but were, in fact, 'hillers' which were, effectively, covers used on the topmost saggars in the oven (Fig. 19).

After the saggars had been filled, they would be carried to the oven and stacked vertically in 'bungs' which were arranged around the interior of the oven. In the large ovens of the 20th century there were between fifty and one hundred and twenty bungs of saggars, each bung comprising between twelve and eighteen saggars; the ovens of the 18th century were considerably smaller in size and their capacity cannot be known. The saggars are sealed at the point where they come into contact with one another by the application of a strip of clay, known latterly as 'wad' clay. Many of the excavated saggars have the remains of the wad clay adhering either to their rims or to their bases. Those saggars at the top of the bung would have been closed with a 'hiller'. The placing or setting in of an oven required great skill, for it was important to know which parts of the oven were best for the different types of ware. Some types needed to be placed in the hottest

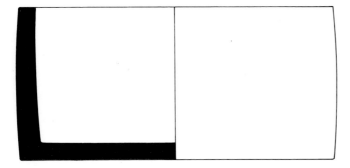

Fig. 19
A typical earthenware saggar and hiller. (Scale 1:4)

parts, others away from the greatest heat. It would have been normal for unfired saggars to be placed at the top of the bungs of fired saggars in order to maintain the necessary supply to the factory.

Little is known about the ovens of the 18th century for none survive and there is little documentary evidence. Even those ovens which have been excavated are not typical of the North Staffordshire Potteries during the second half of the 18th century. The oven base excavated at Samuel Bell's potworks in Newcastle-under-Lyme was circular, brick-built, 2.8 metres in diameter, and with eight fireboxes radiating outwards[36]; it was almost certainly surrounded by a hovel, the encircling chimney which gives the potters' ovens their distinctive bottle shape. This oven pre-dated Bell's death in 1744. Other ovens have been excavated at Longton Hall, Staffordshire, and although they date to a slightly later period than Bell's oven (1751 — 1760), they are likely to be atypical on account of their being for the firing of soft-paste porcelain[37]. The general picture is, however, much the same: brick-built, multi-flued ovens — the Longton Hall biscuit oven had seven fireboxes, the glost oven had five — with a surrounding hovel. These ovens are similar in form to the later 19th and 20th century bottle ovens which are so well-known in the Staffordshire Potteries, but are on a very much smaller scale. Another important point is that there would have been a great variety in the types of ovens used — in size, number of fireboxes, and in construction. This is quite clear from the surviving ovens of later date, with individual builders clearly having their own preferred methods and techniques.

The firing of a potter's oven in Newcastle-upon-Tyne is described in Jars' account of 1765: *The saggars ...are placed one on top of the other in the oven. There are several lines of them on the floor, forming different bungs following the height of the oven. When it is almost full, one closes up the entrance...with bricks and clay; coal is put into the five firemouths distributed around the great oven. After lighting, the flames go not only up the five flues but moreover through small holes which are arranged in each of them. Thus the heat passes equally through parts of the interior of the oven. This heat is to be maintained for 30 hours, after which the fire is baited and, when the oven has cooled, the pottery is drawn out for coating with glaze*[38].

The fuel used in the production of earthenwares and stonewares in North Staffordshire during the 18th century was always coal — Greatbatch refers to this in one of his letters (above, page 55); wood was only used in the firing of soft-paste porcelain. At the end of the 18th century an average firing could burn between twelve and fifteen tons of coal[39].

The biscuit firing cycle was a lengthy process. In the 20th century firing could take sixty hours or more, of which twenty-four hours were needed to slowly bring the oven up to temperature. For biscuit earthenware firings, the required temperature was 1,100 degrees centigrade. The rate at which the oven was cooled varied considerably — sometimes it was cooled slowly, often taking as long as the firing itself; at other times, particularly in the case of the glost firing, it could be rush-cooled. It can be seen that the firing cycle of Greatbatch's oven in 1763 was little different to that of the 20th century — almost three full days:

A Potters Oven when firing or baking, the ware being therein placed in Safeguards, or "Saggers."

Plate 29
Firing the oven.

I shall set the oven in tomorrow and put fire
too on Sunday night — the ware will be ready
on Wednesday by three O'clock afternoon.

Lanedelph Augst. 19th 1763[40]

Problems were clearly to be expected with firing and there was apparently potential for some variation in the way in which this was done, for on 12th October, 1763, Greatbatch writes: *The fire has been too easy I own but think the last oven full was very well on that account, but will fire harder next*[41]. By the early 19th century it was usual for an oven to be fired once a week[42]. There is evidence to suggest that Greatbatch's firing routine was little different to the 19th century practice: in a letter of Wednesday 8th May, 1764, he speaks of wares as if they had just come from the oven and makes a reference to his next firing[43]. Writing during this next firing, he states that the oven is to be drawn on Saturday 18th May, just ten days after drawing the previous oven[44].

Under-glaze Decoration. The introduction of double firings for earthenwares gave the potters the potential for a range of under-glaze decoration, painted or sponged, on to the biscuit body of the ware. The small number of painted creamwares dating to the 1740s have already been referred to (above, page 16), but the first under-glaze decorated wares which can *positively* be shown to have been made by the North Staffordshire potters are the tortoiseshell wares. These were as popular in the time of Greatbatch as they were in the early days of Whieldon's manufacture and the methods of producing the tortoiseshell effect had not changed. The colours used in the decoration were prepared from metallic oxides, powdered and prepared as a liquid; these were then painted or sponged on to the biscuit body and allowed to dry prior to glazing. Many of the sherds recovered from the Greatbatch site were tortoiseshell wares discarded at this stage of manufacture. It is interesting to note how some of the colours had been applied: the under-glaze decorated fruit basket ware had its colours painted on in short brush strokes (Plate XXVI), while the tortoiseshell wares had colours which were

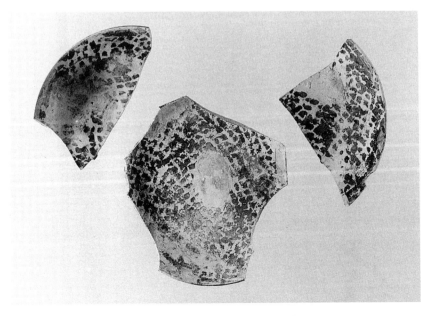

Plate 30
Biscuit tortoiseshell ware with colour applied.

usually dotted on with a brush or else with a small sponge or pad of no more than 2 — 3 mm in width. Some of the flatwares from the site, particularly saucers, appeared to have been decorated while revolving slowly on a wheel, with the dots of colour spiralling towards the centre of the pot (Plate 30). Upon glazing, the colours flowed to simulate tortoiseshell.

A development of this technique is under-glaze blue painted decoration which had been used on English soft-paste porcelains since the 1740s and came to be widely used on creamwares and pearlwares from the mid-1770s. The blue colour was produced from cobalt oxide, in its various states referred to as zaffre and smalt, which was ground to a fine powder and mixed to a liquid with either gum arabic and water, or turpentine. Both methods were used; both had their advantages. Colour mixed with gum arabic and water had the advantage of not requiring hardening-on in a separate firing: it could be air dried and passed direct to the dipper for glazing. However, colour mixed with turpentine had to be hardened-on, for which a firing of 680 — 750 degrees centigrade was required[45]. The advantage of this was a better quality of finish.

Plate 31
Biscuit cream/pearlware with under-glaze blue painted decoration. Left: hardened-on at a low temperature; right: hardened on at a high temperature. Phase III.

It is difficult to interpret the evidence of wasters, but the sherds from the Greatbatch site appear to suggest that Greatbatch used both oil-based and water-based colour in the production of under-glaze blue-painted wares. After hardening-on, the oil-based colour appears black, rather than blue, and may be easily scratched off the surface of the pot, above which it stands slightly proud (Plate 31). Such sherds were recovered in abundance from Phase III of the site, equal in number to those which appear to have water-based colour used in the decoration. The air-dried colour never actually hardens as such and may be smudged if touched with the finger and must, therefore, be handled carefully; the colour appears as

Plate 32
Biscuit cream/pearlware saucer with under-glaze blue-painted decoration which has been air-dried, rather than hardened-on in an oven. Phase III.

a thin grey outline (Plate 32). Many pieces were found on the Greatbatch site which were clearly the work of trainee painters: the amateurish attempts to copy a standard design appear on saucers, teabowls, and plates, often with several failed attempts on a single piece (Plates 33 & 34). A horizontal ground level, crudely painted rocks, and the roof of an Oriental building, floating in mid-air, illustrate the order in which the various elements to the designs were dealt with. These practice pieces are common, but are always of the air-dried type with the colour appearing as a grey outline, easily smudged.

Plate 33
Under-glaze blue practice pieces. Phase III.

Plate 34
Under-glaze blue practice pieces. Phase III.

Very common indeed amongst the excavated blue-painted sherds were biscuit wares whose under-glaze decoration appeared very dense, ranging in colour from dark blue to ink blue or black (Plate 35). The colour had clearly been hardened-on — and is consequently oil-based — and had been fully absorbed into the body of the ware; there was no way in which these designs could be scratched off. Why

Plate 35
Biscuit cream/pearlware saucers with under-glaze blue painted decoration which has been hardened-on at high temperatures. The density of the colours is apparent. Phase III.

132

Plate 36
Biscuit cream/pearlware saucer with under-glaze blue painted decoration which has been hardened-on at high temperature. The warping of the piece suggests that the hardening-on was in an oven which reached the biscuit firing temperature of around 1,100 degrees centigrade or more, thereby causing it to collapse. Phase III.

there should be such a marked variation in the colour of the oil-based blue painted decoration is a problem. We can speculate that higher temperatures may have been reached in some of the hardening-on firings and must assume that this would have resulted in the variation in colour. However could these fluctuations of temperature have caused already fired biscuit wares to warp and collapse? There are several examples of under-glaze blue painted biscuit wares which have suffered in this way (Plate 36) and the only explanation can be that these already fired pieces were placed in a cool part of the oven during a biscuit firing; problems at this stage may well have resulted in a temperature which was far higher than expected, causing already fired wares to warp[46]. This practice is not documented, but if we are interpreting the evidence correctly, it appears that we must consider that the hardening-on of under-glaze blue painted decoration, or at least that which used oil-based colours, took place in a biscuit oven, taking full advantage of the cool spots which occur in any firing. This practice would also serve to economise on fuel, a major consideration in the production process, saving an expensive separate firing.

Glazing. There is no reference in Greatbatch's correspondence to the next stage of the manufacturing process — the glazing of the ware. Jars summarises the processes: *All the glazes in use are based on lead. The mineral, or red lead, or white lead are used according to the quality of the pottery. Some other material is added to vary the colour. To diminish the cost of glazing, some calcined flint is added as well as some of the clay of which the ware is made. As soon as the glaze covering the pots has dried, they are again put into saggars and then into the oven as before, also for 30 hours. They are then ready for selling*[47].

"Glazing" or dipping the ware in a prepared liquid, which produces the glossy surface.

Plate 37
The dipper.

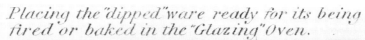

Placing the "dipped" ware ready for its being fired or baked in the "Glazing" Oven.

Plate 38
Glost placing.

As we have seen, by this time the glaze was applied to ware by dipping. Aikin's account is more detailed than that of Jars: *It (the ware) is immersed or dipped into a fluid generally consisting of sixty pounds of white lead, ten pounds of ground flint, and twenty pounds of a stone from Cornwall burned and ground, all mixed together, and as much water put to it as reduces it to the thickness of cream, which it resembles. Each piece of ware being separately immersed or dipped into this fluid, so much of it adheres all over the piece, then when put into other saggars, and exposed to another operation of the fire, performed in the glossing kiln or oven, then ware becomes finished by acquiring its glossy covering, which is given it by the vitrification of the above ingredients* [48].

The placing of glazed wares within the saggars posed far greater problems than the placing of unglazed wares, for it was vital to avoid any more contact than necessary between the vessels, and between the vessels and the saggars. It was also important to prevent excessive flowing of liquid glaze during the firing, for this, too, could lead to wastage as a result of wares fusing together.

Glost firing and placing. The introduction of separate glost firings around 1720 brought with it the need for a completely new range of specialist kiln furniture items. The rough clay 'bobs' used to support the slipwares and other earthenwares of the 17th century[49] would not suffice for the fine wares of the 18th century, whose surfaces would have been scarred by contact with such clumsy items. The kiln furniture which accompanied the introduction of separate firings was based upon the principle of support and separation with the minimum of contact. This usually involved no more than three points of contact, either arranged upon ring stilts, or upon three legged stilts.

The Greatbatch site has produced some of the best examples of kiln furniture of the period, illustrating virtually all the types in use locally. Unlike other groups of kiln furniture from excavations in the area, the material from the Greatbatch site was almost entirely designed for the placing of creamwares. The kiln furniture itself was made from the same white-firing clay used for the earthenware bodies, as any difference in colour might lead to a noticeable scar where kiln furniture touched the vessel. The early material, from Phases I and II, illustrates the importance of the ring stilt to the potter. This consists of three or more points of clay set upon a low ring of rectangular section (Plate 39). Different sizes were used for different wares. Those ring stilts with points only on one, upper face were designed to raise wares from the saggar bottoms, while those with points

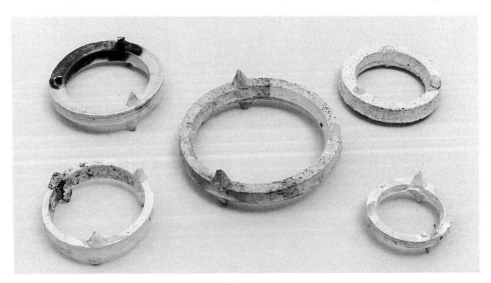

Plate 39
Kiln furniture: ring stilts. Phase II.

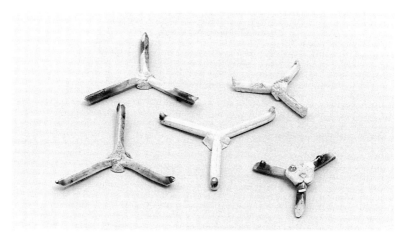

Plate 40
Kiln furniture: stilts, some with traces of colour from the wares they supported, others with scars from contact. Phase II.

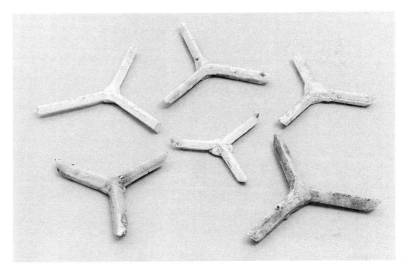

Plate 41
Kiln furniture: stilts, creamware and pearlware (two front). Phase III.

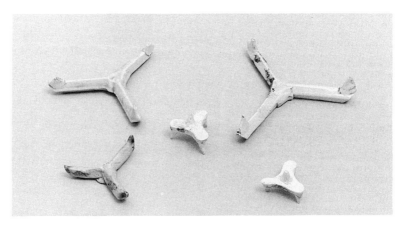

Plate 42
Kiln furniture: stilts with applied points to cut down the area of contact with the ware, and small trivets or cockspurs. Phase III.

on both faces were to form separators within a 'bung' of wares. At the same time, three-legged stilts were used: these were either used as simple supports or separators in their own right, with the topmost edge of their rectangular-sectioned legs serving as the point of contact, or else they were embellished with points at their extremities which cut down the area of contact even further (Plates 40 — 42). Traces of colour on these stilts show that they were used to support a range of both coloured and uncoloured creamwares.

The growing importance in Greatbatch's output during the 1760s of cauliflower, pineapple and other coloured glazed wares, is reflected in items of kiln furniture not yet recognised on other sites in Stoke-on-Trent. Very common amongst the Phase II material are three-legged stilts which have integral drip trays, to catch the fluxed green and yellow glazes, and to prevent excessive contamination of other wares. These stilts with integral drip trays are either of solid, disc type, or of a ring type, with a central hole remaining (Plate 43). Both types are commonly found heavily coated with the thick green and yellow glaze, which flows much more freely than the standard lead glaze, underlining the need for such elaborate supports. Their small numbers amongst the Phase III finds, are an indication of the declining popularity of coloured glazed wares.

The kiln furniture of Phase III is significantly different to that of Phases I and II. This is partly due to the change in the nature of production, and the different emphasis on the various types of ware, but it also reflects some, albeit minor, advances in technology. Firstly, ring stilts almost disappear, their place taken by the multi-purpose three-legged stilts, with or without additional points. A wholly new type appears: this is a small triangular-shaped stilt (Plate 42), not disimilar in function, perhaps, to the small flexible multi-purpose 'cockspurs' of the early 19th century which were often used between plate rims. In Phase III, for the first time, stilts appear which have been designed specifically for the firing of flat ware — plates. This has not been recognised in any of the earlier groups of kiln

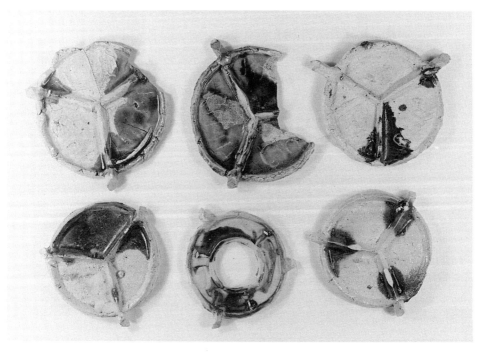

Plate 43
Kiln furniture: stilts with integral drip trays to catch yellow and green glaze. Phase II.

Plate 44
Kiln furniture: saggars with perforated walls and fragments of horizontal bars fused in place. These were used in the glost placing of flatwares. Phase III.

furniture excavated on any of the Stoke-on-Trent sites, and the implication must be that, hitherto, potters had improvised in the placing of their flat wares.

Greatbatch's flat ware kiln furniture is not wholly innovative. The delftware potters of London, Bristol and Liverpool, had for some time made use of short horizontal bars with pointed outer ends in the placing of their tin-glazed plates. These bars were inserted in vertical rows into the already pierced inner walls of the saggars, so that each plate rim rested upon just three small points (Fig. 20). Greatbatch made use of this method of placing his flat wares during Phase III: several perforated saggars have been found together with an assortment of horizontal bars which were of several forms but were all of creamware (Plate 44). This method appears not to have been commonly used, and it may be that it was a late innovation, possibly shortly before production ceased in 1782. It was a variation of this method of flat ware placing which was most commonly used

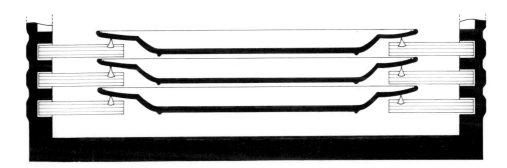

Fig. 20
The placing of flatwares for the glost firing (1). The saggar's walls are perforated to take the horizontal bars which serve as supports for the ware. (Not to scale)

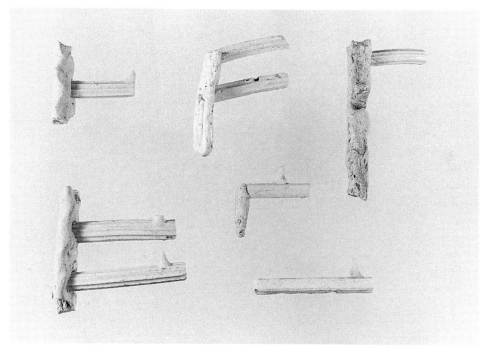

Plate 45
Kiln furniture: horizontal bars, some set into clay strips, used in the glost placing of saggars. Phase III.

during Phase III. Horizontal bars of creamware with pointed ends were pressed into vertical strips of clay which were themselves pressed against the innner walls of the saggars, again in three vertical rows (Fig. 21). Numerous examples of these bars have been found, some still fixed to their clay supporting strips (Plate 45). This method did not require the piercing of the saggar walls to take the horizontal bars.

Saggars used in glost firings needed to be washed with glaze inside prior to use in order to prevent their dry bodies drawing the glaze from the wares which were being fired inside, a process known as glaze starvation. Consequently, it is always possible to identify those saggars used in the glost firings through their glazed interiors. These saggars regularly contain other interesting traces, of kiln furniture, of coloured glazes and of fragments of vessels which have fractured off and have adhered to the saggar's base or sides.

Fig. 21
The placing of flatwares for the glost firing (2). The horizontal bars which support the ware are set into clay strips applied vertically to the inside walls of the saggar. (Not to scale)

Apart from their internal glaze, the glost saggars are characterised by the use of stone and calcined flint, ground into very small pieces, which were thickly strewn about their bases to prevent the kiln furniture from sticking to the saggar. Some examples from the Greatbatch site also have fragments of animal bone mixed in with the small grits.

The glost firing proceeded very much the same as the biscuit firing, except at a slightly lower temperature of about 1050 degrees centigrade, and for a shorter time, of between twenty-four and thirty-six hours in the 20th century. The time difference was the result of there being no need to build up the heat in the slow gradual fashion required in the biscuit firing when it was important to drive off any excess moisture from the ware.

Over-glaze Decoration. After the glost firing, wares were selected for decoration. Over-glaze decoration could be of a superior quality to under-glaze decoration, depending upon the skill of the decorator, and allowed much greater scope for versatility, both in the techniques used and in the range of colours available. The colours employed were produced from the oxides of metals which were fritted, then powdered and mixed to a soft paste with turpentine and fat oil. The coloured patterns were painted on to the ware and were then hardened-on, at temperatures of between seven hundred to eight hundred degrees centigrade in the decorating oven or muffle.

These ovens were very much smaller than the biscuit and glost ovens and were often designed to provide a protective chamber, or muffle, for the wares. It was important that the decorated wares were not contaminated in any way by the fire and, therefore, either the muffle, or the saggars in which the wares might be placed, had to be sealed effectively.

Grinding and preparing the various colours for the Enameller or Painter.

Plate 46
Preparing colours.

Painting and Gilding China or Earthenware.

Plate 47
The painting shop.

It is well-known that different colours harden-on at different temperatures and consequently decorated wares may have required more than one firing. Particularly elaborate pieces, using a wide range of colours and perhaps gilding, would have been through the oven on several occasions, something which would have been reflected in their high price. The simplest method of gilding in the mid-18th century was that known as honey gilding: gold leaf was ground with honey to a paste which was then painted on to the body of the pot. Another low temperature firing was required to harden-on the colour, and afterwards the gold was burnished to brighten its dull colour. The disadvantage with this method of gilding was that the gold colour tended to remain rather dull and to wear off with use.

Many pieces of enamel-painted ware have been recovered from the Greatbatch site and these exhibit a wide range of styles, types of decoration and colours used. The excavated sherds decorated in this way belong almost exclusively to Phase III of the site and are interesting for the large quantity of pieces whose colours have not been properly hardened-on to the body of the pot. The low temperature enamel firing would not have resulted in much loss, except perhaps where discolouration had taken place through contamination from the fire, but why there should be so many pieces whose decoration was not hardened-on is a mystery. Were these pots fired in ovens which did not reach the necessary temperature? This would seem most likely given that any mistakes during the decorating stage could be easily corrected by the painter simply wiping off the pattern and starting again. Additional support for this interpretation may be seen in the way in which these decorated wasters were found on the site, often in large homogenous groups which had clearly been deposited *en masse*.

Over-glaze Printing. In common with many of his contemporaries, Greatbatch made extensive use of over-glaze printed decoration, particularly for his creamwares. Until recently, this technique was commonly believed to have involved the transfer of an image by tissue paper from an engraved copper plate. This is the flat press and tissue paper method, well-known in the manufacture of under-glaze blue printed wares introduced during the 1780s, which is still used today. However, Paul Holdway has questioned the early use of tissue paper-printed designs on creamware. His reassessment of the documentary evidence and study of numerous printed pieces has led him to conclude that the technique employed more or less universally on creamware during the 1760s and 1770s involved the use, not of tissue paper, but of glue bats[50].

During the 18th and 19th centuries, virtually all ceramic printing was from engraved or etched copper plates. From these an image could be reproduced many thousands of times. The medium of transfer is immaterial: both glue bats and tissue paper have their advantages and their disadvantages. What is significant, however, is the overwhelming evidence in favour of the use of glue bats in the printing of creamware and the means by which their use may be determined.

The gluc bats are thin sheets of animal glue in a state midway between rubber and plastic, rather similar to pre-sliced processed cheese. The printer takes an engraved copper plate and applies linseed oil, ensuring that the lines of the design are fully filled, and then removes the excess; the glue bat is brought into contact with the plate and pressed firmly to pick up the outline of the design. The bat is then removed from the plate and pressed on to the pot, leaving behind the oil outline of the design on the glazed surface. The transferred design is then dusted with a fine powdered metallic oxide colour, normally black, but occasionally red, brown or purple, so that the pattern is clearly picked out in colour. Excess colour can simply be blown away. A low temperature firing is needed to harden-on the print.

Engraving designs on Copper Plates, for producing the much admired "blue printed pots", &c.

Plate 48
Engraving.

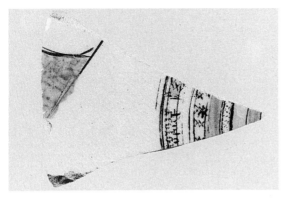

Plate 49
Double image of printed design, caused by careless application of the transfer-bearing glue bat to the body of the pot. Phase III.

John Sadler's own notebook refers to printing with glue in 1760[51] and his use of the technique can be clearly seen from the prints of surviving wares. Glue bats have one great advantage over tissue paper as the medium of transfer, in that they stretch and are ideally suited to printing on round-bodied vessels. Tissue paper, by contrast, does not stretch and when applied to a round-bodied vessel it creases and wrinkles; these creases are apparent on a great many printed wares, appearing as flaws in the pattern. The bat-printed image will distort to the shape of a vessel but is not otherwise impaired; this drawback can be countered to a degree by the design being placed in vignettes which disguise the distortion. Another flaw which is sometimes recognisable in bat-printed designs is a double image, the result of uncertain contact between the bat and the surface of the pot (Plate 49). However, by far the most common flaw in bat-printed designs is one which readily allows us to identify the method of printing: these are small 'eyes' which appear in the prints, and which are usually caused by air bubbles or dirt trapped between the pot and the bat (Plates 50 & 51).

The contemporary name given to this method of printing was black printing, presumably deriving from the colour most commonly used. Greatbatch's black printed creamwares have been examined by Holdway and can all be shown to be printed in the manner described. 'Eyes' and double images are apparent amongst the many hundreds of printed sherds from the Greatbatch site.

Greatbatch's printed wares are particularly noteworthy for the great number of designs which were over-painted in coloured enamels, combining the skills of both printer and enameller. These would have required yet more low temperature firings and would have greatly increased the cost of the wares to the consumer.

Plate 50
'Eye', or bubble in printed design, caused by an air bubble trapped between the pot and the glue bat, or else by dirt on one of the surfaces. Phase III.

Plate 51
'Eye' in printed design, as Plate 50. Phase III.

Enamel Firing. The need for kiln furniture to support ware during the glost firing, as well as the apparent absence of this need during the biscuit firing, have already been discussed (above, page 124). Not discussed, however, is the necessity of supporting wares during the enamel firing when the enamel colours are hardened-on to the surfaces of the glazed wares. Although only a low temperature firing of 700 — 800 degrees centigrade, the heat is sufficient to soften glaze and to result in marking at those points where contact is made with other vessels or with pieces of kiln furniture. Consequently, a similar range of kiln furniture would be required as for the glost firing, although it may be difficult to recognise items used in such a way amongst any excavated assemblage such as that from the Greatbatch site. Stilts which have little or no glaze on them have already been mentioned (above, page 124): these may perhaps have been used to support decorated wares during the enamel firing. In addition, there are a handful of problem saggars which are unglazed, but which have the holes in their sides which have been described in relation to the glost firing (above, page 137). If we accept — and it may be premature to do so — that no kiln furniture was needed during the biscuit firing, then these few saggars are likely to have been used during the enamel firing for the supporting of flat wares.

Salt-glazing. The likelihood that Greatbatch produced white salt-glazed stoneware is great. This has long been suspected, and the quantity of salt-glazed wasters recovered from the excavation would seem to confirm this. It has already been mentioned that the production of salt-glazed stoneware required both a separate oven, which could provide the higher temperatures required of 1,200 — 1,400 degrees centigrade, and a different type of saggar (above, page 106). Finds from the Greatbatch site of salt-glazed saggars were not numerous, reflecting perhaps either the limited importance or the limited period of production of this type. Those saggars which were found, however, are wholly typical of the many examples which are in the City Museum & Art Gallery, Stoke-on-Trent, or which have been found on numerous excavations within the Potteries[52].

A distinctive range of kiln furniture was consistently used during the 18th century in the salt-glazed saggars. These included 'bobs', crudely made cones of clay which have grits set into their tops; ring stilts; and 'prisms' of the type described by

144

Jars: *When the wares are to be placed in saggars, small children prepare supports which are small pieces of the same clay as that of the saggars, cut into rectangular prisms. While they are still moist they are placed on roughly crushed grits which stick all over their surfaces. These grits are placed at the bottom of the saggars and one uses the prisms to support each piece. This is done so that there is no touching. The grits do not stick to the wares and there is not the slightest mark, except on certain pieces which are then to be rejected*[53].

Several examples of this salt-glazed kiln furniture were found on the Greatbatch site, but their numbers reflect the relatively low level of production of salt-glazed stoneware which is suggested by the pottery.

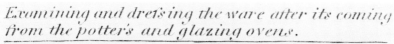

Plate 52
Checking the ware in the warehouse.

Faults. All of the pottery recovered from the Greatbatch site was wasted in some way. Pieces were damaged at every stage of the manufacturing process and many different faults are apparent. Perhaps the most common faults are firecracks, found most frequently in biscuit wares, and warping which occurs in both the biscuit and the glost firing. Excessive heat is the most likely cause of warping, while moisture trapped in the body of a pot would cause firecracking. Discolouration of both biscuit bodies and glazed surfaces is another common fault which could be caused by too little or too much oxygen within the oven. This is apparently referred to by Greatbatch in a communication with Wedgwood:

Sir,

*I hope the above goods will please as
they be Intirely free from the Browning & Don't
doubt they will continue so for future.*[54]

The glazed wares often suffer from glazes which appear to have burnt off, perhaps having been poorly applied in the first instance, or else the result of placing in the wrong part of the oven with incorrect temperatures causing the damage. Another problem encountered during the glost firing is the potential for the ware to pick up dust or dirt from within the saggar or from outside. Consequently it was important that the saggars were of a suitable standard and also that they were properly sealed with wad clay.

Many vessels suffered from contact with others during the firing, either scarring or fusing together. Others bear traces of contact with kiln furniture which would be unacceptable to any purchaser. Others have suffered much more dramatic damage, such as crushing caused by the collapse of a saggar. Several of the saggars have the remains of glazed wares fused to their undersides, illustrating either very poor placing, or the slumping of the saggars during firing.

The difference between wasters and seconds need not be great; seconds were simply those poor quality pieces for which a market could be found. An examination of extant pieces of Greatbatch's wares shows that a great many defects were permissable in the ceramics of the time. Scars and firecracks, blistered glazes, poorly applied prints and shoddy painted decoration are all common faults which have, presumably, been overlooked. At the commencement of business, Greatbatch sets out the price of his wares, including seconds. The seconds are almost half the price of the first quality wares — 2 shillings for seconds of coffee pots and teapots, compared with 3/6d for firsts[55]. In another of his letters to Wedgwood, Greatbatch displays concern about disposing of his seconds: *..their will also be some seconds which you must take for I cannot keep them to look at.* [56]

Packing China and Earthenware in "Crates."

Plate 53
Packing the ware.

Packing the ware is referred to in several of Greatbatch's letters. This was done in basketwork crates which were transported by horse or, more normally by waggon. For these, Wedgwood was charged between one shilling for a simple crate[57], 1/6d for a seven withe crate and 1/10d for a nine withe crate[58]. In addition, reference is made to *horse crates* which were priced at 10d and *large crates* which were 1/5d[59], while hogsheads priced at 3/3d each are mentioned in a single note[60]. The potential for accidents at this late stage of the production process has been described above (page 55) when a crate of ware leaving Greatbatch's factory fell from the waggon[61]. For such damaged wares, and for other wasters from the factory, there was clearly a demand, as shown by an invoice of 24th September, 1763, which lists a *Crate of Pitchers* (i.e. waste sherds) amongst the items supplied to Wedgwood[62]. Such pottery waste could be used as hard core, for drainage or, more likely in this case, for re-cycling within the industry as the grog necessary for the manufacture of saggars.

What happened to the perfect wares between their leaving Greatbatch's factory and turning up in collections today will remain a mystery and is unimportant. It is those discarded wares, the failures in their day, which, through their rediscovery, have become the more important for what they can tell us about 18th century pottery production, and Greatbatch's factory in particular. The survival of documentary material for the years 1762 — 1765 merely reinforces the evidence of the pottery itself.

1. Weatherill 1971, 38.
2. Dossie 1764, 360 — 361.
3. Dated 2nd November, 1764. Wedgwood MSS: 22389-30.
4. Weatherill 1971, 61.
5. Thomas Whieldon's Account and Memorandum Book. City Museum & Art Gallery, Stoke-on-Trent (unpub.).
6. Weatherill 1971, 51 — 52.
7. John Wedgwood's Wage and Hiring Book 1756 — 78. City Museum & Art Gallery, Stoke-on-Trent.
8. Young 1769.
9. Wedgwood MSS: 22325-30.
10. Account edited by Henri-Louis Duhamel du Monceau and incorporated into his work *L'Art du Potier de Terre* (published 1773), where it forms Chapter 3, *Poterie d'Angleterre*. Annotated translation given by Celoria (1976a & 1976b).
11. Celoria 1976b, 25 — 26.
12. Wedgwood MSS: 22349-30.
13. Gabriel Jars quoted in Celoria 1976b, 26.
14. Weatherill 1971, 33.
15. Barker 1990; Barker & Halfpenny 1990, 7 — 10.
16. Wedgwood MSS: 22359-30.
17. *ibid.*: 30136-30.
18. John Proudlove, described by Shaw (1829, 223) as *at that time the best mould maker and turene maker in that part.*
19. Pitt 1817, 418.
20. *ibid.*: 418 — 419.
21. Weatherill 1971, 61.
22. Tait & Cherry 1978, 15 — 17.
23. Elliott 1981, 80 — 86.
24. The workings of, and decoration formed by the engine lathe have been clearly explained in Adeney 1989. John Adeney's excellent work on engine-turning has presented us with a classification for incised decoration which, it is felt, should be adhered to.
25. Josiah Wedgwood's Commonplace Book, Volume I, page 33. Wedgwood MSS: E39-28408.
26. Wedgwood MSS: E.18080-25.
27. *ibid.*: E25-18136.
28. Celoria 1976a, 23.
29. Plot 1686, 123.
30. *ibid.*
31. Brears 1971, 131.
32. Thomas Whieldon's Account and Memorandum Book. City Museum & Art Gallery, Stoke-on-Trent (unpub.).
33. 11th October, 1766, and 7th October, 1767: John Wedgwood's Wage and Hiring Book 1756 — 78. City Museum & Art Gallery, Stoke-on-Trent.
34. Wedgwood MSS: 22341-30.
35. For which I thank Robert Copeland.
36. Bemrose 1973, plate 2.
37. Tait & Cherry 1978.
38. Celoria 1976a, 23.
39. Aikin 1795, 533.
40. Wedgwood MSS: 22344-30.
41. *ibid.*: 30126-30.
42. Pitt 1817, 419.
43. Wedgwood MSS: 22374-30.
44. *ibid.*: 22375-30.
45. Copeland 1980, 24.
46. I am grateful to Robert Copeland for this suggestion.
47. Celoria 1976a, 23.
48. Aikin 1795, 533.
49. Plot 1686, 124.
50. For a preliminary notice of the results of this research see Holdway 1986. A more fully illustrated account will be presented in Holdway forthcoming. A most enlightening demonstration of printing with a glue bat was given at the 1986 Keele Ceramics Summer School.
51. John Sadler's Notebook. City of Liverpool Reference Library.
52. See for example Mountford 1971, figs. 2 — 4.
53. Celoria 1976b, 27.
54. Wedgwood MSS: 30120-30, dated 6th August, 1763.
55. Above, page   . Wedgwood MSS: 22401-30.
56. *ibid.*: 22324-30.
57. For example on 23rd December, 1762. *ibid.*: 30106-30.
58. For example on 14th March, 1763. *ibid.*: 30109-30.
59. For example on 10th January, 1763. *ibid.*: 30107-30.
60. *ibid.*: 22403-30.
61. *ibid.*: 22402-30.
62. *ibid.*: 30124-30.

PLATE I **Creamware coffee pot,** painted over-glaze in enamel colours: red (main designs), and red, yellow and green (handle terminals d knop). *c.* 1765-1770. See page 206, and Plate 90 for reverse. (City Museum & Art Gallery, Stoke-on-Trent)

PLATE II **Creamware teapot,** painted over-glaze in enamel colours, excavated from Phase III. *c.* 1770-1782. See page 209. (City Museum & Art Gallery, Stoke-on-Trent)

PLATE III **Creamware teapot,** painted over-glaze in coloured enamels. The central panels show the Sun (front) and the Moon (reverse). *c.* 1770-1782. See page 209. (The Jacobs Collection. Photography by Gavin Ashworth)

PLATE IV **Creamware teapot,** painted over-glaze in enamel colours; traces of gilding survive on the framing cartouche. *c.* 1770-1782. See page 215, and Plate 98 for reverse. (The Jacobs Collection. Photography by Gavin Ashworth)

PLATE V **Creamware teapot** with applied moulded band and painted over-glaze in enamel colours. *c.* 1770-1782. See page 193. (Norfolk Museums Service. Norwich Castle Museum)

PLATE VI **Creamware teapot,** painted over-glaze in enamel colours with floral patterns, front and reverse. *c.* 1770-1782. See Plate 94 for reverse. (Norfolk Museums Service. Norwich Castle Museum)

PLATE VII **Creamware teapot,** painted over-glaze in enamel colours with floral patterns, front and reverse. *c.* 1765-1770. See page 206. (Walford Collection)

PLATE VIII **Creamware teapot,** painted over-glaze in enamel colours with floral patterns, front and reverse. *c.* 1770-1782. See Plate 97 for reverse. (City Museum & Art Gallery, Stoke-on-Trent)

PLATE IX **Creamware teabowl and saucers,** painted in enamel colours, excavated from Phase III. *c.* 1770-1782. (City Museum & Art Gallery, Stoke-on-Trent)

PLATE X **Creamware teapot,** painted over-glaze in enamel colours with the subject of 'Aurora'; the reverse subject is the rising sun. *c.* 1770-1782. See page 216, and Plate 117 for reverse. (City Museum & Art Gallery, Stoke-on-Trent)

PLATE XI **Creamware teapot,** printed with the subject of *Aurora* and painted over-glaze in enamel colours; other decoration is painted in under-glaze blue. The reverse subject, also printed, is the 'World with Sun, Moon and Stars'. *c.* 1770-1782. See page 233. (The Jacobs Collection. Photography by Gavin Ashworth)

PLATE XII **Creamware teapot,** printed with the subject of 'Captain Cook being directed by Britannia' and painted over-glaze in enamel colours. The reverse subject, also printed, is the 'World with Sun, Moon and Stars'. *c.* 1776. See page 234. (The Weldon Collection. ©1990 Henry H. Weldon. Photography by Gavin Ashworth FBIPP, FRPS)

PLATE XIII **Creamware teapot,** printed with the subject of 'The Fortune Teller' and painted over-glaze in enamel colours; gilding survives on the teapot's rouletted moulding. The reverse subject, also printed, is *The XII Houses of Heaven.* 1778-1782. See page 236. (City Museum & Art Gallery, Stoke-on-Trent)

PLATE XIV **Creamware teapot,** printed with the subject *The Prodigal Son in Excess* and painted over-glaze in enamel colours. The reverse subject, also printed, is *The Prodigal Son in Misery* (Plate 143). *c.* 1770-1782. See page 229. (City Museum & Art Gallery, Stoke-on-Trent)

PLATE XV **Creamware teapot,** printed with the subject of 'a lady, her suitor, and her father in a garden' and painted over-glaze in enamel colours. The reverse subject is 'Harlequin and Columbine discovered in an arbour'. *c.* 1770-1782. See page 233. (Norfolk Museums Service. Norwich Castle Museum)

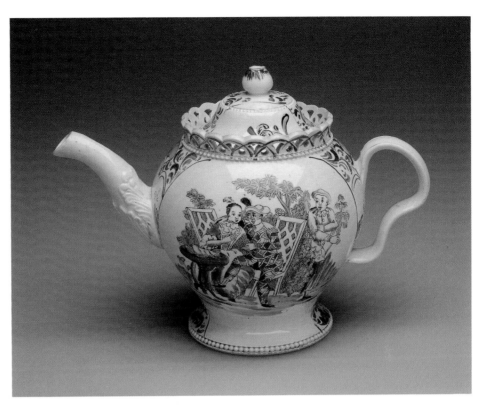

PLATE XVI **Creamware teapot,** printed with the subject of 'Harlequin and Columbine discovered in an arbour' and painted over-glaze in enamel colours. The reverse subject, also printed, depicts 'a lady, her suitor and her father in a garden'. *c.* 1770-1782. See page 232. (The Jacobs Collection. Photography by Gavin Ashworth)

PLATE XVII **Creamware teapot,** printed front and back with Oriental figure subjects, and painted over-glaze in enamel colours. *c.* 1770-1782. See page 237, and Plate 150 for reverse. (City Museum & Art Gallery, Stoke-on-Trent)

PLATES XVIII/XIX **Creamware teapot,** printed with the subjects of *Juno* (front) and 'the World with Sun, Moon and Stars' (reverse) and painted over-glaze in enamel colours. *c.* 1770-1782. See pages 233-234. (Norfolk Museums Service. Norwich Castle Museum)

PLATE XX **Creamware** *tortoiseshell* **teapot,** coloured under-glaze with metallic oxides. *c.* 1770-1782. See page 196. (City Museum & Art Gallery, Stoke-on-Trent)

PLATE XXI **Creamware** *tortoiseshell* **teapot and bowl,** the latter decorated with sprigged reliefs, excavated from Phase II. *c.* 1765-1770. See page 196. (City Museum & Art Gallery, Stoke-on-Trent)

PLATE XXII **Candlestick,** green-glazed creamware, of moulded leaf design and with a band of four owls' heads around the lower stem. c. 1765-1775. See pages 253-254. (City Museum & Art Gallery, Stoke-on-Trent)

PLATE XXIII **Creamware** *cauliflower* **teapot,** press-moulded, with green glaze to lower body. See pages 255-258. *c.* 1765-1770. (The Board of Trustees of the National Museums & Galleries on Merseyside. Liverpool Museum)

PLATE XXIV **Creamware** *cauliflower* **teapot, plate and slop bowl,** excavated from Phase II. *c.* 1765-1770. See pages 255-258. (City Museum & Art Gallery, Stoke-on-Trent)

PLATE XXV **Creamware coffee pot,** press-moulded with clusters of shells to body, coloured under-glaze with metallic oxides. *c.* 1765-1770. See pages 245-247. (The Board of Trustees of the National Museums & Galleries on Merseyside. Liverpool Museum)

PLATE XXVI **Excavated and extant. Fruit basket** teapot body, biscuit, with oxide colours applied prior to glazing. Phase III. *c.* 1770-1782. Fruit basket teapot of Phase II type. *c.* 1765-1770. See pages 241-244. (City Museum & Art Gallery, Stoke-on-Trent)

PLATE XXVII **Pearlware figure of Ceres,** with details highlighted in coloured glazes, flanked by over-glaze painted base sherds comprising lion, rocks and cornucopia excavated from Phase III. *c.* 1775-1782. See page 182. (City Museum & Art Gallery, Stoke-on-Trent)

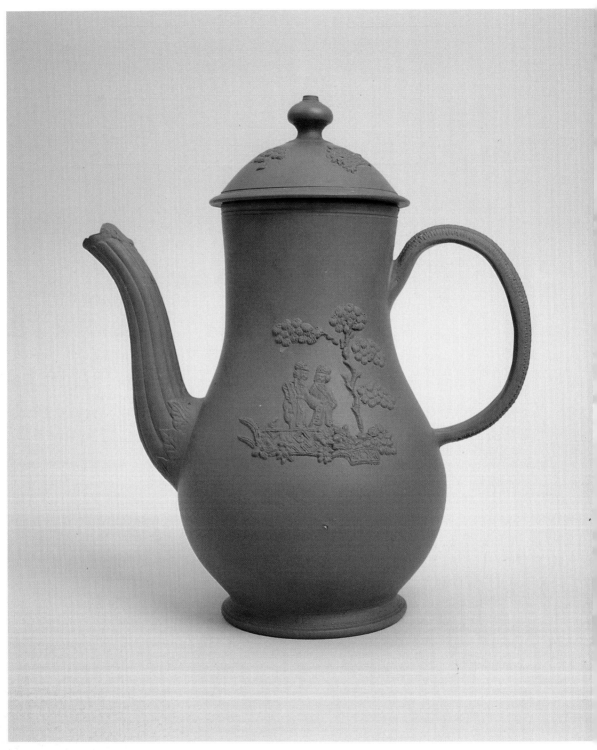

PLATE XXVIII **Red Stoneware coffee pot,** decorated with sprigged reliefs. *c.* 1765-1770. See pages 264-268. (City Museum & Art Gallery, Stoke-on-Trent)

CHAPTER 6

THE POTTERY: EXCAVATED AND EXTANT

Having looked at the documentary evidence for Greatbatch's career and his pottery, we must now turn to the most conclusive evidence for his manufacture — the wasters from his Lower Lane factory. These wasters represent twenty years of production and form the basis for widespread attribution of pieces in museum and private collections, but a closer dating of these pieces must take into account the evidence of the archaeology. Having been deposited in three clearly defined phases, Greatbatch's factory wasters offer us the opportunity to assign dates much more accurately to the creamwares, pearlwares, red stonewares and other important types of ware produced by him. In this chapter Greatbatch's pottery will be discussed by type, rather than by date of manufacture, simply for convenience of recognition. However, the significance of the dating evidence for each of the types will be emphasised. An overview of the pottery from each of the three phases of the Greatbatch site can be seen in Fig. 22 which lists the wares in order of the quantities recovered, and which forms the basis for further discussion in this chapter.

Phase I (*c.* 1762 — 1765)	Phase II (*c.* 1765 — 1770)	Phase III (*c.* 1770 — 1782)
Creamware	Creamware	Creamware
Blackware	Basket and fruit ware	Pearlware
White salt-glazed stoneware	Cauliflower ware	Tortoiseshell ware
Tortoiseshell ware	Tortoiseshell ware	Fruit basket ware
Cauliflower ware	Red stoneware	Cauliflower ware
Pineapple ware	Pineapple ware	Marbled ware
Fruit basket ware	Shell ware	Melon ware
Melon ware	Melon ware	Pineapple ware
Red stoneware	White salt-glazed stoneware	Red stoneware
Shell ware	'Reeded' ware	Glazed redware
Glazed redware	Basket and pineapple ware	Caneware
Basket and pineapple ware	Buff stoneware	Yellow glazed ware
Green glazed ware	Green glazed ware	Black basalt
Yellow glazed ware	'Serpent' moulded ware	White salt-glazed stoneware
'Reeded' ware	Yellow glazed ware	Blackware
'Serpent' moulded ware	Barleycorn moulded ware	Green glazed ware
Hexagonal Chinese moulded	Hexagonal Chinese moulded	Floral moulded creamware
Buff stoneware	Floral moulded creamware	'Reeded' ware
Agate ware	Glazed redware	'Serpent' moulded ware
	Black basalt	Buff stoneware
	Blackware	Agate ware
	Agate ware	

Fig. 22

Pottery types recovered from each of the three phases of the Greatbatch site, listed in decreasing order of quantities recovered. At one end of the scale creamwares comprise between 70-85 per cent of the total while, at the other, agate ware is represented by only a few sherds.

CREAMWARE AND PEARLWARE

William Greatbatch is best known as a producer of creamware. This is suggested by the limited documentary evidence available for his early manufacture and by the surviving pieces which are assignable to his later years. The archaeological evidence supports this: sherds of creamware formed in the region of eighty-five per cent of the total recovered. The proportions vary for each of the three phases, but the evidence is clear: from the very beginning of his operation, Greatbatch was first and foremost a creamware manufacturer.

The creamwares recovered from the Greatbatch site were the first in North Staffordshire to be excavated in any quantity as a production group and, consequently, offered the first clear insight into contemporary manufacture. Previously all our evidence was taken from documentary sources, with the inevitable heavy bias towards the achievements of Josiah Wedgwood, and from marked pieces surviving in collections. The picture was far from complete and was much clearer for those areas for which there was archaeological evidence or good documentary source material, namely the Leeds and other Yorkshire potteries, while the hypothetical Melbourne factory in Derbyshire, for which the evidence was anything but sound, was hailed as a major producer of creamware.

The discovery in Fenton of large quantities of creamware wasters was of great importance at the time because it raised the possibility, indeed the probability, that not all developments in creamware were taking place in Yorkshire or at Wedgwood's factories. Here was an enormous group of creamwares, spanning a period of two decades, whose range of vessel forms, of decoration and of features was wholly unexpected. Here were many types and elements of decoration which had previously been attributed with confidence to Leeds and Melbourne. The most obvious and immediate outcome of the excavation was that previous attributions of pottery of the period could be seen to be in need of a complete re-assessment and that the criteria upon which such attributions were made were clearly shown to be in need of re-definition.

That creamware was present in such quantities on the site is partly due to the fact that this type embraces so many others. Creamware is simply an earthenware manufactured from refined white-firing clays, strengthened and whitened by the addition of calcined flint, which is covered by a lead glaze. Consequently, the term covers all those variations which are coloured under-glaze by the application of slips of metallic oxides, often referred to as tortoiseshell wares. There is a significant overlap between plain cream and tortoiseshell wares and, therefore, the two are for the most part treated together in this volume, with only a short section devoted to tortoiseshell where decoration or forms are specific to this sub-group of creamware.

The introduction of coloured glazes — green, yellow and brown, in this case — is only a minor development of the simple uncoloured creamwares. Green glazed cauliflowers, green and yellow pineapples, melons and other types are all, essentially, creamwares. They were made with the same basic technology, used the same body recipes, were produced alongside the plain creamwares and were fired in the same ovens. The coloured glazed wares are treated separately here simply because of their distinctive range of predominantly moulded forms which it is necessary to examine in detail before a clear understanding of Greatbatch's products can be gained. For the most part, however, we should be aware that, when referring to creamware, we are including a wide variety of superficially different wares.

Closely related to creamware is pearlware. The development of *china glaze*, a lead glaze with a blue tint resulting from the deliberate addition of a minute quantity of cobalt to the recipe, is now well-documented as a result of the work of Miller[1]. However, the pearlwares recovered from Phase III of the Greatbatch site came to light long before the traditional view of the type's introduction by Wedgwood in 1779 had been seriously questioned. Pearlware was present in a significant quantity in Phase III, which in itself seemed to cast some doubt on the traditional date of 1779 for its introduction, particularly as Greatbatch was out of business within three years of this date. Miller's research and the currently favoured date of *c.* 1775 for the development of *china glaze* or pearlware is, therefore, most welcome and reassuring. This allows a sufficient time period within which Greatbatch could have taken on board the recent innovation and have produced the quantities of pearlware necessary to account for the number of wasters present.

Pearlware, too, is treated together with the later creamwares simply because, apart from blue tint of the glaze, there is virtually nothing to distinguish it from the contemporary creamwares. The two types use exactly the same vessel forms and rouletted decoration; handles and spouts are the same; and even the under-glaze blue-painted decoration, which is used on the majority of the pearlwares, is also found on contemporary creamwares. It is often assumed that both creamware and pearlware used similar, if not identical recipes for their clay bodies; certainly there is no obvious means of distinguishing the two when in the biscuit state, short of analysis, and it would seem logical to conclude that a single manufacturer would use the same ingredients for the two types of ware. Just a single sherd of pearlware from the Greatbatch site has been analysed and compared with creamware sherds analysed in the same manner[2]. Two important points were highlighted: that the proportion of flint used in the body was lower in the pearlware sherd than in the creamware sherds, and that a different clay appeared to have been used for the two types. An economy with flint in the body may be explained simply by the diminished need for whiteness in the body of the pearlware which was, after all, to be lost beneath a blue-tinted glaze; it may also be that a slightly inferior quality of clay was acceptable to the manufacturer for the same reason but, if this is so, no difference in quality is discernable in a casual examination.

Although, it is maintained, creamware embraces a variety of sub-types, from the tortoiseshell wares with an almost clear lead glaze, to those wares which use a coloured glaze, creamware in its narrowest sense — uncoloured and undecorated in any way — still makes up by far the highest proportion of the types present on the Greatbatch site, in all three phases. The importance of a pottery production site such as the Greatbatch site cannot be over-estimated. Not only does the clearly defined sequence of tipping allow a chronological framework to be established for the wares' production, but significant deductions about the factory's output can be made. The way in which the material has been deposited enables us to assess the proportions of individual types present within the different phases, and hence within a defined date range, reflecting changes in their popularity with the customer. We can also trace the developments of the pottery itself — changes in form and style, in finish, in decoration, and in the handles and spouts used. Such changes are quite apparent amongst the excavated pottery and, once identified, may be used with confidence for the dating of extant pieces. These developments will be discussed throughout the chapter.

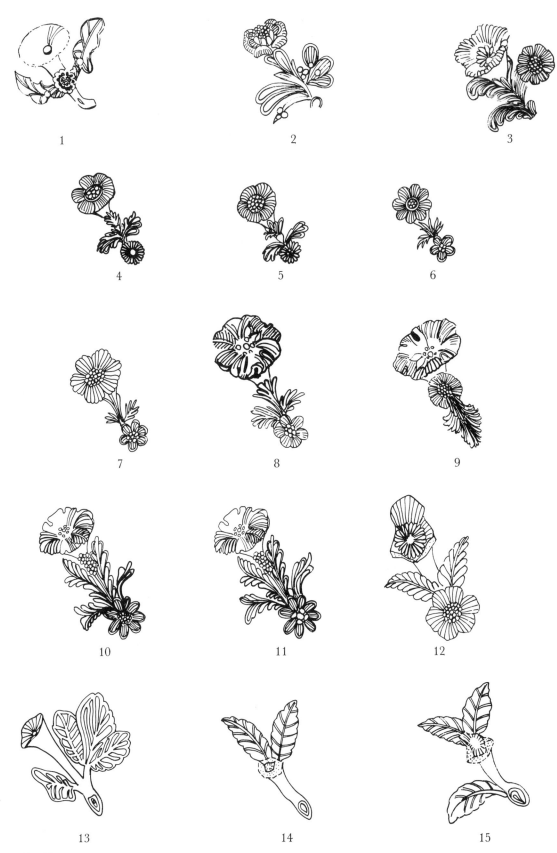

Fig. 23
Floral knops found on the Greatbatch site. Type 13: Phase I; Types 3, 12, 14-15: Phase II; Types 1-2, 4-11: Phase III. (Scale 1:1)

The attribution of any extant piece of pottery is difficult in the absence of makers' marks and, for the period under discussion, the use of such marks is the exception. The attribution of extant pieces which lack distinguishing features will be an impossibility. It may never be possible to attribute with any certainty vessels such as teabowls, saucers, bowls or, often, even plates. Shades of glaze colour, painted decoration, and nicks in footrings have all been used as evidence of manufacture, but are now shown to be meaningless in a situation of industrial production whose complexities we can barely begin to imagine[3]. For an attribution to have any basis, a vessel must have some characteristic or feature which sets it apart from others, and which can be shown to be peculiar to a single manufacturer. Such characteristics may include the details of a moulded body, but even here there are problems associated with the manufacture and trade in block moulds, an area which is as yet far from understood, and a cautious approach to such evidence is called for[4]. The movement of block moulds also affects the reliability of moulded features or details added to a vessel during production — handles, spouts, knops and applied relief decoration. All of these were based upon the use of a block mould which could be passed from manufacturer to manufacturer in the same way as block moulds for the pots themselves. Indeed, there is positive evidence for this, and yet, in the main, such features tend to provide a much more reliable basis for attribution and it has been possible to identify many which are specific to one factory or another. The basis for attribution will be even more sound when moulded features can be studied alongside moulded bodies — the more points of comparison, the better — but this is not always possible.

The sherds from the Greatbatch site have revealed a wide range of features used by Greatbatch on his wares which may be used as a basis for identifying these in collections. There will certainly be others which were not found on the site and which will turn up from time to time on pieces in collections. There are, for example, some fifteen types of flower and leaf knop amongst the excavated material (Fig. 23), while at least two others have subsequently been recognised on extant teapots (Plates 66 & 92). Greatbatch's knops occur on teapot, coffee pot, milk jug, mustard pot, sugar bowl and many other covers. They may all be dated fairly accurately from their position on the site and it is apparent that, in the main, flower and leaf knops are a Phase III phenomenon. Only Type 3 is a common Phase I and II knop. The other early Types, 12 — 15, are rare or unique. Many of the knops are common to a range of creamwares, especially tortoiseshells, and those from Phase III are found on both creamwares and pearlwares. This is also true of the flower handle terminals identified amongst the excavated material.

Fig. 24
Knops found on the Greatbatch site. (Scale 1:1)

Fig. 25
Flower and leaf handle terminals found on the Greatbatch site, 1. Types 1-5, 21-22: Phase I; Types 11, 14, 17-20: Phase II; Types 6-10, 12-13, 15-16, 22: Phase III. (Scale 1:1)

Fig. 26
Flower and leaf handle terminals found on the Greatbatch site, 2. Types 24-25, 28-30: Phase I; Type 26: Phase II; Types 23, 27: Phase III. (Scale 1:1)

Traditionally the majority of flower and leaf handle terminals in creamware have been attributed to the Leeds Pottery. Of course this is now known to be nonsense, and the variety of such terminals now identified on excavations of pottery sites in North Staffordshire testifies to their widespread popularity with both producers and users of creamware over a long period[5]. Greatbatch was no exception in his use of applied flower and leaf terminals to adorn twisted rope or strap handles on a range of vessels (Figs. 25 — 26); although purely decorative in appearance, these terminals also served a practical purpose in hiding the unsightly joins between handles and body. Some thirty types of flower and leaf terminals have been identified on the excavated sherds of all three phases. Most commonly, they belong to the creamwares, the tortoiseshells and, in Phase III, the pearlwares. Some types are more common in one phase than in another, but there is little indication that certain terminals were reserved for particular vessels. Most terminals are used on a variety of forms, from cups to coffee pots. Only the large and elaborate terminals, Types 27 — 30, are reserved for larger vessels such as salad dishes and soup tureens.

Many different handles were used by Greatbatch, of which the most popular was the indented loop handle (Type 18) which has long been recognised on his later creamwares. Towner made the connection between this handle and Greatbatch, or rather the prints used by Greatbatch, but considered that the vessels upon which it occurred were of Leeds manufacture[6]. The indented loop handle is the most abundant of the types found in Phase III of the Greatbatch site, but is absent in Phases I and II. There are slight variations of this type, both in size, according to the size of vessel, and in the style of the ribbing, where present (Fig. 27, nos. 18a-d). However, this handle does present problems in that it was not used solely by Greatbatch. Examples have been noted on pots which were definitely not produced by Greatbatch, and it must therefore be regarded as an unreliable guide to attribution in the absence of any other matching features.

There are other handles which are not specific to Greatbatch, such as the crabstock handle, Type 1, and the simple loop (Type 17). The twisted rope and intertwined strap handles, frequently used by Greatbatch, are also a poor basis for attribution, despite their production by extrusion from a dod box with shaped holes which give a consistent form to the handles; quite simply there are limitations to the shape of rope handles and the style of ribbing which may be used on the strap handles. These were all used by many manufacturers and appear on a wide variety of wares. The more elaborate of the moulded handles have, by contrast, so far only been identified on Greatbatch pieces; they appear to be reliable guides to identification but, ideally, should be supported by the evidence of other features.

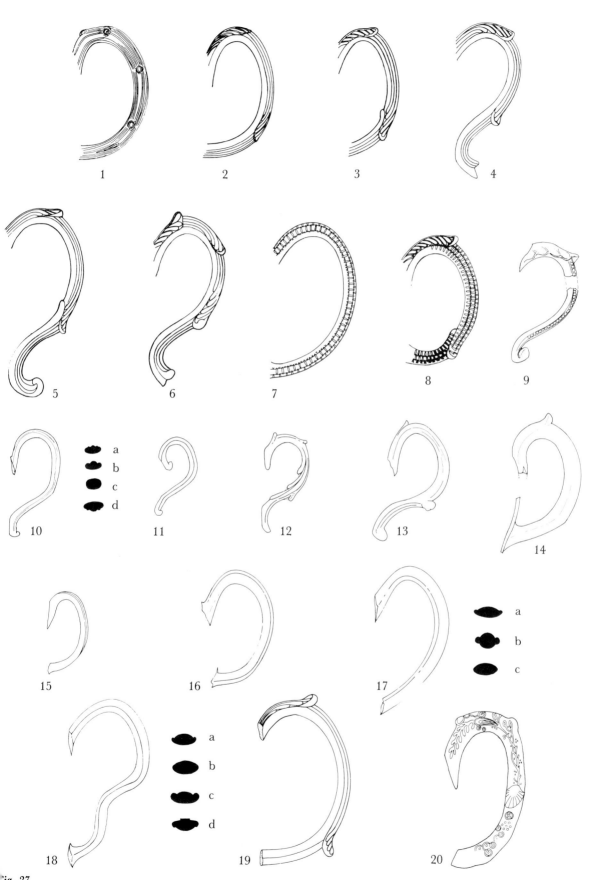

Fig. 27

Creamware handles found on the Greatbatch site. (Scale 1:2)

174

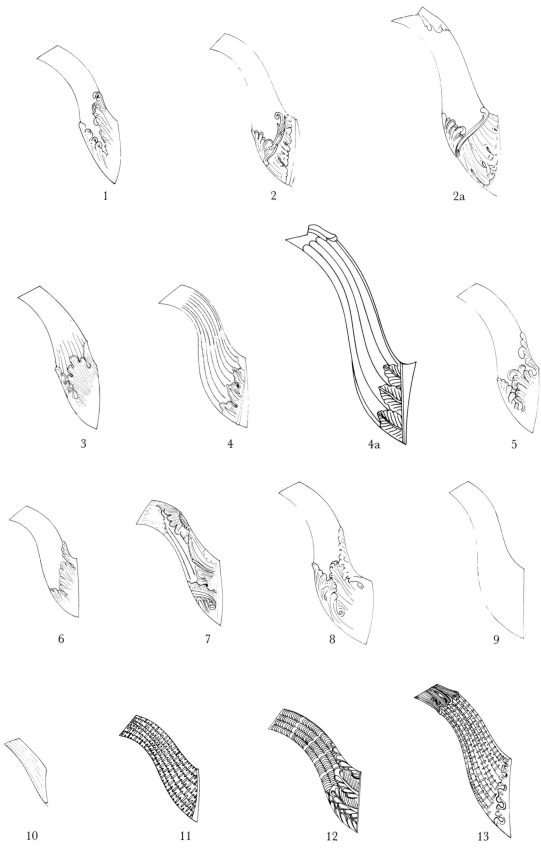

Fig. 28
Creamware spouts found on the Greatbatch site, 1. (Scale 1:2)

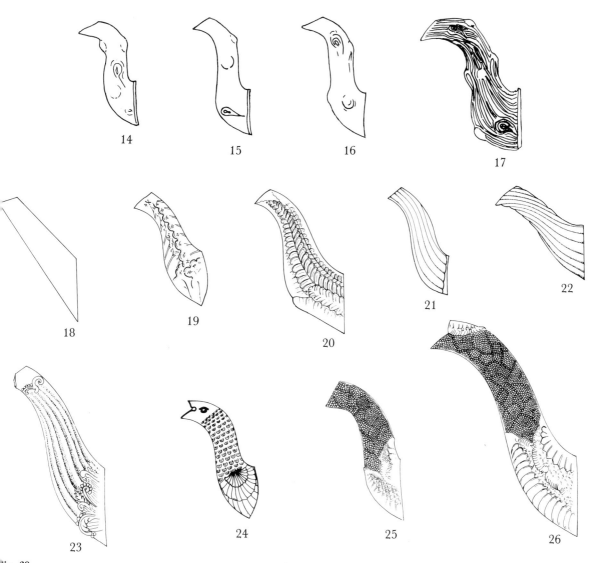

Fig. 29
Creamware spouts found on the Greatbatch site, 2. (Scale 1:2)

The spouts used by Greatbatch on his tea, punch and coffee pots present similar problems. Many are site specific, used only by Greatbatch, while others are far more widely used. Into the latter category falls the fluted spout with acanthus leaves (Type 4), which is perhaps the most common of all creamware spouts. It is used on teapots and, in its elongated form (Type 4a), on coffee pots. The Type 4 spout is common in all three phases of the Greatbatch site and is found on both creamwares and red stonewares. The crabstocks, too, are widely used and examples of all four types have been found on sites throughout the Potteries.

There are, nonetheless, several spouts which have only been identified on vessels produced by Greatbatch and these include types from all three phases. The most common Phase II spout is the ubiquitous Type 21 crabstock, but after this the most frequently used of the early types is the basketwork spout, Type 12, which is found on both creamwares and red stonewares. No other factory has yet been shown to have used this spout. Of the Phase III spouts, three (Types 1, 2 & 3) were linked with Greatbatch by Towner because of their regular occurrence with 'Greatbatch' prints; they were considered to have been Leeds types[7]. These spouts are exclusive to Greatbatch's factory, as are types 5 and 6. These are used on most Phase III creamwares and their related types.

The vessel forms produced by Greatbatch in creamware are far too numerous to be described in detail here and, moreover, many of them bear none of the features which would aid their identification amongst similar pieces in collections. Those types which are in some way distinctive do, however, merit special treatment, whether because of their forms or because of their decoration. A significant number of vessels occur, or at least are predominant in just one phase of the site. The marked differences apparent in the wares of Phases II and III have already been mentioned (above, pages 73 & 77), as has the fact that this has most probably resulted from the abandonment of the site as a waste tip for a short period in about 1770. This horizon is crucial for distinguishing Greatbatch's early and late wares.

The differences in form and features which characterise the three phases of the Greatbatch site are complemented by varying proportions of the types of ware present, by changes in decoration and by a development of a lighter coloured creamware. The lightening of the creamware is in line with improvements made by Wedgwood in the late 1760s (above, page 23) and by other manufacturers at about the same time or somewhat later. There is evidence to suggest that manufacturers did not all make improvements to their creamware at the same time and it would appear that there continued to be a market for the darker creamware long after the introduction of the lighter. For example, creamwares recovered from the cargo of the snow the *Ledbury*, which went down off the coast of Florida in 1769, were of roughly equal proportions of both the light and the dark types[8].

Greatbatch's creamwares change completely from the dark to the light in the short interval which separates Phases II and III, in other words in about 1770. The creamwares from Phases I and II are entirely of a dark, almost butter colour, which can be seen even on those moulded types covered by an external coloured glaze. By contrast, the Phase III creamwares are all of a much lighter colour, almost white in its paleness. This move towards a lighter coloured creamware would have arisen in response to the demands of the market, demands which doubtless increased as a result of Wedgwood's endorsement of the lighter coloured ware. The excavated creamwares show quite clearly that Greatbatch did not produce both light and dark coloured creamwares at the same time, and we may recall here Wedgwood's own inability, or rather unwillingness, to diversify his production in this way. It is difficult to be certain of the exact nature of the improvements made to creamware bodies and glazes during the period in question as these are not adequately documented. At the same time, it would be naive to assume that individual manufacturers were making exactly the same improvements to their wares, even if the desired end result was shared. There were doubtless many different solutions to the problem of how to produce a lighter ware, achieved by individual manufacturers at different times. Sherds of creamware from each of the three phases of the Greatbatch site have been analysed and marked differences in both the bodies and the glazes of the three have been detected[9].

The changes in the colour of Greatbatch's creamwares complement the stylistic development of vessel forms which is apparent in the three phases. The new lighter coloured creamware of Phase III coincided with the introduction of new vessel forms, new decorative techniques, and a new range of spouts and handles; in short, production at Greatbatch's factory was drastically overhauled and brought up to date in the short interval between Phases II and III. At the same time, however, significant elements of production remained much as they had been, with, for example, cauliflower and fruit basket wares still in production, and still based upon the same set of block moulds, but with these wares the significant distinction is the lightening of the cream colour in Phase III.

Throughout, Greatbatch's production comprised primarily teapots and plates, with slightly smaller proportions of teabowls, saucers, bowls, jugs and mugs. Coffee wares, while common in all phases, were much less numerous than teawares. Cream and sauce boats were consistently an important element of the factory's output, as were sugar bowls and canisters. Other forms, and there were many of them, from plain dishes to soup tureens, from pickle dishes to stirrup cups, formed a relatively small percentage of the total number of types produced.

The invoices emphasise the fact that Greatbatch was a major producer of teapots and this is borne out by the excavated evidence. The predominant vessel form in most of the ware types identified was the teapot. Greatbatch's Phase III creamware teapots are well-known from the large number of extant pieces with printed or painted decoration which have been illustrated, and the recovery of a great quantity of these types was no surprise. The Phase III teapots, with their light cream coloured glaze and distinctive range of handles and spouts, are immediately identifiable and few could be confused with the products of other manufacturers. The more common teapot forms of Phase III are illustrated throughout this volume; their decoration, both turned and rouletted, may vary according to the manufacturer's requirements, or may be omitted altogether. Similarly, any of the Phase III handles and spouts may be used in whatever combination happens to have suited at the time of manufacture; sometimes a double twisted handle is used instead of the indented loop or plain loop, and with this the range of possible terminals is great. All those combinations which were possible for the creamware teapots were also used for the pearlware teapots.

The teapots of Phases I and II are less familiar to us, as they have not previously been attributed to Greatbatch by writers on ceramics. There was actually a greater variety of cylindrical teapots produced during Phases I and II than in Phase III, although there appears to have been little variation in the use of the plain, straight spout (Type 18), and of double twisted strap of rope handles; handle terminals are usually of Types 17 — 22. The cylindrical teapot bodies are either left undecorated or have rouletted bands.

The majority of the Phase I and II teapots are round-bodied types. These use a much wider range of spouts (especially Types 4, 12 and 21) and handles (especially Types 1 — 4, 6 and 8), as well as the double twisted rope and strap handles. The use of crabstock handles and spouts is very common indeed and many of the round-bodied teapots from these phases appear as tortoiseshell wares. Rouletted moulding of a variety of patterns is common and turned decoration is also found (Fig. 30).

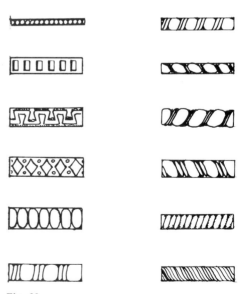

Fig. 30
Rouletted decoration used by Greatbatch. (Scale 1:1)

Fig. 31
Greatbatch's backstamps. Phase III. (Scale 2:1)

Second to teapots, plates were by far Greatbatch's most numerous products. This is not apparent in the invoices, which suggest that plates were an insignificant part of the total output during the years 1762 — 1765. Even the evidence from Phase I of the excavation contradicts this, for creamware plates, biscuit and glazed, formed a significant proportion of the wares recovered. By Phase II, however, the proportion had fallen considerably, although the number of individual moulded types was still great. By Phase III plate production was massive and comprised an even greater number of moulded edges than in the previous phases.

Just as the proportions of flatwares recovered from the excavation change from phase to phase, so do the wares themselves develop. The most obvious development is that apparent in all of Greatbatch's creamwares, the move towards a light coloured ware in Phase III, and, alongside this, we see the introduction in Phase III of the *WG* monogram backstamp (Fig. 31 no. 1) which is used only on flatwares. A second backstamp is also found only in Phase III. This is an impressed mark containing a five-pointed star, surrounded by dots (Fig. 31 no. 2), of which a few examples have been found, but only amongst the excavated material; no extant examples have been identified. A third Phase III mark, rather more common than the second, but still very much in a minority, is an impressed asterisk (Fig. 31 no. 3) which is similar to one identified on a very small number of Phase I creamware plates.

The great majority of Greatbatch's Phase III flatwares are marked and yet only two extant examples have been recognised (Plate 54). The use of backstamps on pottery during the 1770s was not common and Greatbatch's mark is certainly unusual. It compares only with the *WB* backstamp, identified on some creamwares, which has been tentatively attributed to Greatbatch's neighbour and contemporary in Lower Lane, William Bacchus (above, page 84).

Plate 54
Creamware plate with moulded 'Chinese lantern' edge and impressed *WG* backstamp. *c.* 1770-1782. (Paul Fox)

Figs. 32 — 33 illustrate the more common moulded plate edges used by Greatbatch during his twenty years of production. Many are well-known and are unlikely to be particularly helpful in providing attributions, especially when there is no backstamp. Others of the edges have been identiifed on the wares of a number of factories, but have minor variations of detail which may distinguish the wares of individual manufacturers. Consequently, it is important to illustrate the common types which we now know to have been produced by Greatbatch, not only to highlight the range of his products, but also to stress that many of the types had a very wide currency and were not necessarily the preserve of a single factory.

The excavation has produced evidence for the dating of individual plate edges, evidence which is lacking from other sources. The most common pattern overall, present in all three Phases, is the feather edge (Type 10). Feather edge plates are most numerous in Phase I, but are still present in significant quantities during Phase III. An eight barb feather pattern is often used on the larger plates and platters, while several minor variations of the standard seven barb feather pattern indicate that a range of block moulds was used. The occurrence of these variations together on one site rules out the possibility of this edge being used as a basis for attribution. The developed feather edges (Types 11 and 12) are specific to Phase III and clearly a late development. The Queen's shape is also present in all three Phases, but is especially common in Phases I and II. Very common and specifically Phase III types are the pendant leaf edges (Types 17 and 18), the foliate edge (Type 14), the Royal edge (Type 9), the various shell edges (Types 20 — 22), the reeded edge (Type 16) and the 'Chinese lantern' edge (Type 15). Variations on many of these edge patterns are known from other manufacturing sources, both in North Staffordshire and beyond. The pendant leaf, for example, has been identified locally in many groups of late 18th century wasters, while a variation of the 'Chinese lantern' is known from the Swinton factory in Yorkshire[10]. Some of the variations of these edge patterns have been found in dark, as well as light coloured creamware. The cargo of the *Ledbury*, already referred to, included numerous sherds of 'Chinese lantern' plate edges which were in a mid to dark creamware which must have been produced shortly before September, 1769, when the ship was wrecked[11]. Much more evidence of this sort is required before a complete picture of the manufacture and date of the various plate edges can be built up. Greatbatch's pearlwares, by contrast, seem to have made use of a much narrower range of plate edges, which include the Royal edge (Type 9) and the three shell edges (Types 20 — 22).

One final feature which may distinguish the flatwares of the different phases is the use, or otherwise of a footring. Three types of underside are encountered. The first is a simple low, rounded footring, formed during pressing by the use of a shaped profile of the sort illustrated in Fig. 15. These are very common on Phase III flatwares, even on those oval platters whose footrings could not have been made in the same simple fashion[12]. In Phases I and II footrings are much less common and tend to be of a lower, less rounded profile. The second type is the inset base, easily produced by removing a thin layer of clay from the underside. In Phase III, this inset base tends to be quite pronounced, but is not common. The flatwares of Phases I and II make frequent use of this type. The third type is the plain base, either rounded or sharply angled, which has neither

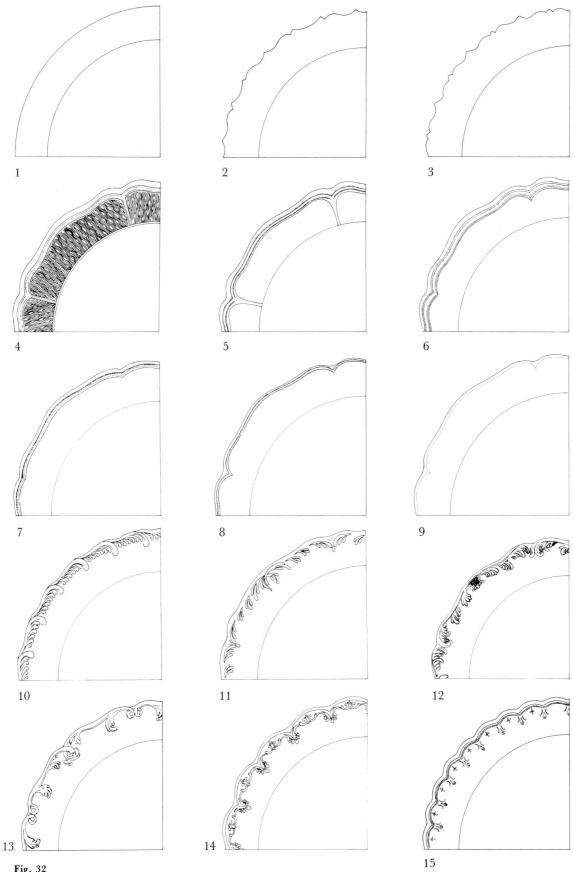

Fig. 32
Common plate edges used by Greatbatch 1. (Scale 1:3)

181

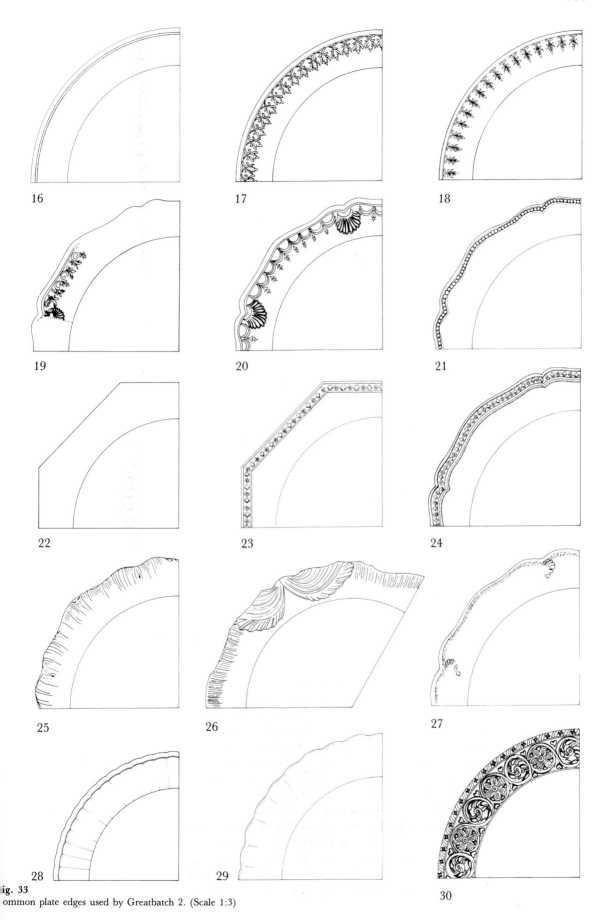

16

17

18

19

20

21

22

23

24

25

26

27

28

29

30

Fig. 33
Common plate edges used by Greatbatch 2. (Scale 1:3)

Plates 55a & b
Moulded figures of birds in glazed and unglazed creamware. Phase II. (Ht. 75 mm)

footring nor the inset; this is quite well-used in Phases I and II, but is virtually unknown in Phase III. Worthy of note is the almost complete absence, in Phase III, of backstamps on those flatwares with inset bases.

The plates are found in a variety of sizes, of which the most common diameters are 245 mm (10 inch), 205 mm (8 inch) and 155 mm (6 inch). Larger sizes of round plates are found, up to 450 mm (18 inch), in many, but by no means all of the edge patterns. Soup plates (10 inch), too, are less frequently encountered, as are oval plates and platters.

While a high proportion of Greatbatch's production comprised teapots and flatwares, the range of other vessel forms was wide. These were almost entirely useful wares, rather than ornamental wares, although amongst the latter may be included a small number of figures. These are mostly fragmentary, but from matching sherds the pearlware figure of Ceres illustrated in Plate XXVII has been attributed to Greatbatch. The cornucopiae which have been traditionally linked with Greatbatch (above, page 95) may also be considered ornamental and a single sherd of a green-glazed piece suggests that he did indeed produce some, but by no means all, of this type (Plate 56).

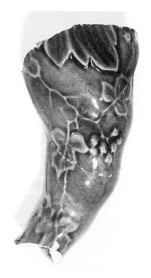

Apart from these we have *useful* wares which are similar in form and style to those of many of the 18th century Staffordshire potters. In the range of forms produced Greatbatch was typical of his contemporaries, but for the quality of his wares he is outstanding. But neither quality nor form will enable us to positively identify Greatbatch's wares in collections. Scores of vessel forms will never be attributable, lacking any of the features which may suggest manufacture by Greatbatch.

Plate 56
Fragment of green-glazed cornucopia, matching the block moulds illustrated in Plate 8. Phase I.

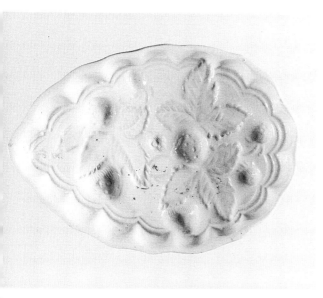

Plate 57
reamware jelly mould. Phase III. (L. 111 mm)

Plate 58
Creamware Bacchus cup, painted over-glaze in enamel colours. Similar pieces were found in pearlware. Phase III.

The range of moulded vessel forms is wide, from sauce boats to tureens, from pickle leaves to Bacchus cups (Plate 58). The moulded features of vessels must be viewed cautiously when attempting to identify the wares of a particular manufacturer for, as we have already seen, block moulds may travel or be copied. Ideally, we must recognise other features which link the piece in question to a manufacturer.

We turn, once again, to handles, handle terminals and applied relief decoration. With these features, we can hope to recognise mugs, jugs, mustard pots, cups, chamber pots, sauce boats, salad dishes, tureens, and other handled forms. Applied reliefs are more likely to be found on teabowls, saucers, bowls, canisters and, of course, on teapots, jugs and coffee pots. All of these pots were produced by Greatbatch, in a variety of forms, and with a variety of finishes.

Plate 59
Creamware sauce tureen. Phase I.

184

1

2

3

4

5

6

Fig. 34
Creamware forms: thrown jugs with distinctive handle terminals and moulded sauce boats. Phase II — 1, 2 & 4; Phase III — 3, 5 & 6. (Scale 1:2)

METHODS OF DECORATION

Greatbatch's pottery exhibits decoration of many types — moulded, which is essentially a production method; turned, engine-turned and rouletted by which the unfired clay body of a vessel is partially removed or impressed; applied reliefs, fixed to the body of a vessel in the clay state; sponged or painted, which involves the addition of colour to the surface of a vessel, either under-glaze or over-glaze; slip-decorated — at this period marbled; printed; or, in many cases, a combination of several of these. Coloured glazes, too, may be considered a form of decoration and will be dealt with below. Many of these different methods of decoration are common to a variety of different creamwares. Some of the methods may be more typical of one phase of Greatbatch's production than another, but most are used on creamware in at least one of its various guises.

Turned and rouletted decoration

Lathe-turned decoration is used in all three phases and is common throughout. This may comprise nothing more than simple incised lines to break up the monotony of a plain surface, or the turning of a large part of a vessel's surface to produce a very distinctive decorative pattern.

The most simple extension of the incised line is the covering of the entire surface of a vessel with incised decoration. 'Reeded ware' is the name given here to a small but distinctive class of creamwares, invariably round-bodied teapots and covers or, to a much lesser extent, small jugs, whose exteriors are completely covered with incised lines (Plates 60 — 61). This limited range of wares has an unsophisticated appearance; the vessels are sometimes coloured under-glaze with patches of metallic oxide colours which border on tortoiseshell in style or, more commonly with thin splashes of a light green coloured glaze. The 'reeded wares' are predominantly a Phase II type, with only small quantities recovered from Phases I and III. Teapot spouts, where they have been found, are Type 17 crabstocks; no handles survive.

The removal of bands of clay from a vessel's surface to produce an overall decorative effect was very common in Phases I and III, but reserved largely for creamwares and, to a much lesser degree, pearlwares. The width and number of bands removed was infinitely variable, depending upon the skill and preference of the turner; there appears to be no regular pattern to the banded wares recovered. The vessels most commonly decorated in this way are cylindrical mugs (Phases I and III) and teapots (Phase III), round-bodied jugs (Plate 62) and chamber pots in Phase III, and large jars in Phase I.

Plates 60-61
Reeded creamware teapot covers with patches of light green coloured glaze. Phase II.

Plate 62
Lathe-turned 'banded' creamware jug, painted over-glaze in enamel colours. See also Plate 124. *c.* 1776. (Published by Permission of Northampton Central Museum & Art Gallery)

Plate 63
Creamware teapot, lathe-turned with raised central band which has incised chevrons. Painted over-glaze in enamel colours. Type 23 handle terminals. *c.* 1770-1782. (Walford Collection)

Plate 64
Creamware teapot with engine-turned vertical ribbed decoration in relief to lower body. Painted over-glaze in enamel colours. *c.* 1770-1782. (Norfolk Museums Service. Norwich Castle Museum)

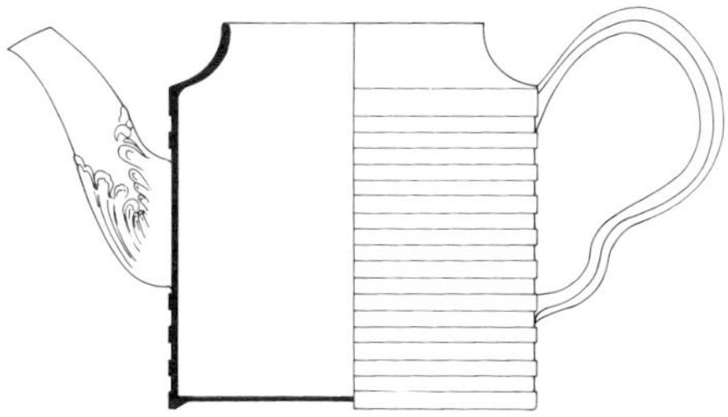

Fig. 35
Lathe-turned 'banded' teapot. Phase III. (Scale 1:3)

Rather than removing bands of clay by turning, another method used by Greatbatch is the removal of some of the surface of the vessel, while still retaining a central band which then stands proud; this band itself is then decorated with incised cross-hatching (Plate 24). This method of decoration is quite common on Phase II creamwares and tortoiseshell wares, but has not been found on any of the Phase III wasters. Just one extant piece of creamware from Greatbatch's later phase of production is known with this style of decoration and this is, itself, a most unusual piece (Plate 63).

The use of rouletted decoration is ubiquitous in the form of the various types of beading which are used on Greatbatch's creamwares and pearlwares. These types include simple beading, large oval beading, the Greek key moulding, linear moulding, and diamond beading. Beading is commonly applied to the rims, shoulders and bases of vessels, as well as to the interiors of saucers and the edges of covers.

Other forms of rouletted decoration tend to be more restricted in their use. Only the melon wares consistently use rouletted decoration, either in the form of continuous lines of simple dots or the zig-zag pattern. Apart from this there are only a few sherds of red stoneware from Phases I and II which have bands of simple rouletted decoration.

Engine-turned decoration is normally associated with red stonewares and glazed redwares as wavy, diagonal and curved reeds. However, a small number of engine turned creamwares have been found with wavy reed decoration, together with a single sherd of black basalt. Fluted and ribbed decoration were also produced on an engine lathe, used the lateral motion (above, page 119). This came to be used extensively by Greatbatch on wares other than creamwares, mainly in Phase III.

Fluted creamwares and pearlwares are extremely prolific in Phase III, embracing most common vessel forms — teabowls, saucers, cylindrical teapots, round-bodied teapots, jugs, bowls and others. Many of these bear additional decoration, either under-glaze or over-glaze. The fluted decoration is most commonly of the concave fluted type, running vertically up the side of a vessel, or else running from a central point, as in a saucer, to the rim. Vertical ribs in relief, apparently always in pairs, are also known; sherds of teabowls, saucers, jugs, teapots and coffee pots have been found in Phase III, but only one extant piece has so far been identified (Plate 64).

Applied relief decoration

The use of applied moulded reliefs was common to all fine earthenwares and stonewares of the mid-18th century, whether as sprigged reliefs from plaster of Paris moulds, or as mould-applied reliefs from metal dies. The large number of relief-decorated pieces surviving in collections today bears witness to the popularity of the technique as a means of decorating wares, while excavated evidence is slowly enabling us to link specific reliefs with known factories. Greatbatch, too, made use of both mould-applied and sprigged decoration, but not extensively.

The finds from the Greatbatch site suggest that Greatbatch, at least, had to a large extent moved away from applied decoration by 1770 and had turned to other methods of ornamenting his wares. Very little pottery decorated in this way was recovered from Phase III of the site, while even in Phases I and II there were clearly other preferred methods of decoration. It is difficult to know to what extent Greatbatch was typical in this move towards other forms of decoration, whether he was in a minority, or whether he was, to some extent, leading the way.

Greatbatch's limited reliance on applied decoration is evident from the very small number of reliefs which have been identified on his wares. Just forty different types have been identified (Figs. 36 — 37), compared with over one hundred from a similar, but much smaller waste tip excavated in Town Road, Hanley, which dates to about 1755 — 1760[13]. Nevertheless, a number of Greatbatch's reliefs are quite distinctive and are themselves a fairly reliable aid to the attribution of his wares.

Contemporary applied decoration was either mould-applied or sprigged. The use of mould-applied reliefs gave the manufacturer considerable flexibility in the range of finely detailed human and animal figures which could be used; by contrast, sprigged reliefs tended to be of flowers, leaves, berries and vine stems, for which fine detail was not so critical. Greatbatch clearly had a preference for sprigged reliefs which were of a quality far in excess of that identified on contemporary wares. His sprigged decoration was not restricted to flowers and leaves, but encompassed a limited range of finely modelled human figures, rococo scrolls, trees and bushes. The detail of these is extremely delicate and works well either unglazed or glazed.

The majority of Greatbatch's applied relief decoration is from Phases I and II. It commonly occurs on red stonewares, rather less so on tortoiseshell wares, and on a small number of green-glazed wares, melon wares and plain creamwares; a few pieces of early blackware also have sprigged decoration, but this is so hidden by a thick glaze that identification of the designs is impossible. By far the most common reliefs are the sprigged Types 8 — 40, while just seven mould-applied reliefs are known.

The sprigged relief Types 13 and 14, and 24 — 27 are used, almost without exception, upon tortoiseshell wares and are very much in the style of the flowers and trailing vine stems of the wares of the mid-18th century. Other sprigs are commonly used to form a framing cartouche: the two Oriental ladies (Type 38), for example, are often surrounded by a cartouche formed of Type 29 sprigs (Plate 72), while the sprigged figures of Minerva (Type 35), and of the seated Chinese man (Type 39), are flanked by flowers, Types 30 and 32, and trees (Type 40) respectively.

189

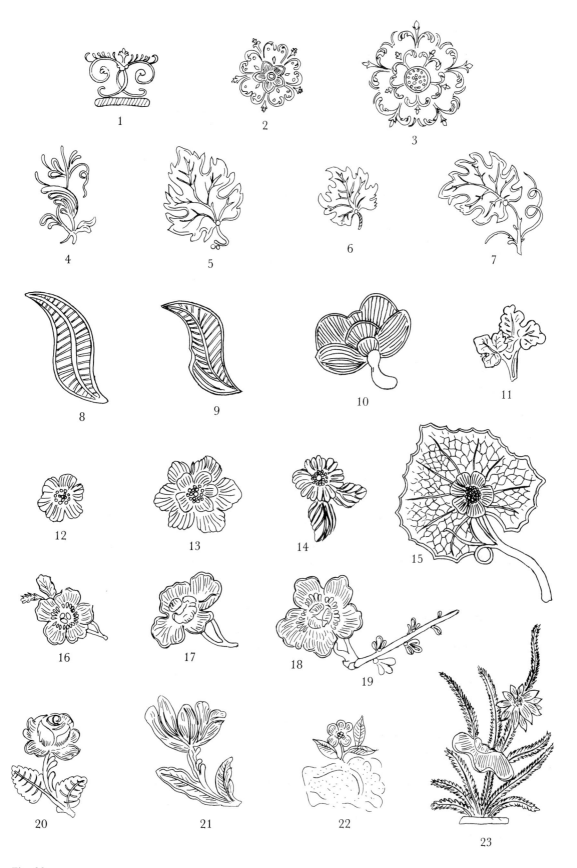

Fig. 36
Applied decorative reliefs used by Greatbatch, 1. Types 1-7: mould-applied; Types 8-23: sprigged. (Scale 1:1)

Plate 65
Plate 175 of *The Ladies Amusement* by Robert Sayer. The Oriental ladies are the source for Greatbatch's Type
38 sprigged relief.

The pair of Oriental ladies (Type 38) is a common subject of decoration used
by the manufacturers of red stoneware and tortoiseshell ware and is usually mould-
applied[14]. Greatbatch's Oriental figures differ slightly from other versions and
are sprigged, taken from a plaster of Paris mould which itself took the relief from
a ceramic block mould. The source for this design is Robert Sayer's *The Ladies
Amusement: or, Whole Art of Japanning Made Easy* (its full title), which was published
in at least two editions of 1759 or 1760, and 1762. The book was lavishly illustrated
with two hundred copper plate engravings by Jean Pillement and others depicting,
as the title page explains, *Flowers, Shells, Figures, Birds, Insects, Landscapes, Shipping,
Beasts, Vases, Borders, &c.* The fifteen hundred individual illustrations include both
European and Oriental subjects and scenes, the Oriental being pure Chinoiseries
— views of the Orient from the European imagination. The title page also tells
us that *The above Work will be found extremely useful to the PORCELAINE, and other
Manufactures depending on Design,* and the use of subjects from this volume in the
decoration of English porcelains is well-known. Decorators of tin-glazed
earthenware, white salt-glazed stoneware and porcelain drew inspiration from
its pages, as clearly did the manufacturers of metal dies for mould-applied reliefs
and, in our case, a block maker who was probably Greatbatch himself.

Plate 175 of *The Ladies Amusement* shows the two figures, one holding a fan,
standing side by side, behind an open-work fence within a stylised Oriental
landscape (Plate 65). No immediate source can be cited for this anonymous print
in Sayer's volume, but the figures are very much in the style of the *lange lijzen*,
the ladies who occur regularly on Oriental blue and white porcelain of the 17th
and 18th centuries. It is significant that the print here is given the title *Painted
on Jars and other Large Vessels*.

Greatbatch's sprigged relief comprises the two ladies and the fence; it differs
little from the source print, even in its size, and is only slightly smaller as a result
of shrinkage during firing. The figures may occur within a surrounding cartouche

Fig. 37
Applied decorative reliefs used by Greatbatch, 2 - sprigged. (Scale 1:1)

of Type 29 sprigs, flanked by Type 30 and 32 flowers (Plate 7) or by Type 40 trees (Plate XXVIII), or without any surround (Plate 201). The Oriental ladies are used primarily on red stonewares and tortoiseshell wares, although they do occur on some creamwares in which only the reliefs, rather than the whole vessels, have been coloured in under-glaze oxides.

The Oriental ladies occur on excavated sherds from all three phases of the Greatbatch site, although the quantities from Phases I and III are insignificant; they are predominantly a Phase II type, dating to *c*. 1765 — 1770. It is surprising, therefore, that the very same figures should be found adorning early 19th century wares. In 1989, a black basalt cream jug, impressed with the *EASTWOOD* mark of William Baddeley of Hanley (1802 — 1822), was sold at a Stoke-on-Trent sale room; the sprigged decoration of this was the pair of figures used by Greatbatch in the 1760s and came, without a doubt, from the same block mould. A second piece with this sprigged relief has been identified: this is a caneware vase of about 1810, again marked *EASTWOOD*[15]. The conclusion is clear, that somehow Greatbatch's block mould found its way to Baddeley's Eastwood factory where it continued to have a useful life. The means by which the block mould arrived there is, of course, unknown, but it is important to remember that upon Greatbatch's bankruptcy in 1782 the entire stock of his factory, tools and equipment, would all have been sold at auction, thereby complicating further the attempts of ceramic historians to attribute wares on the basis of decorative features alone.

This figure of Minerva (Fig. 37, Type 35), leaning upon her Gorgon-headed shield, is the relief most commonly found on the excavated sherds. It is primarily a Phase II type, but its use is restricted almost entirely to red stoneware; only one biscuit creamware sherd with this relief has been found. Surprisingly few Greatbatch pieces with this design have been identified in collections and the subject does not seem to have been widely used in relief decoration by other factories. Indeed, only one other variation of Greatbatch's Minerva is known, occurring on a red stoneware teapot by an unidentified maker[16]; the details of the relief are slightly different to that of Greatbatch, but the source is undoubtedly the same. No source for the design is known, although Minerva, the goddess of wisdom, was a popular subject with artists and decorators during the Age of Reason.

The seated Chinese man (Fig. 37, Type 39) is a subject which occurs on a wide variety of wares, but rarely in isolation. He appears, for example, on those moulded hexagonal teapots which carry Oriental figures in each of the body panels against a background of square spirals; these are known in red stoneware and in creamware bodies, the latter decorated either under-glaze with coloured oxides, or with coloured glazes[17]. These teapots have sometimes been attributed to Greatbatch, but there is no evidence that he produced anything of the sort. The single sprigged Chinese man is without doubt taken from the same source as the decoration of these teapots but whether Greatbatch used him in isolation, sitting beneath his tree, or as part of a larger group of figures, is not known: very few sherds of this relief were found on the excavation and no extant vessels with this figure have been identified. The relief occurs in red stoneware and in biscuit creamware.

The sprigged flower reliefs, Types 20 and 21, are interesting for the quality of their manufacture, and for the fact they they are uniquely Phase III types. They are also reserved solely for use on melon wares, primarily coffee cups, and are unknown elsewhere.

A variation of the sprigged relief is the applied moulded band of trailing flowers and foliage which appears to have been popular with Greatbatch's customers. Several sherds of this type have been recovered from Phase III of the site and several extant vessels decorated in this way, also of the 1770s period, are known. The vessel to be decorated was first of all turned on the lathe and a central horizontal band of 1 — 2 mm depth and 19 mm width was removed. The sprigged band was then applied into the turned depression in the normal manner, apparently in short strips, and a close inspection of the pieces will reveal where the joins in the applied strips occur. The teapots with these applied bands are exceptionally fine pieces, elaborately decorated in over-glaze colours (Plates V, 66 — 67).

Plate 66
Creamware teapot with applied moulded band to body. Painted over-glaze in enamel colours. Type 23 handle terminals; the flower knop is a variation of Type 10 not recognised amongst the excavated sherds. *c.* 1770-1782. (ex Towner Collection)

Plate 67
Creamware teapot with applied moulded band to body. Painted over-glaze in enamel colours. Type 23 handle terminals. *c.* 1770-1782. (ex Towner Collection)

Under-glaze sponged and painted decoration

The technique of decorating under-glaze with coloured metallic oxides prepared as slips has been discussed above (page 128). Colours could be applied to the biscuit body of a pot either by sponge or by brush. Best known of the wares decorated in under-glaze oxides are the tortoiseshells, but the technique was also used for a variety of moulded types such as the fruit basket and the shell wares described below.

Tortoiseshell ware was one of Greatbatch's main lines of production throughout his twenty year career. The vessels decorated under-glaze are simply those which appear in contemporary plain creamware, with the same variations of handles and spouts being used, and as such require no extra discussion. A lightening of the creamware colour is apparent in the Phase III tortoiseshells, just as in the plain creamwares of that period.

For the most part, the colour of Greatbatch's tortoiseshells has been applied either by brush or by a very small sponge, with occasional larger patches of a contrasting colour applied by sponging or else as a touch of coloured glaze. The colours used vary considerably: light and dark shades of brown are by far the most common colours, although we also find, alongside these or used alone, shades of grey, green, yellow and orange. The darker colours are more typical of Phases I and II, when they would have complemented the darker colour of the ware; by Phase III lighter brown spots with patches of light green is more normal.

Tortoiseshell tea and coffee wares far outnumber the flatwares, with teapots, teabowls, bowls and saucers being the most numerous vessel types. This is rather less noticeable in Phase II, when plain creamware plates are poorly represented and teapots predominant, but in Phase III the difference is more striking on account of the very large quantities of plates present in plain creamware. A limited range of plate edges has been found in tortoiseshell, particularly the feather edge, the barleycorn pattern, the plain circular type and the Queen's pattern.

It is during Phase II that the tortoiseshells appear to enjoy their greatest popularity; at this time they are present in quantities almost as great as the moulded wares, the fruit basket and cauliflower wares. There is certainly a decline in the quantities produced during Phase III, but tortoiseshell remained a significant part of Greatbatch's production throughout the 1770s.

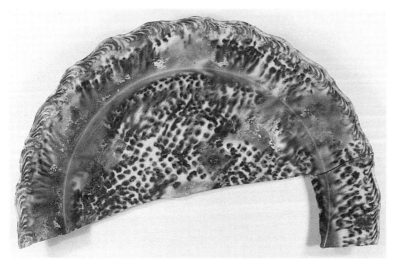

Plate 68
Tortoiseshell plate with feather edge. Phase II.

Plate 69
Tortoiseshell cup and saucers. Phase II.

Plate 70
Round-bodied tortoiseshell teapots. Phase II.

Plate 71
Round-bodied tortoiseshell teapots. Phase III.

Plate 72
Tortoiseshell coffee pot decorated with sprigged reliefs. *c.* 1765-1770. (Delhom Collection, The Mint Museum of Art, Charlotte, North Carolina. Photographer: Bill J. Moretz)

Tortoiseshell wares are generally known for their heavy reliance upon applied decoration in the form of sprigged or mould-applied reliefs. Greatbatch, too, made use of these to decorate his wares, a much greater use, in fact, than with any other of his products except red stonewares. Even so, the number of sprigged or mould-applied pieces is comparatively small and most of the tortoiseshells depend solely upon their under-glaze colours for their decoration. Sprigging is more common on the wares of Phase II, when the Oriental ladies (Plate 72) and flower and leaf reliefs, Types 13 and 14, and 25 — 27, were popular upon bowls, saucers and jugs, teapots and coffee pots. Just seven mould-applied reliefs have been identified on Greatbatch's wares and these are only found on Phase III wares, biscuit creamware and tortoiseshell (Types 1 — 7), and melon ware (Type 2). So very few mould-applied sherds have been found amongst the excavated material that the survival of a Greatbatch tortoiseshell teapot with mould-applied decoration in the collection at Stoke-on-Trent is something of a surprise (Plate XX).

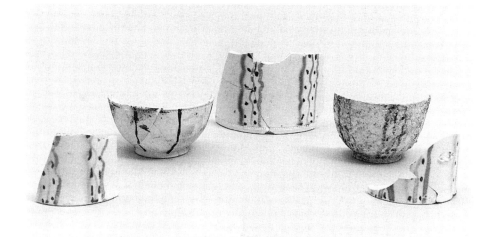

Plate 73
Creamware mug and teapot sherds, painted under-glaze in brown, grey, yellow and green. Phase III.

A small number of tortoiseshell sherds have turned decoration, of the raised and cross-hatched band type as in Plate 63. These are round-bodied teapots of Phase II, the phase during which the style of decoration appears to have been most popular.

Another less common type of under-glaze decorated ware was encountered in Phase III. This was creamware in a range of common forms — teabowls, saucers, teapots, mugs, etc. — which was decorated with stripes and dots of metallic oxides in brown, yellow, blue-grey, and green, painted on to the biscuit body (Plate 73). Several unglazed pieces enable us to see the decoration in its unfinished state (Plate 74). Pieces of this type are known in collections and it is clear that many manufacturers were decorating in this way. Should any of Greatbatch's under-glaze painted wares survive in collections, they will be recognised by their handles and spouts which, on the excavated pieces, are of the common Phase III types.

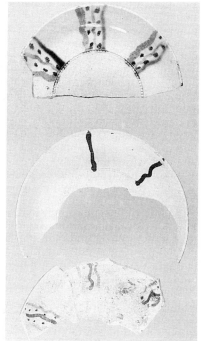

Plate 74
Under-glaze painted creamware saucers in different stages of production. Top: glazed; centre: biscuit and part-painted; bottom: wasted during the glost firing. Phase III.

Under-glaze blue painted decoration

On the Greatbatch site under-glaze blue painted decoration is a Phase III phenomenon which is found on very large quantities of both creamwares and pearlwares. Evidence for an interest in under-glaze painted decoration is present in Phase II: a handful of biscuit sherds were found with crude blue painted floral designs which appear to be practice pieces, prefiguring the great surge of popularity of under-glaze blue designs during the 1770s.

Plate 75
Pearlware plate with moulded 'Chinese lantern' edge and under-glaze blue painted decoration. Unmarked. *c.* 1775-1782. (The Lockett Collection)

Plate 76
Pearlware teabowls, biscuit (left) and glazed (centre and right), with under-glaze blue painted decoration. Phase III.

Plate 77
Biscuit cream/pearlware teabowls and saucer, with under-glaze blue painted decoration which has been air-dried. Phase III.

Evidence that Greatbatch's blue painted creamwares and pearlwares were decorated at his factory may be found in the large numbers of practice pieces which were recovered from the excavation (Plates 33 and 34). The designs which the trainee painters were attempting to copy were reasonably simple and straightforward which should have posed few problems. Greatbatch's most common under-glaze blue patterns are variations on the Oriental-style 'tree-fence-house-fence-tree' theme which seems to have been used by many manufacturers at this time, in response to the continuing popularity of chinoiserie subjects and of Oriental porcelain. Several of the Oriental landscape scenes are repeated time and again on certain types of pot, while others appear to be unique variations which perhaps reflect a degree of autonomy allowed to the decorators. It is impossible to detect the work of different painters in Greatbatch's under-glaze painted wares.

Some of the under-glaze blue painted wares of contemporary manufacturers made use of figure subjects, European or Oriental, often set within stylised landscapes. Greatbatch appears not to have done so and his only concessions to variety are floral designs which, in fact, are generally painted to a much higher standard than his landscapes. One of these floral patterns is illustrated in Plate 78. The plate, in this case creamware, is not marked but the 'Chinese lantern' edge pattern matches excavated pieces exactly, while the painted design is also paralleled on a number of pieces from the Greatbatch site. Here, a match in decoration is simply strengthening an attribution based upon identical moulded details.

Plate 78
Creamware plate with 'Chinese lantern' moulded edge and under-glaze blue painted decoration. Unmarked. *c.* 1770-1782. (Private Collection)

Plate 79
Pearlware sauce boat with under-glaze blue painted decoration. *c.* 1775-1782. (City Museum & Art Gallery, Stoke-on-Trent)

Plate 80
Pearlware sauce boat with under-glaze blue painted decoration. Phase III.

Plate 81
Biscuit cream/pearlware plate with moulded shell edge
and under-glaze blue painted decoration. Phase III.

Plate 82
Biscuit cream/pearlware bowl with
under-glaze blue painted decoration.
Phase III.

Plate 83
Pearlware teapot with under-glaze
blue painted decoration. Phase III.

Plates 84a & b
Pearlware teapot with under-glaze blue painted decoration which has flown during glazing. *c.* 1775-1782. (Courtesy of Lindsay Grigsby)

Greatbatch's under-glaze blue painted decoration is used on many of the Phase III vessel forms in both creamware and pearlware. Particularly common in under-glaze blue are teapots, teabowls, saucers, milk jugs, sauce boats, mugs, bowls and punch bowls. These latter carry a variety of Oriental landscape subjects, buildings, bushes and often an inscription on the inside. Amongst these inscriptions, we find *One more, Lads Drink, It's Out*, and other such well-known mottoes. Mugs, too, have been found with inscriptions in under-glaze blue, but are too fragmentary to permit a full reconstruction. Creamware plates have also been found with inscriptions on their undersides: *Wardroom* and *Gunroom* occur on several sherds, while one plate inscribed *S.I.C. / S.C.* has been recovered.

Marbled or surface agate decoration

The use of slip decoration on creamwares and pearlwares is not encountered until Phase III on the Greatbatch site. This method of decoration may possibly be seen as a relatively late innovation as the majority of the marbled wares are pearlwares, rather than creamwares, suggesting a post-1775 date for its introduction.

The decoration is produced by trailing three slips of different colours on to the unfired surface of a pot, and then swirling the colours together in the manner of marbling paper. Sometimes the colours are combed, or broken with a feather in the manner well-known on the slipwares of the late 17th — mid-18th centuries. The colours used on Greatbatch's wares include pink, white, and various shades of brown, which are darkened somewhat after glazing. The marbled effect is often enhanced by lathe turning of rims, particularly of mugs, beakers and teabowls, which may then be touched with a little green coloured glaze. The effect is bright, cheerful, but a little less subtle than that achieved by the majority of Greatbatch's creamwares. A few vessels, saucers, show that marbled exteriors were sometimes combined with under-glaze blue painted interiors, with the usual Oriental landscapes being depicted.

A limited range of standard vessel forms is used. Most common are cylindrical mugs, flaring beakers, bowls, teapots, teabowls, saucers, dishes, and flower pots and stands. Plates, sugar bowls, coffee pots and cups have not been found, and the more elaborate tureens and sauce boats are also absent. Even so, a reasonably large quantity of this type of ware has been found.

Plate 85
Biscuit cream/pearlware teapot with 'marbled' slip decoration. Phase III.

Plate 86
Biscuit cream/pearlware teabowls with 'marbled' slip decoration. Phase III.

Plate 87
Biscuit cream/pearlware mugs and a beaker with 'marbled' slip decoration. Phase III.

Over-glaze painted decoration

The use of enamel-painted decoration on ceramics was widely practised by the time that Greatbatch's manufacturing business was under way towards the end of 1762. Its use on creamwares of the period is well-known, but rather too much significance has been attached the styles of decoration used and their potential as a means of attribution. The futility of this is underlined by the simple fact that very little is known about the decorators of creamware during the 1760s and 1770s; indeed, it is not even known which manufacturers might have employed in-house decorators, in preference to sending their glazed wares to specialist decorating shops. Very little is known about those specialist decorators who existed alongside the pottery industry, and far too much emphasis has been placed on the work of David Rhodes and Jasper Robinson of Leeds on account of their connection with Wedgwood. This is not the place to discuss the often flawed reasoning which has led to pieces being attributed to Wedgwood on the evidence of enamelled decoration which is in the *style* of Rhodes and Robinson. Suffice to say that there is no positive evidence for what their style may have been, and that the oft-repeated assertion that the use of red and black enamel colours is 'tantamount to a signature' is nonsense.

Greatbatch made extensive use of over-glaze enamel painted decoration on his creamwares and the most common patterns are of flowers coloured in red and black which are wholly in what has traditionally been known as the 'style' of Rhodes and Robinson. What writers on ceramics have generally ignored is the ability of a decorator to copy a standard design which makes any discussion of style superfluous. Examples of Greatbatch's creamwares which would previously have doubtless been attributed to Rhodes and Robinson may be seen in Plates VII and IX and the similarity of their decoration to that used by other manufacturers is striking.

Many surviving examples of enamelled decoration are known on the range of typically Phase III type creamware teapots which have long been attributed to Greatbatch. Very many different styles are represented which would not, themselves, suggest a single manufacturing source. Fortunately Greatbatch's teapots are quite distinctive and we have a large body of excavated evidence to support observations made of extant pieces. Enamelled wares were extremely numerous amongst the excavated pottery and, in many instances, the patterns identified match those used on the extant wares. Other designs have yet to be recognised on surviving wares and, for the present at least, the sherds from the Greatbatch site provide our only evidence for these.

Enamelled decoration on the excavated sherds belongs almost exclusively to Phase III and occurs on both creamwares and pearlwares. Only a handful of enamelled sherds have been recovered from Phases I and II, suggesting that this method of decoration was not important in the years before *c.* 1770 and that little,

Plate 88
Creamware saucer, painted over-glaze in red enamel which has failed to harden-on properly. Phase III.

Plate 89
Creamware teapot, painted over-glaze in enamel colours. Type 23 handle terminals and Type 3 knop. *c.* 1765-1770.
(Courtesy of the Colonial Williamsburg Foundation)

Plate 90
Creamware coffee pot (reverse to
Plate I), painted over-glaze in
enamel colours. Types 17-19
handle terminals and Type 3
knop. *c.* 1765-1770. (City
Museum & Art Gallery,
Stoke-on-Trent)

if any, over-glaze painting was carried out at Greatbatch's factory. The situation
in Phase III is very different. The quantity of enamel painted ware recovered
effectively proves that decorating was carried out in-house for, otherwise, wasters
from this stage of production would not have been represented in any numbers
on Greatbatch's factory waste tip: these would almost certainly have been hardened
on at the decorator's and, if wasted, would have been discarded elsewhere. There
were also numerous pieces from the excavation whose painted decoration had
not been properly hardened-on (Plate 88). Such pieces were beyond redemption
and were discarded immediately; they were certainly not brought in from outside.

Plate 91
Creamware teapot, painted over-glaze in enamel colours. The inscription *Spencer Howe/And Liberty* is a reference to the 1768 'spendthrift' election in Northamptonshire when Lord Spencer is reputed to have spent £160,000 to ensure the election of his candidate Mr. Howe. *c.* 1768-1770. (Published by Permission of Northampton Museums & Art Gallery)

While the absence of enamel painted sherds from Phases I and II suggests that Greatbatch was not heavily involved in the production of over-glaze decorated creamwares, the evidence of extant wares provides a contradiction to this. Many pieces of creamware of Phase I and II types have been identified in collections, decorated in over-glaze enamel colours in a variety of styles (Plates I, VII, 89 — 91). The absence of decorated wasters in Phases I and II of the excavation make it highly unlikely that these very competently painted wares were decorated at Greatbatch's factory and we must, therefore, conclude that prior to *c.* 1770 Greatbatch sent his creamwares elsewhere for specialist decoration. There is, in fact, a possible reference to this in Greatbatch's correspondence with Wedgwood, for on 12th July, 1763, Greatbatch wrote: *I shall send Mr. Courzen's ware to his painting shop to night*[18]. There are two possible Mr. Courzens in Stoke-on-Trent, both described as painters. Henry Curzon is described as such upon his marriage to Ann Ball on 13th April, 1762, as is John Curzon upon his marriage to Elizabeth Hunt on 17th December, 1763[19]. Upon the baptism of their first child on 15th August, 1762, Henry and Ann Curzon are listed as being of Penkhull[20]. A further reference to a painter, this time not named, occurs in a letter from Greatbatch to Wedgwood of 9th January, 1765:

Sir,

the painter will be over at Burslam next week
and will make a tryal of his hand if you will have
the Coulers in readiness.[21]

Plate 92
Creamware teapot (reverse to Plate 114), painted over-glaze in enamel colours. This knop has not been recognised amongst the excavated sherds. *c.* 1770-1782. (Delhom Collection, The Mint Museum of Art, Charlotte, North Carolina. Photographer: Bill J. Moretz)

Plate 93
Creamware teapot, painted over-glaze in enamel colours. Type 23 handle terminals. *c.* 1770-1782. (Courtesy of Lindsay Grigsby. Photographer: Katherine Wetzel)

Plate 94
Creamware teapot, of unusual form (reverse to Plate VI), painted over-glaze in enamel colours. *c.* 1770-1782. (Norfolk Museums Service. Norwich Castle Museum)

Plate 95
Creamware teapot (reverse of Plate 121), painte[d] over-glaze in enamel colours. *c.* 1770-178[2] (Norfolk Museums Service. Norwich Cast[le] Museum)

Plate 96
Creamware teapot (reverse of Plate 122), paint[ed] over-glaze in enamel colours. *c.* 1770-178[2] (Norfolk Museums Service. Norwich Cas[tle] Museum)

Plate 97
Creamware teapot (reverse to Plate VIII), pain[ted] over-glaze in enamel colours. *c.* 1770-1782. (C[ity] Museum & Art Gallery, Stoke-on-Trent)

Plate 98
Creamware teapot (reverse to Plate IV), painted
over-glaze in enamel colours. *c.* 1770-1782. (The
Jacobs Collection)

There were probably other specialist decorators working in the area at this time, about whom we know nothing. By about 1770, however, Greatbatch clearly had over-glaze painters working for him at his factory in Lower Lane. The enamel-painted wares of the period *c.* 1770 — 1782 are extremely varied. Creamwares of all forms are decorated in this way and even enamel painted plate edges are found. Floral patterns are by far the most common of the designs used: these often occur as simple flower sprays in red monochrome, red and black or in red and black with added detail in yellow, green or mauve. Other more complex designs are found, including flowers in a two-handled vase (Plate 98). The floral decoration is not reserved solely for creamware, and a range of fluted pearlware vessels has been excavated with pink floral patterns (Plate 99). Considerable use is also made of trailing flowers or leaves which may be intertwined with drapes or swags. These may be very finely done (Plate 100), while other examples are rather more crude (Plate 103). A very distinctive style of floral decoration may be seen in Plates II and III, and 104. These have various sprays of flowers set against an olive green ground, within which are plain panels decorated with trailing leaves and, in the case of one piece, the Sun and the Moon. A relatively late date is suggested for these pieces as they occur in both creamware and pearlware.

Plate 99
Creamware and pearlware teabowls and saucer, painted over-glaze in pink enamel. Phase III.

Plate 100
Creamware teapot fragments, painted over-glaze in enamel colours. Phase III.

Plate 101
Creamware teapot fragments, painted over-glaze in enamel colours. Phase III.

Plate 102
Creamware teabowl and saucers, painted over-glaze in enamel colours. Phase III.

Plate 103
Creamware teapot and saucer, painted over-glaze in enamel colours. Phase III.

Plate 104
Creamware teapot, painted over-glaze in enamel colours. *c.* 1770-1782. (Courtesy of Lindsay Grigsby)

Figure subjects are also very common and the most important of these appear to have been Chinese figures who occur alone, in pairs, holding parasols or wands, but invariably pointing. Particularly common are teapots which contain individual pointing Chinamen, often accompanied by large jars, in panels framed by painted scrolls (Plates 109 — 110). Other figures are more unusual, such as the infant satyrs, or Bacchic cherubs of Plates 111a and 111b, or the seated figure of Asia with her camel, jewels and crescent moon (Plate 112). The seated figure of a fox, together with the inscription *Beware of / the Fox* (Plate 113), has a political flavour, being a reference to the reforming Member of Parliament Charles James Fox. Fiercely anti-monarchist and hated by George III, Fox was a favourite of the people and the inscription on this teapot is clearly intended as a warning to the King at a time of increasing pressure to limit the power and privilege of the Crown[22].

Plate 105
Creamware teapot, painted over-glaze in enamel colours. Type 22 handle terminals. *c.* 1770-1782. (Courtesy of Jonathan Horne)

Plate 106
Creamware teapot, painted over-glaze in enamel colours. Reverse — Plate 126. *c.* 1770-1782. (Nancy Gunson Collection)

Plate 107
Creamware teapot, painted over-glaze in
enamel colours. Reverse — Plate 125.
c. 1770-1782. (Courtesy of Jonathan Horne)

Plate 108
Creamware teapot (reverse of Plate 120),
painted over-glaze in enamel colours.
c. 1770-1782. (Norfolk Museums Service.
Norwich Castle Museum)

Plate 109
Creamware teapot, painted over-glaze in
enamel colours. c. 1770-1782. (Courtesy of
Jonathan Horne)

Plate 110
Creamware teapot, painted over-glaze in enamel colours. *c.* 1770-1782. (The Jacob Collection)

Plates 111a & b
Creamware teapot, painted over-glaze in enamel colours. *c.* 1770-1782. (The Jacob Collection)

Plate 112
Creamware teapot, painted over-glaze in
enamel colours. The subject of the design is
clearly Asia. Reverse — Plate 128.
c. 1770-1782. (City Museum & Art Gallery,
Stoke-on-Trent)

Plate 113
Creamware teapot, painted over-glaze in
enamel colours. The inscription is a reference
to the politician Charles James Fox. Reverse
— Plate 127. *c.* 1780. (Royal Pavilion Art
Gallery & Museum, Brighton)

A number of painted subjects may be linked by their use of a similar framing
cartouche, and by the fact that they have the appearance of theatrical characters.
The first of these is the bust of a most impressive-looking Turk (Plate 114) who
is perhaps the character Mahomet, from Miller's play of the same name, who
appears in printed form on tin-glazed tiles[23]. The second subject is the bust of
an equally impressive-looking lady who has flowers in her hair and whose
appearance, again, suggests a character from the theatre (Plate 115). Who the
lady might be is not known. A third subject within this cartouche is a lady, full-
length, carrying a basket (Plate IV) about whom we can say nothing, except that
she appears on another pot in the same attitude, but without the cartouche
(Plate 116).

Plate 114
Creamware teapot, painted over-glaze in enamel colours.
The subject within the cartouche is possibly Mahomet, from
Miller's play of the same name. Reverse — Plate 92.
c. 1770-1782. (Delhom Collection, The Mint Museum of
Art, Charlotte, North Carolina. Photographer: Bill J.
Moretz)

Plate 115
Creamware teapot, painted over-glaze in enamel colours.
Reverse — Plate 98. *c.* 1770-1782. (Walford Collection)

Greatbatch's best-known figure subject is undoubtedly that of Aurora in her
chariot drawn by two winged horses (Plate X). She appears on many teapots
with the reverse either of Dawn, shown in Plate 117, or else with an accompanying
inscription. Plate 118 shows a teapot with the inscription *Ann / Heath / 1776*
accompanying a painted Aurora. Another Aurora teapot at Temple Newsam
House has the reverse inscription *C.G. / 1775*[24]. Yet another painted Aurora,
identical to those on the teapots, is known on an elaborate creamware jug which
bears the inscriptions *J C* and *AURORA Goddess / of the Sun / 1775*[25]. The reverse
design to this piece is identical to that shown in Plate 117. Given the exact match
of the decoration of this piece and the teapots already mentioned, it is extremely
tempting to suggest manufacture by Greatbatch. It is important to remember,
however, that decoration and manufacture are not always synonymous and, in
this case, the elaborate and particularly distinctive handle of the jug does not match
anything recovered from the Greatbatch site. If there is a Greatbatch connection,
it cannot be confirmed.

Plate 116
Creamware teapot, painted over-glaze in enamel colours. Reverse — Plate 129. *c.* 1770-1782. (Courtesy of Lindsay Grigsby. Photography: Katherine Wetzel)

Plate 117
Creamware teapot (reverse of Plate XI), painted over-glaze in enamel colours. *c.* 1770-1782. (City Museum & Art Gallery, Stoke-on-Trent)

Plate 118
Creamware teapot, painted over-glaze in enamel colours. *c.* 1770-1782. (Family of Ann Heath)

Peter Walton has pointed out that the stylistic details of the *Ann Heath* and *C. G.* inscriptions of the Aurora teapots are sufficiently close for them to be grouped together and has noted the Greatbatch connection[26]. The script is indeed very distinctive and other pieces inscribed in the same style include a creamware teapot with the inscription *M M / 1775* (Plate 120), which is, without doubt, by Greatbatch. Jugs, however, are more of a problem in the absence of features which may be specific to Greatbatch. A creamware jug at Temple Newsam House with the inscription *Daniel Potter / Barton Mills / 1775* (Plate 119), and a jug in the Harrogate Museum with the inscription *John Avey / Welnetham / 1775* are both inscribed in the above style. Barton Mills and Welnetham are in Suffolk, and the individuals named on these two pieces have been idenitifed by Sheila Bidgood as a result of her excellent biographical work on named and dated creamwares[27]. Whether or not we can confirm a consistent Greatbatch connection is open to debate. Both of the jugs have the indented loop handle which is very frequently used by Greatbatch, but which is also used by other manufacturers, and which cannot, therefore, be used as a basis for attribution. Moulded face mask pouring lips are more likely to be exclusive to an individual factory and, indeed, that of the *Daniel Potter* jug can be matched exactly by a mask excavated from Phase III of the Greatbatch site. This jug, at least, was made by Greatbatch.

Other inscriptions occur on Greatbatch teapots, but in completely different styles to those described above. These include the inscriptions *Let your conversation / Be upon the / Gospell of Christ* (Plate 121) and *When this you See / Remember me tho / Many miles We / Distant be* (Plate 122). A very crude inscription appears on a creamware teapot between a pair of very badly painted buildings in an Oriental style: *Green / Tea / 1777* (Plate 123). These buildings are similar in style to those which occur frequently as under-glaze blue painted designs and are far from being some of Greatbatch's best work. On the reverse of this teapot is an unusual tower which appears once again on a large jug with the inscription *Richard Roberts / 1776* (Plates 62 and 124). This jug has typical Greatbatch handle terminals, Type 13, and a moulded face mask pouring lip which is paralleled in a smaller size amongst the excavated material. Production by Greatbatch is, therefore, a strong possibility.

Plate 119
Creamware jug, painted over-glaze in enamel colours. Inscription *Daniel Potter / Barton Mills / 1775.* Daniel Potter was landlord of the The Bull inn at Barton Mills, Suffolk, and consequently we have the bull design on the jug. *c.* 1775. (Leeds City Art Galleries. Temple Newsam House)

Plate 120
Creamware teapot, painted over-glaze in
enamel colours. Inscription *MM / 1775* in
black enamel. Reverse — Plate 108. *c.* 1775.
(Norfolk Museums Service. Norwich Castle
Museum)

Plate 121
Creamware teapot, painted over-glaze in
enamel colours. Inscription: *Let your
conversation / Be upon the / Gospell of Christ.*
Reverse — Plate 95. *c.* 1770-1782. (Norfolk
Museums Service. Norwich Castle Museum)

Plate 122
Creamware teapot, painted over-glaze in
enamel colours. Inscription: *When this you See
/ Remember me tho / Many miles We / Distant be.*
Reverse — Plate 96. *c.* 1770-1782. (Norfolk
Museums Service. Norwich Castle Museum)

Plate 123
Creamware teapot, painted over-glaze in enamel colours. Inscription: *Green / Tea / 1777.*
c. 1777. (City Museum & Art Gallery, Stoke-on-Trent)

Plate 124
Creamware jug with turned decoration, painted over-glaze in
enamel colours. Inscription: *Richard Roberts / 1776.* See also Plate
62. *c.* 1776. (Published by Permission of Northampton Museums
& Art Gallery)

A variety of buildings are depicted on Greatbatch's enamel-painted creamwares.
These include single storey houses and towers in an Oriental style, as well as
structures which have a more European feel to them. The windmill shown in
Plate 129 is rather more recognisably European than other buildings.

Plate 125
Creamware teapot (reverse of Plate 107),
painted over-glaze in enamel colours.
c. 1770-1782. (Courtesy of Jonathan Horne)

Plate 126
Creamware teapot (reverse of Plate 106),
painted over-glaze in enamel colours.
c. 1770-1782. (Nancy Gunson Collection)

Plate 127
Creamware teapot (reverse of Plate 113),
painted over-glaze in enamel colours.
c. 1770-1782. (Royal Pavilion Art Gallery &
Museum, Brighton)

Plate 128
Creamware teapot (reverse of Plate 112), painted over-glaze in enamel colours. *c.* 1770-1782. (City Museum & Art Gallery, Stoke-on-Trent)

Plate 129
Creamware teapot (reverse of Plate 116), painted over-glaze in enamel colours. *c.* 1770-1782. (Courtesy of Lindsay Grigsby. Photography: Katherine Wetzel)

Plate 130
Creamware teapot, painted over-glaze in enamel colours. *c.* 1770-1782. (ex Towner Collection)

Printed creamwares

Greatbatch's manufacture of printed creamwares is well-known. The printed designs which have previously been attributed to Greatbatch, although mistakenly as engraver, have already been referred to (above, pages 100-102). These all occur on extant vessels which are typical of Phase III of Greatbatch's production; in other words they post-date *c.* 1770. The printed wares excavated from the Greatbatch site likewise belong exclusively to Phase III and the range of vessel forms upon which they occur matches those of the extant pieces. However, the excavation did produce a much greater number of printed designs than had hitherto been anticipated, many of which have no known parallels on surviving pieces.

The excavated evidence implies that none of Greatbatch's wares were printed during Phases I and II and no extant printed pieces of this earlier period have been identified to contradict this. It is, of course, quite possible, that Greatbatch transported some of his wares to market via a specialist pottery printer, in which case, there would be no trace of printed wares on Greatbatch's factory waste tip. This practice is documented in the 1760s: Wedgwood himself, for example, sent his wares to Liverpool to be printed by John Sadler and Guy Green, some of them being decorated there and then shipped on to their final destination[28]. For the present, the fact that no early printed wares have been attributed to Greatbatch is a strong indicator that, at least, they were not a significant part of his production.

By the time that Greatbatch was producing large quantities of printed creamwares, the technique of transfer-printing on pottery had been in use for almost two decades, and on creamware for almost one. Greatbatch's prints have all been produced by the use of glue bats and exhibit those minor faults which occur with this method (above, pages 142-143). Who might have carried out Greatbatch's printing is an open question, despite the traditional association with Thomas Radford which has already been referred to in Chapter 4. What is clear, however, is that Greatbatch had access to a good number of copper plates, most of which had been engraved to a high standard. The majority of Greatbatch's prints were of a very good quality[29], with just a few being somewhat poorer in their execution.

Two quite different styles of engraved design were required by Greatbatch. Many of his prints are over-painted in enamel colours, a practice which obviated the need for elaborately detailed prints. These enamel-painted prints are therefore little more than outlines which were subsequently filled in by the painters; detail and shading were largely irrelevant here. The discovery on the excavation of black printed sherds which were not over-painted was not expected. Black printing necessitated the extra detail and this may be seen in the several designs which have been identified, mainly in black, but with a small number of pieces printed in red. The majority of these prints are well-executed with line-engraved and stippled detail.

Just one extant piece of Greatbatch's black-printed creamware has so far been identified. This is a teapot which carries, on one side, a print of John Wesley, with the inscription *John Wesley A.M. Fellow of Lincoln College Oxford,* and on the other the inscription *Let your Conversation be as becometh the Gospel of Christ* (Plates 131a & b). These two prints are of a very high standard, and are amongst some of the most competent work apparent on Greatbatch's wares. Other versions of the print of Wesley are known: there is one which bears the inscription *Green Liverpool* beneath it[30], and another without the second inscription which is found on a marked Wedgwood teapot[31]. The detail of these prints is very similar indeed; the major difference between the Greatbatch print and the others is the use in the former of predominantly lower case letters in the inscription, whereas the others use upper case letters throughout. This is far from being the only example of Greatbatch using a printed design which was a popular subject at the time and which was more widely used by other manufacturers.

Plates 131a & b
Creamware teapot, printed over-glaze in blac
Front: John Wesley and the inscription *Jo
Wesley A. M. Fellow of Lincoln College Oxford.* Bac
the inscription *Let Your Conversation Be as Becom
the Gospel of Christ,* framed within a scroll
cartouche. *c.* 1770-1782. (Reproduced b
courtesy of the Board of Trustees of the Victori
& Albert Museum)

Another of Greatbatch's black printed designs is of merrymaking ouside a tent, a print not hitherto identified on creamwares. Nevertheless, the quantity of excavated sherds printed with this design suggests that it enjoyed a certain popularity (Plate 132). Once again, the quality of the engraving for this design is very high. The print depicts a scene from the popular opera Flora, or Hob in the Well by John Hippisley and has been taken from the volume *Songs from the Opera of Flora with Humerous Scenes of Hob Design'd by ye Celebrated Mr. Gravelot; & Engraved by G. Bickham jun.,* which appeared for sale in 1737[32]. The print (Plate 133) reappears in George Bickham's *Universal Penman,* which was published in

Plate 132
Creamware sherds, printed over-glaze in black with a scene from
Songs from the Opera of Flora. Phase III.

201

Plate 133
Page 25 of *Songs from the Opera of Flora with Humerous Scenes of Hob Design'd by ye Celebrated Mr. Gravelot; & Engraved
by G. Bickham jun.* (1737), reproduced as Plate 201 of George Bickham's *Universal Penman* of 1743. (Dover
Publications, Inc.)

1743[33], and is identical to that on the excavated sherds, save for the reversal of
the image which has occurred, and for the loss of the surrounding cartouche which
does not appear on Greatbatch's print.

Such popular subjects taken from operas or plays were commonly used by the
manufacturers of pottery and porcelain in the decoration of their wares. Their
widespread availability ensured that they were copied by engravers throughout
the country, many of whom supplied the pottery factories with copper plates.
Other scenes from *Flora* have been identified as painted designs on the porcelains
of the Chelsea factory[34], but none of these have yet been identified on
creamware.

Plate 134
Creamware sherd, printed over-glaze in black with the subject known as 'The Exotic Birds'. Phase III.

Another printed subject which was popular with the manufacturers of creamware was that known today as 'The Exotic Birds'. It is no surprise, therefore, that Greatbatch used this subject on his wares and that several sherds printed with this pattern were found (Plate 134). This is another very good quality print, comparing favourably with other examples of the same subject.

Plate 135
Creamware sherds, printed over-glaze in black with a rustic landscape subject. Phase III.

Rather less competent, is a print of a rural scene which occurs on several of the excavated creamwares (Plate 135). The subject comprises, in the foreground, a shepherd sitting amongst his sheep, while across a lake there stands a farm with a circular tower; the scene is very much in the genre of the landscape subjects which were popular at that time. The print occurs in black and sepia, and all the sherds recovered are of cylindrical teapots.

Plate 136
Creamware sherd, printed over-glaze in black with an unknown subject. Phase III.

Plate 137
Creamware saucer, printed over-glaze in red with a design depicting Venus and Cupid. Phase III.

Two black printed subjects were used together on vessels, although neither can be identified. The first subject appears to depict Venus walking in a garden and striking at a flying bird. She is accompanied by cupid, who is in tears, with a broken bow, part of which lies on the ground with his quiver and a number of broken arrows. The second subject shows a male figure in classical drapery, with helmet and breast plate, standing in a garden in front of a large turreted house; a winged *putto* with lighted torch hovers overhead, while cupid's broken bow appears once again on the ground in this print.

These two black printed subjects appear on both cylindrical and round-bodied teapots, coffee pots, bowls, teabowls and saucers. They are also used as red prints on both teabowls and saucers (Plates 136 & 137). They are the only red printed subjects identified amongst the Greatbatch sherds and we must conclude that red was a colour little used by Greatbatch for his printed wares. Both the teabowls and saucers with these two designs are decorated additionally in over-glaze red enamel colour: the rim interiors have the common scalloped bands with leaves. Although the subject of neither print is known at present, it is interesting to note that the Venus and Cupid design has been identified elsewhere on a piece not produced by Greatbatch: in the Victoria and Albert Museum is a pearlware jug of about 1790 which is decorated with this same printed subject, this time in pink[35].

228

The print of a man of war in full sail has long been recognised as one of the subjects used on Greatbatch's teapots together with the subject of Admiral Keppel (Plates 147a & b). The extant pieces identified to date have prints which have been over-painted in enamel colours, in the style of Greatbatch's Prodigal Sons and other enamelled prints. Surprisingly, no sherds of an enamelled man of war were found on the Greatbatch site, although this need cause no concern as losses during this stage of production would have been very small indeed. However, three sherds of an uncoloured man of war of the same print were identified; the prints are from a full engraving which would stand on their own without additional colouring, but with detail which is not too strong to prevent the use of colour. It is impossible to know from these waste sherds whether over-painting was intended, although the evidence of the extant prints would seem to suggest that it was.

Another well-known printed subject on Greatbatch's wares is that of Captain Cook being directed by Britannia (Plate XII). This print, too, appears on surviving vessels only in over-painted versions and, indeed, several enamelled sherds of the subject were found on the excavation. In addition there is an uncoloured sherd of a Captain Cook print in a sepia colour which is, significantly, taken from a different engraving to that used for the coloured prints. The designs of the two are generally very similar, but with additional detail and stippling on the sepia print; when the two are seen together these differences are immediately apparent (Plate 138).

Plate 138
Creamware sherds, printed over-glaze with the subject 'Captain Cook being directed by Britannia'. Different engravings have been used for the uncoloured sepia print (bottom) and for the over-painted prints (rest). These differences can be seen in the details of the child in the left of the print. Phase III.

A number of other black printed subjects have been found, but most can neither be reconstructed in their entirety, nor positively related to other surviving prints. The only recognisable subject amongst these printed sherds is a version of the print known as the 'Tea Party' (Plate 139).

Plate 139
Creamware sherds, printed over-glaze in black with a subject known as the 'Tea Party'. Phase III.

To judge by the large number of pieces in collections today, Greatbatch was a prolific producer of creamwares with printed and enamelled subjects. Shaw saw fit to mention this in 1829, referring to the Prodigal Son series, and many others have been identified in recent years through stylistic comparisons with the Prodigal Son printed wares[36]. The large number of enamelled printed sherds found on the Greatbatch site supports the view of Greatbatch as a manufacturer of numerous elaborately decorated wares which enjoyed a widespread popularity. All those printed subjects which had been attributed to Greatbatch by Towner were identified amongst the excavated sherds of Phase III creamwares, as well as several other subjects which had either not been seen before, or else had not been connected with Greatbatch. These subjects will all be dealt with below.

The Prodigal Son series comprises a set of six prints in a distinctive style which generally appear in pairs: *The Prodigal Son Receives his Patrimony* with *The Prodigal Son Taking Leave; The Prodigal Son in Excess* with *The Prodigal Son in Misery*; and *The Prodigal Son returns Reclaim'd* with *The Prodigal Son Feasted on his Return*. One example of *The Prodigal Son in Excess* standing alone, without its companion print, is found on a teapot in Birmingham City Museum and Art Gallery[37]; rather than a printed subject on the reverse, the teapot has the painted inscription: *When this you see Remember me / And keep me in your mind / let all the World say what they will / Speak of me as you find*, a curious combination. The prints are most commonly found on teapots, although examples on coffee pots are known.

The parable of the Prodigal Son was a popular subject with the English public from the mid-18th century, after a set of six engravings of paintings by the French artist Sébastien le Clerc II was published in Paris in 1751 as the *Histoire de l'enfant prodique*[38]. English copies, one set by Richard Purcell and another by an unknown printmaker, appeared over the next few years, which were still being advertised for sale twenty years later in 1775[39].

The Prodigal Son prints which appear on Greatbatch's tea and coffee pots follow closely the set of six mezzotints by Purcell. Hairstyles and dress have been updated on Greatbatch's prints, but the general position, posture and attitudes of the figures are the same, as are the furniture and other items. The subjects of Greatbatch's *Taking Leave* and *returns Reclaim'd* are reversed from the originals, but are otherwise very similar in detail to Purcell's prints; *Excess, Misery* and *Feasted* are close copies in every respect, while *Patrimony* differs considerably from Purcell's in its overall composition, although retaining certain small details.

Plate 140

Creamware sherds, printed with the subject *The Prodigal Son Feasted on his Return* and painted over-glaze in enamel colours. The sherds have prints from two different engravings, as is shown by different detail on the column to the left of the print, and by the presence, or absence of a necklace on the lady to the right of the host. Phase III.

Plates 141 a & b
Creamware teapot, printed with the subjects *The Prodigal Son Receives his Patrimony* (front) and *The Prodigal Son Taking Leave* (reverse), and painted over-glaze in enamel colours. *c.* 1770-1782. (The Jacobs Collection)

Plate 142
Creamware teapot, printed with the subject *The Prodigal Son in Excess* and painted over-glaze in enamel colours. *c.* 1770-1782. (Private Collection)

Plate 143
Creamware teapot (reverse of Plate XIV), printed with the subject *The Prodigal Son in Misery* and painted over-glaze in enamel colours. *c.* 1770-1782. (City Museum & Art Gallery, Stoke-on-Trent)

Plates 144a & b
Creamware teapot, printed with the subjects *The Prodigal Son returns Reclaim'd* (front) and *The Prodigal Son Feasted on his Return* (reverse), and painted over-glaze in enamel colours. *Feasted* is an excellent example of the double image which sometimes resulted from the use of a glue bat; this is clear in the figures of the lady at the left of the table and of the orchestra above. *c.* 1770-1782. (The Jacobs Collection)

Towner noted second versions of both *Patrimony* and *Taking Leave* occurring on creamwares, which he also attributes to Greatbatch although, as with the other prints, as engraver[40]. These are very different in style to the prints used by Greatbatch but are irrelevant to the present volume as they are on vessels which were not produced by Greatbatch and whose provenance is uncertain.

The enamel colours used to over-paint the Prodigal Son prints are consistent with those used on the other printed subjects, and with those used in over-glaze painted decoration generally, namely: red, pink, mauve, yellow, green and a lighter red/orange. Gilding was also commonly applied, particularly where a vessel has one or more rouletted bands which required highlighting. As with many of the other printed subjects, front and back designs are separated by bands of mauve sponged decoration, outlined in red, which extend vertically from the base to the rim. Inset within these vertical bands we commonly find panels of red painted scrolled or foliate decoration around the junctions of both handles and spouts, together with oval panels of green sponged decoration which often occur on the shoulders of vessels, or beneath handles and spouts. In the main, there is a strong uniformity in all of Greatbatch's printed wares, a uniformity which is heightened by the distinctive vessel forms and the repeated use of a limited range of handles and spouts.

Several of the over-painted printed subjects used by Greatbatch were popular with the potters of the period. One of these is a scene from the *Comedia del Arte*, Harlequin and Columbine discovered in an arbour by Pierrot. The print used by Greatbatch is lively and, when painted, extremely colourful (Plate XVI). The print often contains the imprint *Greatbatch* (Plate 145) which, as has been pointed out, does not mean that he was the engraver. Where this imprint does not appear, we may assume that the printer has simply wiped away this part of the design immediately after the print had been transferred to the pot. However, why this should have sometimes been desirable is not known. Harlequin and Columbine appear primarily on teapots, but a rather more unusual vehicle for the print is a cylindrical mug which is in the the Mint Museum of Art, Charlotte[41]. The excavated sherds of this subject appear all to be from teapots and there are several examples of the *Greatbatch* imprint.

Plate 145
Detail of imprint *Greatbatch* from the print Harlequin and Columbine. (Delhom Collection, The Mint Museum of Art, Charlotte, North Carolina. Photographer: Harold Allen)

The same scene appears on tin-glazed earthenware tiles[42], reflecting the popularity of the *Comedia* as a source for ceramic decoration: the characters from the *Comedia* were much-used by potters as figure subjects, especially in porcelain, while scenes such as Harlequin and Columbine provided subjects for printmakers. This particular scene derives from an engraving in the John Bowles Drawing Book, from a sheet bearing the date 24th November, 1756[43], which differs only in minor details from the print used by Greatbatch.

The companion print to Harlequin and Columbine is a subject of uncertain significance (Plate XV). A young man, perhaps a suitor, approaches a young lady who is clearly distressed and has placed herself behind an older man, perhaps her father. The three are outside in a garden. Given the theatrical nature of the accompanying print, it would be logical for this, too, to derive from a theatrical source, although what this may have been is not known at present.

We have already looked at Greatbatch's frequent use of Aurora, the goddess of the Dawn, as an enamel-painted subject; the over-painted printed version of this subject is equally common on his wares and several examples are known on tea and punch pots. The printed Aurora rides in a four-wheeled car, pulled by a pair of winged horses; winged *putti* look down from the clouds above and the goddess's name is framed overhead (Plate XI). Another, almost identical version of this print is known on contemporary creamwares produced by Wedgwood[44].

The companion print to the printed *Aurora* is usually that known as The World with Sun, Moon and Stars, although one piece is known upon which the second print is of the goddess Cybele[45]. The World with Sun, Moon and Stars (Plate XIX) is an interesting subject which occurs in slightly different versions on other creamwares of the period. In the centre of the print, a map of the World is laid out within concentric circles; the continents are named — *EUROPE, ASIA, AM.* and *AF.* Flanking the World are the Sun, to the left, and the Moon with stars to the right. In the top right-hand corner of the print a winged Justice flies with scales in one hand; in the top centre of the print, just below coloured clouds, is the Hebrew word *Shmayim*, meaning Heavens. The meaning of the subject of this print is not known, although a possible Masonic connection has been discussed[46].

Plate 146
Creamware teapot, printed with the subject *Cybele* and painted over-glaze in enamel colours. *c.* 1770-1782. (Leeds City Art Galleries. Temple Newsam House)

This was indeed a popular subject with Greatbatch and his customers, and is one of the prints most widely used by him. In addition to its use with *Aurora*, it also occurs with *Cybele*, *Juno*, Captain Cook, and another as yet unnamed subject. The large number of sherds of this subject excavated on the Greatbatch site provides additional proof of its great popularity.

As a companion to The World with Sun, Moon and Stars, the print *Cybele* is another popular subject (Plate 146), although as we have seen there is at least one teapot upon which this subject features with *Aurora*. As a subject for pottery decoration, this print appears to have been used exclusively by Greatbatch; no comparable prints have yet been recognised. The print shows *Cybele*, wearing a mural crown, holding a key, and seated in a four-wheeled car which is drawn by a pair of lions, the lovers Hippomenes and Atalanta who had their human form taken from them for offending the goddess. The name of the goddess appears above.

Juno is well-known on Greatbatch's teapots (Plate XVIII). The goddess, crowned, sits in a four-wheeled car which resembles a shell and is drawn by two peacocks; her name is framed in a similar manner to that of Aurora. The companion to this subject is invariably the World with Sun, Moon and Stars. Several sherds of this design were found on the Greatbatch site; all are of teapots.

Captain Cook being directed by Britannia has already been discussed on account of the two versions of the subject which were used by Greatbatch: the plain black print, and the over-painted print (Plate 138). Both are slightly different in their details, which reflect the intended use to which the prints were to be put. The print intended for over-painting required less detail from the engraver and would suffice mainly in outline. The print shows Captain Cook studying a book which is being shown to him by Britannia, while two *putti* stand waiting for him to embark upon the waiting ship whose mast and sail are visible. One of the *putti* leans upon a box or crate which bears the inscription *WRO No. 129*; the meaning of this is not known.

Captain Cook made three voyages between 1768 and 1779, becoming the first European to reach Australia in 1770 during his first voyage. His second voyage began in July, 1772, while his final voyage began in June, 1776. It is suggested that it was Cook's final voyage which most probably inspired Greatbatch's production of teapots bearing this subject. The reason for this is simply that the dates, stated or implied, of other printed wares manufactured by Greatbatch are consistently within the second half of the decade 1770 — 1780.

The print depicting Admiral Keppel (Plate 147a) which is used by Greatbatch can be dated with some degree of certainty. Admiral Augustus Keppel was court martialled in February, 1779, for his failure to win a naval victory at Ushant. He was acquitted and the incident fired the popular imagination; Keppel's notoriety was such that numerous prints of the man appeared. Wedgwood himself was aware of the commercial value of Keppel in the sale of ceramics and wrote to Bentley stressing the potential value of wares depicting the admiral to their business[47]. Wedgwood did indeed make use of this subject and marked wares bearing Keppel's head in a plain black print are known[48]. The composition of the Wedgwood print is rather different to that used by Greatbatch, but it is interesting to see the two manufacturers capitalising on this event each in his own way. The Greatbatch print, over-painted in enamel colours, carries the inscription *The Honble. Augtus. Keppel*.

The companion to this subject, the man of war in full sale (plate 147b), we have already discussed on page 228.

Plates 147a & b
Creamware teapot, printed with the subjects *The Honble. Augtus. Keppel* (front) and a man of war in full sail (reverse), and painted over-glaze in enamel colours. *c.* 1779. (The Jacobs Collection)

236

The Fortune Teller, in many different forms, was a popular subject for the printmakers of the mid-18th century and consequently it is no surprise to find that Greatbatch made use of a version on his teapots. Greatbatch's Fortune Teller (Plate XIII) sits at a table, surrounded by the tools of his trade, and hands his clients — both ladies — sheets with their fortunes written clearly upon them: *Never Married, A Husband Desir'd*. The print is very well-executed, lively, colourful and witty. Versions of the Fortune Teller are known on both creamware and pearlware which are very close in their detail to Greatbatch's[49], suggesting either a common source used by the engravers or copying.

The companion to the Fortune Teller is always *The XII Houses of Heaven* (Plate 148). The print is particularly significant in that it carries the imprint *Published as the Act directs Jany. 4. 1778 by W. Greatbatch Lane Delf Staffordshire*, further evidence for the late date of Greatbatch's printed wares. Variations of this print were used by many potters at the time, but Greatbatch's version is quite distinctive.

Plate 148
Creamware teapot, printed with the subject *The XII Houses of Heaven* and painted over-glaze in enamel colours. The print bears the imprint *Published as the Act directs Jany. 4. 1778 by W. Greatbatch Lane Delf Staffordshire. c. 1778-1782.* (The Jacobs Collection)

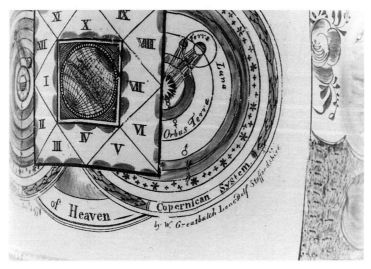

Plate 149
Detail from the imprint of *The XII Houses of Heaven*.

Plate 150
Creamware teapot (reverse of Plate XVII), printed with an Oriental figure subject and painted over-glaze in enamel colours. *c.* 1770-1782. (City Museum & Art Gallery, Stoke-on-Trent)

In the light of the excavation of the Greatbatch site, it has been possible to attribute a number of other prints to Greatbatch on the evidence, largely, of the vessels upon which they occur. Only one of these recently identified prints has been found on the Greatbatch site. First, there is a print which depicts an Oriental lady, in a splendid dress with large sleeves, talking to a child (Plate XVII). The reverse print is of a second Oriental lady with basket and parasol, walking away from a multi-storeyed pagoda (Plate 150).

The remaining over-painted printed subjects which have not been identified on the Greatbatch site include an unknown print depicting, it would appear, Europe, in the guise of Minerva, and Asia surrounded by instruments of navigation and discovery, a globe, and an artist's palette with brushes (Plate 151); the reverse to this print is the World with Sun, Moon and Stars. A second pair of subjects relates to the War of American Independence, occurring on just one teapot. The first of these is a portrait of *Lord Cornwallis* (Plate 152a), the second a battle scene in which British troops are clearly driving off the enemy above the inscription *Success to the British Arms* (Plate 152b). This pair of prints may be dated with some degree of certainty. Cornwallis's reputation during the war in America had grown considerably since his victory at the Battle of Camden, in South Carolina, in 1780. The print depicting Cornwallis is almost certain to post-date this event, and may indeed commemorate his success. An equally plausible event to merit popularising in printed form was Cornwallis's advance from Charleston in January, 1781, which was aimed at securing control of Virginia for the British forces. The outcome of this campaign is well-known — the surrender of the British army at Yorktown in October, 1781. Our Greatbatch printed teapot is most unlikely to be any later in its date of manufacture than this event.

Plate 151
Creamware teapot, printed with a subject which is possibly Europe and Asia and painted over-glaze in enamel colours. *c.* 1770-1782. (Nancy Gunson Collection)

Plates 152a & b
Creamware teapot, printed with the subjects *Lord Cornwallis* (front) and a battle scene with the inscription *Success to the British Arms* (reverse), and painted over-glaze in enamel colours. *c.* 1780-1781. (Royal Pavilion Art Gallery & Museum, Brighton)

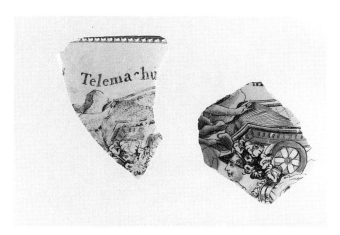

Plate 153
Creamware sherds, printed with the subject *Telemachus* and painted over-glaze in enamel colours. Phase III.

A number of printed subjects have been identified on the excavated creamwares which are, as yet, unknown on extant pieces. The most mysterious of these is of an incomplete classical subject which bears the inscription, itself possibly incomplete, *Telemachu(s)* (Plate 153). Two other printed subjects, Minerva, and the arms of the Society of Bucks, were found on sherds from the Greatbatch site. Neither of these has been identified on extant Greatbatch pieces, although slightly different versions of the prints are known on the wares of other manufacturers.

Plate 154
Creamware sherds, printed with the subject of Minerva, with the inscription *LET WISDOM UNITE US,* and painted over-glaze in enamel colours. Phase III.

The first of these subjects, Minerva, is seated amongst the clouds; in the foreground are three winged *putti* holding what appears to be a globe. Beneath the oval central panel containing these figures is the inscription *LET WISDOM UNITE US* and surrounding the whole is a wreathed cartouche (Plate 154). Game trophies, suspended, flank the central panel and complete the subject of the print. The sherds from the Greatbatch site do not complete the design, but the details are known from a print of the same subject engraved by Thomas Rothwell which is known on creamwares[50].

The second subject, the arms of the Society of Bucks, is represented by several sherds (Plate 155). The print depicts sporting gentlemen flanking a stag and a plough amid rococo scrolls, within which are the mottoes *FREEDOM WITH*

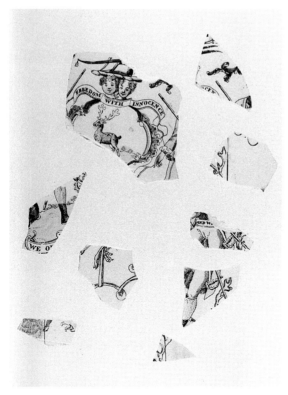

Plate 155
Creamware sherds, printed with the arms of the Society of Bucks and painted over-glaze in enamel colours. Phase III.

INNOCENCE, INDUSTRY PRODUCETH WEALTH, WE OBEY and *UNANIMITY IS THE STRENGTH OF SOCIETY*. The details of the print are very similar to one of the same subject which bears the imprint *Sadler Liverpool*[51].

We have seen that a number of the printed subjects used by Greatbatch often occur on the pottery of other manufacturers in slightly different versions. This suggests that the potters were receiving copper plate engravings from a variety of sources, particularly the numerous engravers who made their living by copying popular pictures. Only rarely, however, are we able to learn anything about the engravers, but at least one North Staffordshire engraver appears to have been capitalising upon Greatbatch's success. A very interesting, if rather crude, pair of the Fortune Teller and *The XII Houses of Heaven* has recently come to light which, it might be argued, could have been copied from a Greatbatch printed piece[52]. They occur upon a cylindrical creamware teapot of uncertain origin which has been decorated in over-glaze colours in exactly the same style and colours as Greatbatch's printed wares. The prints, too, have been over-painted in manner of Greatbatch's Fortune Teller and *XII Houses* prints. The decorator of this teapot was without a doubt familiar with Greatbatch's work and a deliberate attempt at copying seems likely. The *XII Houses* print of this creamware teapot carries the imprint *J. Aynsley — Lane End*. John Aynsley appears to have been involved in many areas of pottery production, as an engraver, an enameller and as a manufacturer[53]. He is documented in Lane End between 1790 and 1829, the year of his death.

Others of Greatbatch's prints appear to occur on non-Greatbatch vessels in an identical form, in other words taken from the very copper plate that Greatbatch himself had used; these prints include *Juno*[54] and the Fortune Teller. It must be stressed that none of the pots with apparently Greatbatch prints has been studied in the detail necessary to confirm a match in the engraving, but at the same time such a situation is far from unlikely. Copper plates were small, valuable and portable items for which there would always be a market amongst pottery manufacturers; they are likely to have been amongst the the equipment sold after, for example, a bankruptcy, and hence the prints from them are highly likely to be found on the wares of more than one factory. Indeed, we have already noted this occurrence with regard to the block mould for Greatbatch's sprigged Oriental figures which have been recognised on early 19th century wares from the Eastwood Factory. Once more, the importance of seeking several points of comparison between wares in matters of attribution is emphasised.

MOULDED CREAMWARES — CLEAR GLAZE

Fruit Basket Ware

The largest group of all of Greatbatch's moulded wares, fruit basket ware is most closely associated with tortoiseshell ware on account of its predominantly under-glaze coloured decoration. Present in all three phases of the Greatbatch site, fruit basket ware attained the height of its popularity, along with the other moulded wares, during Phase II when it was clearly produced in very large quantities. The scale of production is reflected in the rate of survival: numerous examples have been recognised in present day collections, and it appears that Greatbatch was the manufacturer of them all. The distinguishing features — the handles and spouts — of the many vessels studied to date are all Greatbatch types and there can be no doubting that they originate from his factory.

It is most interesting that such a common type of ware can be attributed to just one manufacturer, and extremely fortunate that the opportunity has arisen for this manufacturer to be identified. The moulded details of this type are quite distinctive and there is no possibility of confusion with any other moulded ware. Essentially, the design comprises a band of tightly woven basketwork, above which is a looser trellis work band. Fruit of various sorts is piled into the basket and, in places, spills over the sides. The handles of the basket rise vertically upwards in a tight basketweave to the top of the vessel. Where the vessel has a cover, the tight basketweave of the 'handles' continues to provide the decoration for this, without any of the accompanying fruit. The two sides of hollow ware vessels are not identical and present a slightly different disposition of fruit motifs within the basket. Equally, slight variations in detail are apparent in vessels of different sizes.

The association of this type with the *basket work'd teapot* sent to Wedgwood by Greatbatch on 21st January, 1765[55], has already been tentatively suggested (above, page 90). However, Greatbatch was producing more than teapots. The range of forms produced in fruit basket ware is limited, but remains consistent throughout, being primarily tea and coffee wares, and comprises teapots and covers in various sizes; coffee pots; plates, which may perhaps be stands; milk jugs and covers; sugar bowls and covers; slop bowls; canisters and covers; teabowls; coffee cups; saucers; cream boats; and beakers. The details of the moulded decoration are equally consistent and reflect the continued use of the same block moulds throughout the entire period of production.

It is quite possible to differentiate between the fruit basket wares of the different phases. The handles and spouts are those used on other creamwares and are readily identifiable as early or late types. For example, in Phases I and II the spouts most commonly used on fruit basket teapots were Types 4 and 12, while the larger teapots sometimes have Type 7; the Phase III spouts are invariably of Types 1 to 6 and were used in conjunction with the indented loop handle, Type 18. A greater variety of handles was used during Phase II and includes Types 2, 3, 4 and 8. The spout favoured for use on coffee pots of all three phases was Type 4a.

In addition to the type of handle and spout used, the early and late fruit basket wares are distinguishable by their cream colour. The early pieces, of Phases I and II, are characterised by the dark cream colour which is typical of Greatbatch's earlier creamwares generally, while the later, Phase III wares are of the pale colour which is equally typical during the last decade of production.

Plate 156
Creamware fruit basket
teapot. *c.* 1765-1770. (ex
Towner Collection)

Plate 157
Creamware fruit basket teapot,
coloured under-glaze with metallic
oxides. *c.* 1770-1782. (The Jacobs
Collection)

Plate 158
Creamware fruit basket sugar
bowl, coloured under-glaze with
metallic oxides. *c.* 1770-1782.
(Reproduced by courtesy of the
Board of Trustees of the Victoria
& Albert Museum)

Shell Ware

The *shell teapots* supplied by Greatbatch to Wedgwood in 1764 have already been referred to (above, pages 98-99), as has the occurrence amongst the excavated material of a distinctive range of shell decorated ware. Greatbatch's shell ware, like the fruit basket ware, is a press-moulded creamware with the decoration in relief highlighted in under-glaze oxide colours. The design comprises various clusters of sea shells and sea weed or, in the case of smaller pieces, individual shells set between bands of vertical fluting which have been lathe-turned on the models, rather than on the vessels themselves. The vertical seams where the two moulded halves of certain pots have been joined together can usually be seen. In joining the two halves of a vessel, the workmen often caused a certain amount of damage to the moulded decoration, particularly the fluted bands, which lie in the way of the joins and which are often smudged over at this point. The shells, together with the narrower bands of fluting, are highlighted in under-glaze colours — green, brown, grey and yellow — in exactly the same way as the fruit basket wares. Again, the colours were prone to severe running during glazing and firing.

The shell wares are primarily tea and coffee wares, comprising teapots and covers in several sizes; coffee pots and covers; milk jugs and covers; sugar bowls and covers; slop bowls; canisters and covers; tea bowls; coffee cups; and saucers. There are also butter dishes and covers, small jugs or cream boats, and small plates with shell panels on the rim are most probably butter dish, teapot or coffee pot stands. The range of vessel forms was limited, as was the quantity of this type amongst the finds from the Greatbatch site. Distinctive amongst these shell-moulded vessels were a number of cylindrical butter dish sherds which were green-glazed.

Shell ware is predominantly a Phase II type, with only very small quantities found in Phases I and III. This corresponds with the suggested date of its introduction, at some time during the early part of 1764 when Greatbatch writes of having completed a shell teapot block mould (above, page 56). The archaeological evidence indicates that by *c.* 1770 shell ware's short-lived popularity was very much on the wane, with only a handful of sherds assignable to Phase III. The overall quantity recovered from the excavation, together with the fact that very few pieces survive in collections suggests that shell ware was never one of Greatbatch's major lines of production.

Plate 162
Creamware canister, moulded with shell designs and coloured under-glaze with metallic oxides. *c.* 1765-1770. (City Museum & Art Gallery, Stoke-on-Trent)

Plate 163
Plate 26 of Robert Sayer's *The Ladies Amusement*. The central cluster of shells forms the main element of Greatbatch's shell decoration.

The shell wares are quite distinctive and the source for the moulded designs used upon them has been identified[57]. Plate 26 of *The Ladies Amusement*, published by Robert Sayer in two editions of 1759 or 1760 and 1762[58], details several clusters of shells depicted amongst seaweed engraved by the artist Kenton Couse (Plate 163). The largest, central cluster of shells exactly matches the shell cluster used most frequently by Greatbatch on his shell wares, particularly for the larger vessels, except that the modeller has preferred to use the design upside-down. Even the size of the designs matches, with just a little variation occurring as a result of shrinkage during firing.

Other shells from Sayer's Plate 26 are used by Greatbatch to decorate smaller vessels or the covers of the various vessels. A variation of the most commonly used shell cluster is found on Greatbatch's cylindrical butter dishes. The butter dish shell cluster is formed out of the smaller shell clusters which are found around the edge of Sayer's Plate 26 and Fig. 38 identifies the individual elements which make up this design: the shells *a-a* are those at the bottom left-hand corner of the print; *b-b* matches those in the top right-hand corner; while *c* is the smaller of the shells in the bottom right-hand corner; *d* and *e*, however, are taken from the following plate of *The Ladies Amusement*, Plate 27 (Plate 164), which is presumably also from an engraving by Couse, although in this case the artist is not named.

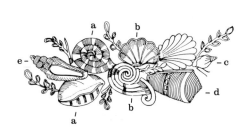

Fig. 38
Detail of shell cluster used on Greatbatch's butter dishes, indicating the individual elements which make up the design.

The appearance of Greatbatch's shell ware during the decade 1760 to 1770 reflects the widespread fascination amongst gentlemen of the period with shells and shell collecting, a result of the growing interest in awareness of the natural world. Josiah Wedgwood himself is known to have possessed a collection of shells and his own interest may have provided the inspiration for the well-known Wedgwood wares which were produced in the form of shells, and for the range of printed wares which drew upon these same plates of *The Ladies*

Plate 164
Shells from Plate 27 of *The Ladies Amusement* used as
elements of Greatbatch's shell decoration.

Amusement. Shell collecting was not confined to native species and, indeed, the
shells illustrated in *The Ladies Amusement* are, in the main, types which are foreign
to England's shores. These are shells which gentlemen collectors would have striven
to acquire. Amongst the shells depicted there are just two which are out of place:
the first is a land snail (top right-hand corner of Sayer's Plate 26), and the second
is a sea urchin (Sayer's Plate 27, not illustrated here). A final peculiarity of the
prints is that the shells are depicted in reverse to nature, that is as mirror images,
the inevitable result of the engraver copying original material. This reversal of
the image is repeated in Greatbatch's moulded wares.

The use of *The Ladies Amusement* as a source of inspiration by the decorators
of pottery and porcelain has already been noted. We have seen, also, that
Greatbatch copied the Oriental ladies of Plate 175 for use as a sprigged relief.
It is no surprise, therefore, that Greatbatch should have used *The Ladies Amusement*
as a source for one of his moulded pottery designs, although he is the only
manufacturer known to have done so[59].

The shell wares, being early in date, are characterised by the darker cream
colour which is typical of the pre-1770 phases. In addition, they make use of a
restricted range of handles and spouts which are Phase II types. The spouts found
on teapots of this ware are Types 4 and 12, while on coffee pots Type 4a is used.
Handles are Types 2 — 4, 6 and 8, while the basketwork handle, Type 7, is
one which is widely used by Greatbatch on coffee pots in a variety of different
bodies. Everything about the shell wares is typically Greatbatch and, although
very few pieces have been identified in collections to provide a good sample of
complete pieces, all the evidence points to Greatbatch as the one and only
manufacturer of this type of ware.

Plate 165
Creamware sugar bowl cover, moulded with shell designs
and coloured under-glaze with metallic oxides. Phase II.

Plate 166
Creamware milk jug cover, moulded with
shell designs and coloured under-glaze with
metallic oxides. Phase II.

248

Floral

A handful of sherds from Phases II and III indicate the existence of a type of press-moulded creamware not hitherto recognised in collections, and not wholly open to reconstruction from the excavated pieces. Four creamware covers and a small number of body sherds of teapots, biscuit and glazed (Plates 167 — 169), are our only evidence for this type.

The design clearly comprises sprays of flowers and leaves, with the lower body of the teapots decorated with turned vertical concave fluting which derives from the block mould. The covers display two similar, but not identical designs of flower sprays within a reeded border, and these, too, are press-moulded. The glazed pieces are all without colour and it seems likely that this floral moulded type was intended to stand without any additional colour.

Plate 167
Creamware sherds, biscuit and glazed, with moulded floral decoration. Phases II-III.

Plates 168-169
Biscuit creamware teapot covers with moulded floral decoration. Phase II.

Basket and Pineapple Ware

Vessels with a press-moulded basketwork body with a central panel containing a pineapple surrounded by rococo scrolls are well-known. They occur with a variety of handle and spout types and were clearly made by a number of different manufacturers. Greatbatch's basket and pineapple wares are not numerous, but occur in all three phases of the site, with slight differences in the range of types recovered from each of these. They predominate in Phase II, when teapots are the only form found. These occur with Type 12 spouts and the remains of typical Phase II handles. There are two quite different moulded teapot bodies, one of which is shown in Fig. 39, and two types of moulded cover (Plates 170 & 171). Unfortunately, no pieces have been completely reconstructed, which makes a full understanding of moulded details difficult. The teapots are all of plain creamware without any additional colouring.

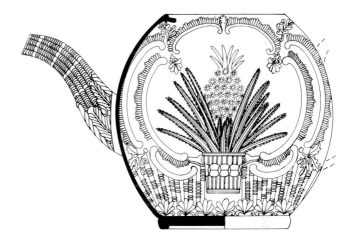

Fig. 39
Basket & pineapple teapot and cover. Phase II. (Scale 1:2)

Plates 170-171
Creamware teapot covers from moulded basket and pineapple ware. Phase II.

The Phase III basket and pineapple wares, by contrast, occur in a much wider range of forms, including large numbers of coffee cups, several large saucers with a diameter of about 20 cm, bowls and teapots. All of these forms have only been recovered as biscuit wares, which is most surprising; we have no idea of their intended finish. On the other hand, pieces of three or four smaller saucers were also found: these were glazed and were coloured under-glaze in brown, green and yellow metallic oxides (Plate 172).

Very few sherds of this type were found in Phase I, but amongst these were a single green-glazed body sherd and fragments of several sugar bowl covers coloured under-glaze in dark brown, yellow and green.

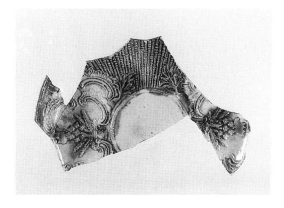

Plate 172
Creamware basket and pineapple moulded saucer, coloured under-glaze with metallic oxides. Phase III.

Barleycorn Moulded

Barleycorn moulded bodies were used by many local manufacturers and are well-known in salt-glazed stoneware, in tortoiseshell ware, in plain creamware, and in green-glazed creamware. Greatbatch used this moulding for plates and platters in each of these types, but beyond this it is conspicuous by its absence. The only vessels, apart from plates, which have barleycorn moulded bodies are a number of saucers from Phase II. Unfortunately, these saucers are all unglazed and consequently we have no idea of their intended finish.

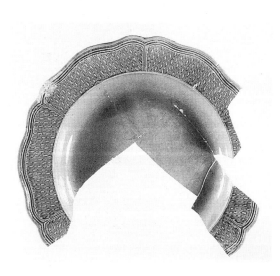

Plates 173-174
Creamware plates, green-glazed, with moulded barleycorn edge pattern. Phase II.

COLOURED GLAZED CREAMWARES

The introduction of coloured glazes has traditionally been attributed to Wedgwood. His Experiment book details his efforts towards producing a green glaze and a yellow glaze during the years 1759 and 1760 (above, page 20), but this alone does not prove that he was the first to introduce these. Indeed, it seems likely that a green glaze, based upon a lead glaze formula with a very small proportion of calcined copper added, was available to potters before Wedgwood's well-known experiment, and that Wedgwood was motivated by the need to improve upon this. Other evidence shows that within two years of Wedgwood's yellow glaze experiments of 1760, if not before, other potters including John Baddeley of Shelton, were making use of coloured glazes[60], as was Greatbatch himself shortly after commencing production in 1762. There was clearly no monopoly on the use of these glazes by any manufacturer.

Green-glazed Ware

It is difficult to define green-glazed ware as a particular type since the coloured wares are essentially simply creamwares which occur in a limited range of standard forms. Although few green-glazed pieces were recovered, they occur in each of the three phases with the greatest number in Phase II. The two circular barleycorn plates illustrated in Plates 173 and 174 are typical Phase II types, as is the canister illustrated in Plate 175 with its sprigged floral decoration. Besides sprigged decoration, a few sherds have been found with engine-turned wavy reed decoration. The most unusual Phase I piece is a fragmentary barber's bowl.

Plates 175
Creamware canister, green-glazed, with sprigged decoration. *c.* 1765-1770. (Private Collection. Photographer: Bob Munro)

Plate 176
Creamware saucer, glazed green and yellow. Phase II.

Plate 177
Fragment of green-glazed candlestick. Phase II.

Plate 178
Creamware candlestick sherds, biscuit and green-glazed, after a design by William Kent. Phases II-III.

We have seen that green-glazed examples of both shell ware (excavated) and fruit basket ware (extant) are known. Other pieces which combine both green and yellow glazes in the manner of melon ware, but without the rouletting, are also known (Plate 176) but these are rare. Much more significant amongst the green-glazed wares are the 'owl' candlesticks, of which several examples have been identified in collections (Plate XXII). These candlesticks are press-moulded, of an elongated baluster form, with a spreading foot moulded as overlapping acanthus leaves. Four owls' heads are located at the base of the stem and the nozzle is shaped as the head of a Corinthian column. The candlestick has been taken directly from English silver prototypes of the 1740s which were based upon a design by William Kent (1685 — 1748)[61]. Both biscuit and green-glazed sherds of this type have been recovered from the Greatbatch site from all three phases (Plates 177 and 178). The rich green colour of the glaze has seen these pieces traditionally attributed to Wedgwood.

A very interesting Phase I sherd is from a press-moulded tile with the well-known design of a heron fishing. This design is known in salt-glazed stoneware[62] and lead-glazed sherds have been excavated on the Whieldon site at Fenton Vivian. The discovery of a green-glazed fragment from the Greatbatch site suggests that production of these tiles was more widespread than has previously been assumed.

Plate 179
Creamware title fragment, green-glazed, of the heron fishing design. Phase I.

Yellow-glazed Ware

As with the green-glazed ware, yellow-glazed ware is not easily defined as a particular type. A few sherds have been found from each of the phases, with Phase II having a predominance of bowls with a yellow glaze on the outside only, and Phase III having sherds of a plate of Type 30 and the deep feather-edged plate or dish illustrated in Plate 180, both of which were yellow-glazed internally and externally. Also from Phase III is a base sherd from a large soup tureen with feather moulding. Other sherds of yellow-glazed ware are not diagnostic, but include fragments of teapot covers from Phase I.

Plate 180
Creamware plate with moulded feather edge, yellow-glazed. The eighth feathered barb creeps into the pattern of larger vessels such as this. Phase III.

Melon Ware

Melon wares are well-documented in invoices and other records of the 1760s as being amongst the products of many factories. They are characterised by green and yellow coloured glazes which are predominantly, but not always, used together, and also by rouletted decoration. They are well-known in collections and include the usual tea and coffee wares, together with tureens, plates, toys, and other small items.

Greatbatch's melon wares conform to the overall pattern and are quite varied in their colouring and decoration. They occur in large quantities in Phase II and in lesser quantities in Phases I and III. Saucers and teabowls are common amongst the Phase II finds as both standard size vessels and as toys; there are also small jugs which can only have been toys. Barrel-shaped jugs of various sizes are equally common, although it has proved difficult to reconstruct complete profiles. Small teapots have been partially reconstructed from Phase II, while Phase III has regular size teapots and their covers. Also common amongst the Phase III melon sherds are cylindrical mugs, jugs, sugar bowls and covers, saucers, teabowls, and coffee cups, some of which are decorated with sprigged or mould-applied reliefs, or with turned bands.

Despite the quantity of melon ware recovered, we can point to few features which would help to identify Greatbatch pieces in collections. None of the excavated sherds have been found with distinctive handles and the only spouts identified are of Type 4, occurring on Phase III teapots. At present, only the applied decorative reliefs used on a small number of sherds can be cited as possible guides to attribution; these are sprigged Types 14 and 15 on Phase II wares, and Types 20 and 21 on Phase III wares, and mould-applied Type 2, also on Phase III wares. The applied decoration of the Phase III melon wares appears to be restricted to use on coffee cups. It may be that typical Greatbatch handles and spouts will come to be recognised on extant vessels, but at present no surviving Greatbatch melon wares are known.

Plate 181
Creamware melon teabowl and saucers, glazed green and yellow. Phase II.

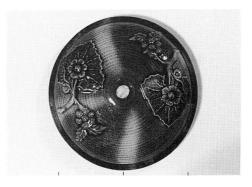

Plate 182
Creamware melon strainer, glazed green and
yellow. Phase II.

Plate 183
Creamware melon sugar bowl cover, glazed green and
yellow, with sprigged decoration. Phase II.

MOULDED CREAMWARES — COLOURED GLAZES

Cauliflower Ware

Throughout the whole period of his manufacture, Greatbatch produced very large
quantities of cauliflower ware. Greatbatch's written references to the production
of cauliflowers from at least as early as September, 1763, are supported by their
presence in Phase I of the Greatbatch site. By Phase II production was clearly
at its peak, a reflection of the wider popularity of cauliflower wares with the
consumer. After this, there is a definite decline in the numbers produced, although
not in the quality, but it appears that Greatbatch continued to make cauliflower
ware until shortly before his bankruptcy in 1782.

As with all the creamware types, Greatbatch's cauliflowers make use of the
handles and spouts which are favoured in the different phases and, equally, reflect
the change from a dark to a light creamware on their uncoloured interior surfaces.
Constant throughout, however, is the use of a range of block moulds which is
rarely added to. In short, both the modelling and the features of Greatbatch's
cauliflowers are distinctive.

Cauliflower wares generally occur primarily as tea and coffee wares. In this
Greatbatch's cauliflowers are no exception. The most common forms are teapots,
coffee pots, coffee cups, teabowls, saucers, jugs, bowls, sugar bowls, tea canisters
and plates. Much less common are cylindrical beakers, trays, cream boats, punch
pots and tureens. Teapots and coffee pots are the most distinctive of the forms,
having the greatest number of points of reference. In all three phases, the most
common spouts are those moulded as cauliflowers, Types 25 and 26, although
in Phase III just a few examples of standard creamware spouts have been
recognised on teapots. The handles for both tea and coffee pots are those which
are typical of the particular phase of production.

Plate 184
Creamware cauliflower teabowl, cup and saucer, glazed green and white. Phase II.

Plate 185
Creamware cauliflower slop bowl and sugar bowl, biscuit. Phase III.

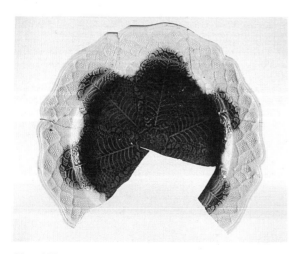

Plate 186
Creamware cauliflower plate, glazed green and white. Phase II.

Plate 187
Creamware cauliflower milk jug,
glazed green and white.
c. 1770-1782. (Leeds City Art
Gallery. Temple Newsam House)

Plate 188
Creamware cauliflower teapot,
glazed green and white. *c.*
1765-1770. (Delhom Col-
lection, The Mint Museum
of Art, Charlotte, North
Carolina. Photographer:
Bill J. Moretz)

Plate 189
Creamware cauliflower teapot,
glazed green and white. *c.*
1770-1782. (Courtesy of the
Trustees of the British
Museum)

Plate 190
Creamware cauliflower coffee pot, glazed and white. *c.* 1765-1770. (Delhom Collection, The Mint Museum of Art, Charlotte, North Carolina)

Pineapple Ware

Pineapple ware, coloured with green and yellow glazes, was again produced by Greatbatch over the whole of his twenty years as a manufacturer, although never, it appears, in the same quantities as cauliflower. The larger tureens and punch pots which were produced in cauliflower ware are not found in pineapple. The excavated sherds are all of tea and coffee wares with a marked preference shown throughout for a single style of moulding.

The taste for coloured and moulded wares during the 1760s sees pineapples produced in their greatest numbers in Phase II, with a marked decline in output by Phase III. Unfortunately, few complete vessel profiles have been reconstructed from the sherds and the very numerous, but fragmentary teapots are best recognised by the typical Greatbatch handle and spout forms which are always glazed green. As yet, no Greatbatch pineapple wares have been identified in collections.

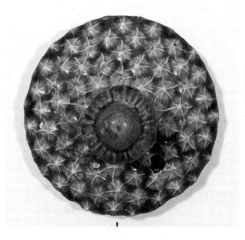

Plate 191
Creamware pineapple teapot cover, glazed green and yellow. Phase II.

Plate 192
Creamware pineapple saucers, glazed green and yellow. Phase II.

Plate 193
Creamware pineapple bowl, glazed green and yellow. Phase II.

Plate 194
Creamware pineapple coffee pot, glazed green and yellow. Phase II.

Hexagonal Chinese Moulded Ware

The traditional attribution of this type to Greatbatch has been discussed above (pages 93-94), an attribution which originally arose out of an over-enthusiastic reading of one of Greatbatch's invoices. This indicated that Greatbatch had supplied Wedgwood with a block mould for *1 Chinese Teapot* for which he received payment of 10/6d on 11th January, 1764[63]. Many wares of this period exist which could be described as 'Chinese' and the identification of this block mould with the well-known hexagonal teapots which have Oriental figure subjects in individual panels is open to some debate.

Excavation has shown, at least, that Greatbatch made hexagonal moulded teapots, but by no means all of them. Just as pieces of this type are well-known in collections, so too are they known from several excavations in North Staffordshire including the Greatbatch site, the Whieldon site at Fenton Vivian, and Town Road, Hanley. Hexagonal Chinese teapots may be found with a variety of handles and spouts and this fact alone suggests that several manufacturers were involved in their production. There are also tea canisters in this type, although only one of the sherds from the Greatbatch site is of a canister.

The hexagonal Chinese sherds are all from Phase II, save for the single canister sherd which is from Phase I, and are found in biscuit creamware, coloured glazed creamware and red stoneware. They are not numerous and no complete vessels have been reconstructed. The coloured glazes, green, yellow and brown, are applied in vertical bands which do not necessarily respect the individual panels or the subjects within them. The only complete handle which has been found associated with the hexagonal Chinese teapots is of Type 6 and is typical of Greatbatch's Phase II wares; only two related spouts have been found, but these were the only examples on the site of the otherwise common cabbage spout (Type 19) which was used by many factories at this time.

No extant examples of Greatbatch's hexagonal Chinese moulded teapots have been recognised, despite many pieces of this type surviving. All those studied so far have handles or spouts which make an attribution to Greatbatch unlikely.

Plate 195
Sherds of hexagonal teapots with moulded Oriental figure subjects in creamware and red stoneware. Phase II.

'Serpent' Moulded Ware

An unusual moulded type, yet one for which a good number of sherds have been found, is that referred to here as 'serpent' because of the sea monster head and tail which occur as teapot spouts and handles. In fact, only teapots have been found in this type, their round bodies moulded in a series of connected circular bosses, possibly intended to suggest the scaly body of a sea monster. The flat covers are moulded in the same manner. The glaze consists of vertical bands of colour, of greens, light and dark, and yellows, against a cream ground which has been further embellished by patches of under-glaze brown oxide colour. Handles and spouts are green-glazed. There are also a few sherds which are totally covered outside by a dark green glaze, although these are the exception. The handle and spout types are also found in red stoneware, but there are no body sherds to suggest the existence of red stoneware serpent teapots. The sherds of 'serpent' ware are confined almost entirely to Phase II of the site, with just a few sherds in each of Phases I and III.

Plate 196
Creamware 'serpent' moulded cover, coloured under-glaze and with coloured glazes. Phase II

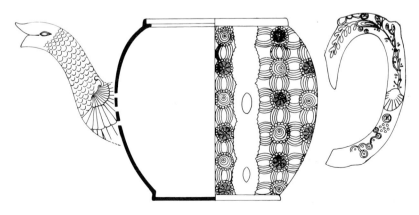

Fig. 40
'Serpent' teapot. Phase II. (Scale 1:2)

DRY-BODIED WARES

Buff Stoneware

Not a common type of pottery generally in the 18th century, buff-bodied stoneware is only a minor type on the Greatbatch site. Not to be confused with caneware, it is used only for teapots and is almost completely restricted to Phase II, with just one sherd from each of Phases I and III. Although no extant pieces are known, the type is of interest because of its consistent use of distinctive pseudo-Chinese seal marks which might, at some future time, enable us to identify examples in collections. The seal marks are illustrated in Fig. 42; No. 1 has only been found on the insides of covers and has no known parallels elsewhere, while No. 2 is used on the undersides of teapots and is very much in the style of contemporary seal marks used by other manufacturers[64], although with its own distinctive details.

The buff stoneware teapots occur in a variety of finishes. The shades of the buff bodies of the teapots vary, and some have been given a white slip coat on both internal and external surfaces. Spouts, handles and knops are often in a red stoneware body, which can provide a striking contrast of colour; sometimes, though, these too are covered by a white slip coat, thereby disguising any difference in colour. The handles and spouts are simple in form, a plain straight spout and a simple, loop handle of circular section being used on all the vessels. There is no additional decoration and, with the exception of the seal marks, Greatbatch's buff stonewares are little different to those of his contemporaries.

Fig. 41
Buff stoneware teapots and covers. Phase II. (Scale 1:2)

1   2

Fig. 42
Impressed seal marks used by Greatbatch on buff stoneware covers (1), and on buff stoneware and red stoneware teapots (2). Phase II. (Scale 2:1)

Red Stoneware

Red stonewares are a distinctive type produced by many, if not most, of the pottery manufacturers during the middle and later years of the 18th century. They are, however, generally restricted to tea and coffee wares, with only a few other forms known. Many of the pieces in collections today are quite distinctive, characterised sometimes by elaborate handles and spouts, by mould-applied or sprigged decorative reliefs, or by a wide variety of pseudo-Chinese seal marks which have been identified on a fair proportion of these wares. On the basis of these features it has been possible to group related pieces[65], but further evidence is needed before they can be positively linked to manufacturers. No positive attributions of red stonewares had been possible until pieces came to be recovered from excavations of known factory sites. The situation today is very different, with red stonewares being attributed to Thomas Whieldon, Humphrey Palmer and Thomas Barker; in this context, the red stonewares from the Greatbatch site are of great importance. Not only can they be attributed to a known manufacturer, but the nature of the site enables their stylistic development and their popularity within the wider market to be charted.

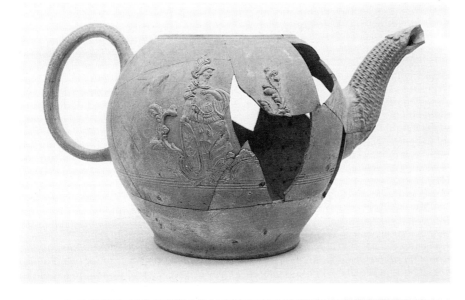

Plate 197
Red stoneware teapot with sprigged decoration. Phase II.

Plate 198
Red stoneware teapot with sprigged decoration. Phase II.

Plate 199
Red stoneware jug and bowl with sprigged decoration. *c.* 1765-1770. (Zähringer Museum, Neues Schloss, Baden-Baden, Germany)

Plate 200
Red stoneware coffee pot with sprigged decoration. *c.* 1765-1770. (Zähringer Museum, Neues Schloss, Baden-Baden, Germany)

We have already referred to the documentary evidence for Greatbatch's red stonewares, namely his *China* teapots and saffron pots which were supplied to Wedgwood in 1764 and 1765 (above, pages 92-93). The excavated evidence points to red stoneware's period of greatest popularity as being Phase II, *c.* 1765 — 1770, and to a much lesser extent Phase I. The wares of this period are well-made and quite distinctive on account of their handles and spouts, and, more particularly, the sprigged decoration which is used on about half of the vessels recovered from the site.

Plate 201
Red stoneware sugar bowl and cover with sprigged decoration. *c.* 1765-1770. (Zähringer Museum, Neues Schloss, Baden-Baden, Germany)

Plate 202
Red stoneware teapot with sprigged decoration. *c.* 1765-1770. (Plymouth City Museum & Art Gallery)

Plate 203
Red stoneware teapot with sprigged decoration. *c.* 1765-1770. (Olive Talbot Collection)

The teapots from Phases I and II use a range of spouts, with a predominance of basketwork (Types 11 — 13) and plain straight types (Type 18); Type 7 also occurs to a lesser extent, particularly on the larger teapots. Handles are generally basketwork Types 7 and 8, the former being found on coffee pots; the coffee pot spout is Type 4a.

The sprigged reliefs used are few in number, comprising Types 29 — 40 illustrated in Fig. 37. The most common reliefs amongst the excavated pieces are the sprigged figure of Minerva (Type 35) and the pair of Oriental ladies (Type 38), already referred to. These occur on teapots, coffee pots, milk jugs, bowls and sugar bowls, while other individual reliefs are used to form framing cartouches or isolated designs of covers. Examples of both figure reliefs are known on extant pieces, while the third sprigged figure used by Greatbatch is not. This is the seated Chinese man (Type 39), of whom very few pieces have been found; the complete pattern to which the figure belongs cannot be reconstructed. No mould-applied reliefs have been found on Greatbatch's red stonewares.

None of the excavated vessels from Phases I and II which have been reconstructed are marked in any way. There are, however, two isolated base sherds from Phase II which bear the impressed pseudo-Chinese seal mark (Fig. 42, No. 2) which is found on the buff stoneware teapots. They do at least indicate that some of Greatbatch's red stonewares were marked and that perhaps they will, in due course, be identified in collections. This is in marked contrast to the Phase III red stonewares which all appear to be marked. The Phase III wares use an impressed seal mark which has clearly been based upon that used on the Phase II buff stonewares and the two sherds of red stoneware, except that the bottom right-hand corner of the mark has been modifed to incorporate Greatbatch's initials *WG* in the same style as the monogram backstamp used on his flatwares at this date (Fig. 43).

This is not the only difference between the red stonewares of Phases II and III. Firstly, use of sprigged decoration seems virtually to disappear, to be replaced by engine-turned decoration; secondly, the range of vessel forms seems to contract dramatically, with teapots dominating; thirdly, the proportion of red stoneware produced during Phase III decreases almost to insignificance; and finally, there is a marked decline in the quality of the Phase III wares. Significantly, no extant wares of Phase III type have been identified.

Engine-turned decoration is found on a fair number of sherds from Phases I and II and is mainly of the wavy reed variety. The quality of these early engine-turned pieces is very good, comparable to that of the sprigged wares, but no complete pieces have been reconstructed. Given the number of sprigged red stonewares from Greatbatch's factory which have been recognised in collections, it is rather surprising that no engine-turned vessels have been identified. This may simply be due to the absence of distinguishing characteristics on these wares; an engine-turned teapot, without a seal mark at this stage, with a straight, engine-turned spout, and with a undiagnostic handle, leaves little by which the piece may be recognised.

Fig. 43
Impressed seal mark used by Greatbatch on red stoneware, black basalt, caneware and glazed redware. Phase III. (Scale 2:1)

The Phase III engine-turned wares would be easily recognised, if any survive, by their seal mark. Apart from this, however, they bear a strong resemblance to the majority of contemporary products. The wares themselves comprise almost entirely cylindrical teapots in several sizes, using straight engine-turned spouts and distinctive reeded handles. The decoration is different to that of the Phase I and II red stonewares, being primarily of the diagonal reeded type and, to a much lesser extent, of the curved reed type.

The recovery from Phase II of the excavation of the serpent handle, Type 20, and spout, Type 24, and of a bamboo handle and spout, all in red stoneware, suggest the production of distinctive types which have yet to be recognised in collections.

Several sherds were recovered from Phase II of a single press-moulded type, the well-known hexagonal teapots moulded with Oriental figures which have been described above (pages 93-94). These have generally been attributed to Greatbatch on the flimsy evidence of a reference to a block mould for a Chinese teapot in Greatbatch's correspondence with Wedgwood[66]. Sherds of this type have also been found in creamware from Phase II but, as has already been stated, it is clear that Greatbatch was but one of several local potters producing these hexagonal teapots.

Plate 204
Red stoneware cover, engine-turned. Phase II.

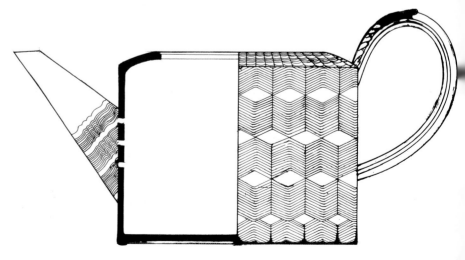

Fig. 44
Red stoneware teapot, engine-turned. Phase III. (Scale 1:2)

Caneware

Greatbatch's canewares are unique. Nothing quite like them has been encountered before and no extant examples have been identifed. Thirteen vessels have been reconstructed from Phase III sherds, and several more are represented by the loose sherds. They are unlike anything else produced by Greatbatch and are of a very high quality.

The introduction of caneware is generally credited to Wedgwood. His correspondence shows quite clearly that he was experimenting with caneware, or *Fawn colour*, from 1771 but he seems to have had little success[67]. Even as late as 1779 he was having major problems with his *cane-colour* which, he states, was porous and apt to stain[68]. It appears that Wedgwood had not perfected his caneware until the mid-1780s[69], and yet here we see Greatbatch with an extremely fine product which, we must assume, was marketed. There is no reason to suspect otherwise, since the majority of the caneware wasters which have been recovered were not discarded until after the decorating stage.

Greatbatch's canewares are extremely fine pieces, but this is not say that he too did not experience problems in their manufacture. The interior of every piece found has been given a lead glaze, suggesting that Greatbatch's wares were porous in the same way as Wedgwood's, the body not having vitrified sufficiently to produce the impervious stoneware which would have allowed him to dispense with an internal glaze.

All the vessels recovered were teapots, in a variety of forms (Fig. 45), but with an emphasis upon the 'boat' shape which is otherwise found only in black basalt and in one or two fragmentary creamwares. The majority of the teapots are engine-turned with concave vertical fluting and a variety of horizontal reeds in relief. Handles, spouts, and the fluted covers are unique to the canewares. All of the teapots are decorated in enamel colours — dark red, mauve, and white with a blue tint — either to define details of the body, or to provide additional designs which are apparently trophies. The decorated canewares have clearly experienced problems during the enamel firing, the mauve and white colours having blistered, sometimes quite badly. The initialled seal mark (Fig. 43) is impressed into the underside of every one of these teapots, providing the means to distinguish these splendid vessels, should any survive today.

Plate 205
Caneware teapots with engine-turned and enamel painted decoration. Phase III.

270

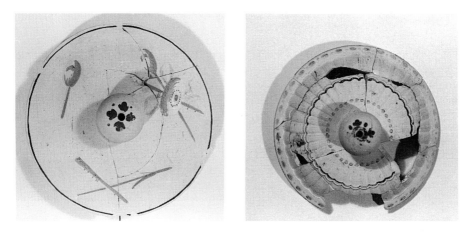

Plates 206-207
Caneware teapot covers with enamel painted decoration. Phase III

Fig. 45
Caneware teapots and covers. Phase III. (Scale 1:3)

Black Basalt

The origins of black basalt are still open to debate, but it is clear that Wedgwood had been involved in its production prior to his move to Etruria in 1769. He was certainly not alone in this, and many of his contemporaries were manufacturing similar black bodied stonewares under the more common name of *Egyptian Black*. Wedgwood's improvements of the body enabled him to develop his reproductions of antique vases and he gave to this improved ware the name *Black Basaltes*.

The basalt sherds from the Greatbatch site suggest that this was never an important line for him, and that he steered clear of vases and other ornamental wares. Tea, and perhaps coffee wares are all that are represented, and these in very small numbers. Greatbatch's basalt is largely a Phase III type, with just five sherds from Phase II, one of which is an engine-turned sherd with wavy reed decoration. None of the other sherds from either phase is decorated in any way. The recognisable forms are cylindrical and round-bodied teapots of the boat shape, some of which have an internal glaze. Incomplete fragments of widow finials have been identified on covers, but the only clearly diagnostic feature of Greatbatch's basalts is the initialled seal mark which is found on those pieces from Phase III (Fig. 43). No extant pieces have yet been recognised.

WHITE SALT-GLAZED STONEWARE

In common with most of his contemporaries, Greatbatch produced white salt-glazed stoneware in the traditional styles. Despite very large quantities recovered from Phase I, and smaller quantities from Phase II, there is nothing to distinguish Greatbatch's wares from those of other manufacturers. We find the same range of plate edges — barleycorn, basketwork, star/dot and diaper, gadrooned and feather patterns — the same range of vessel forms, and the same styles of scratch blue decoration. It is important to note, however, that smaller quantities of white-dipped salt-glazed stoneware were found alongside the finer white-bodied ware, particularly as mugs, jugs and porringers. Handles are traditional reeded loops with pinched terminals and spouts are plain. Greatbatch's salt-glazed stoneware is significant only for the marked decline in the quantity recovered from Phase II, and for its virtual disappearance by Phase III.

EARTHENWARES — COLOURED BODIES

Glazed Redware

Glazed red earthenware, also commonly known simply as redware, had a very long life in the repertoires of many North Staffordshire manufacturers. Introduced during the 1720s, it was probably the first of the locally-produced wares to have both biscuit and glost firings. The range of types associated with Samuel Bell of Newcastle-under-Lyme in the period 1724 — 1744, and subsequently identified by excavation on his factory site[70], changed little until the 1760s. The round-bodied teapots decorated with bands of white slip and mould-applied reliefs in white firing clay continued in production until this late date, along with a limited range of tea and coffee wares decorated in the same manner. The factory waste tip excavated in Town Road, Hanley, and dated to the years 1755 — 1760[71], illustrated the very great popularity of red earthenwares at this time and produced examples of all the common vessel forms.

The evidence from the Greatbatch site suggests that by the early 1760s a major manufacturer could effectively dispense with glazed red earthenware in order to concentrate on other types. The sherds of red earthenware constitute a minute proportion of the total recovered, which seems to show that the type was not long in production, or that the quantities produced were very small. There is nothing distinctive about the few vessels identified amongst the sherds from Phases I and II: they are common forms, such as round-bodied teapots, bowls with white slip decoration, but neither having the mould-applied relief decoration which had been ubiquitous during the 1750s.

The evidence from Phase III of the site points to something of a minor revival of popularity for glazed redwares, although in a completely different style. These later redwares are not only in the style of contemporary red stonewares — they are engine-turned, use the same handles and spouts as the red stonewares and, significantly, the same impressed seal mark (Fig. 43) — but they themselves appear to have a stoneware body. This is surprising since the biscuit sherds recovered are in an earthenware body, suggesting that the vitrification took place during the glost firing. The production of engine-turned redwares during the 1770s is well-known. Many extant examples from different factories are of a quality which suggests that they were not aimed at the top end of the market; Greatbatch's glazed redwares do, at least, display a certain quality and are finely thrown and decorated. The forms include cylindrical and globular teapots, and coffee pots, but although a renewed popularity for these wares is implied, the quantity of pieces from the Greatbatch site is not great; by this time Greatbatch was almost wholly preoccupied with the production of creamwares and pearlwares.

Blackware

Blackwares formed a significant proportion of the ceramics recovered from Phase I of the Greatbatch site, second in quantity only to creamware. This is as one might expect in the early 1760s, for it is clear that the popularity of blackware extended throughout most of the decade. The largest of the excavated sites in North Staffordshire which are almost contemporary with Greatbatch have illustrated the importance of blackware to the potter's production: on both the Whieldon site at Fenton Vivian and the Town Road site, Hanley — the former effectively unstratified, the latter dating to 1755-1760 — blackwares were, along with white salt-glazed stoneware, the most numerous of the pottery types found. Other, much smaller groups of pottery dating to the 1760s, also include significant quantities of the type alongside various creamwares[72].

The Greatbatch site is important for the dramatic decline in production of blackware which has occurred by Phase II. The blackware forms found on the Greatbatch site are wholly typical of those recognised on other sites and those which survive in collections, and are essentially tea and coffee wares. Teapots, coffee pots, bowls, sugar bowls, teabowls and saucers, cups, salts and milk jugs make up almost the entire range of vessels. The majority of Greatbatch's blackwares are undecorated, a situation similar to that identified in other excavated groups. The use of sprigged relief decoration is very much in the style of contemporary wares from other manufacturers, but is used sparingly. Flowers, leaves, berries and trailing vine stems are the motifs used, but the details are so hidden by the thick glaze that it has been impossible to reproduce them. Consequently we cannot determine which few reliefs were used by Greatbatch. The handles and spouts are often crabstock types whose exact details are also hidden by the thick glaze, although the Type 13 basketwork spout can be recognised on several pieces.

Plate 208
Blackware milk jug with sprigged decoration. Phase I.

Agate Ware

It is difficult to determine whether or not Greatbatch actually made agate ware. Just two sherds from vessels were recovered from the site — a knife handle fragment from Phase I and a bowl fragment from Phase II. A number of unglazed agate marbles were found in all three phases, but can represent little more than playthings made by workers at the factory.

1. Miller 1987.
2. Optical microscope examination of the body and X-ray fluorescence analysis of the glaze, undertaken in 1986.
3. Lockett 1986a; Barker & Halfpenny 1990, 7 — 11.
4. Barker & Halfpenny 1990, 7 — 9; Barker 1990.
5. Lockett 1986a, 56.
6. Towner 1957, 68.
7. *ibid.*, 66.
8. I would like to acknowledge the help of Ken Wild in enabling me to study the material from this wreck, which is held by the Florida State Parks Service, Tallahassee, Florida.
9. Results of X-ray fluorescence semi-quantitive comparative analyis of the glaze of creamware and pearlware sherds:

	CREAMWARE Phase I	CREAMWARE Phase II	CREAMWARE Phase III	PEARLWARE Phase III
SILICA (SiO_2)	39	36	40	38
TITANIA (TiO_2)	0.2	0.2	0.15	0.15
ALUMINA (Al_2O_3)	6	5.5	5.7	3.4
FERRIC OXIDE (Fe_2O_3)	0.3	0.3	0.2	0.2
LIME (CaO)	0.15	0.2	0.4	0.5
MAGNESIA (MgO)	0.3	0.3	0.3	0.2
POTASH (K_2)	0.4	0.3	0.3	0.8
SODA (Na_2O)	0.3	0.3	0.2	0.3
LEAD MONOXIDE (PbO)	40	43	40	39
PHOSPHORUS PENTOXIDE (P_2O_5)	TRACE	TRACE	TRACE	TRACE

10. Cox 1983, plate 129d, where it is referred to as *fleur de lys*.
11. See footnote 8.
12. On oval flatwares, it was necessary to form the footring around a mould or template which was of the size and shape of the vessel's underside.
13. Barker & Halfpenny 1990, 17 — 18.
14. Barker 1989, 38 — 39.
15. Lockett & Halfpenny 1982, 103 no. 195, plate 175.
16. British Museum, Cat. No.: G27.
17. For example, Reilly 1989 I, 173 plate 145.
18. Wedgwood MSS: 22341-30.
19. Stoke upon Trent Parish Register IV.
20. *ibid.*
21. Wedgwood MSS: 30136-30.
22. A serious challenge to Royal authority was made by Opposition Members of Parliament in April 1780. This was almost successful.
23. Ray 1973, plate 57, F1-4.
24. Cat. No.: 10.7/38. See Walton 1976, 199 no. 807.
25. Horne 1990, no. 280.
26. Bidgood & Walton 1990, 4.
27. For Daniel Potter see Bidgood 1985; for John Avey see Bidgood & Walton 1990, 4 no. 39.
28. Reilly 1989 I, 211.
29. Comments on the quality of the printing have been made to me by Paul Holdway, an engraver at the Spode factory trained in the traditional way.
30. Towner 1978, 63 plate 22B.
31. Buten 1980, 28 plate 11.
32. Page 25.
33. Bickham 1743, 201.
34. Adams 1986, 94 no. 1, and 96 no. 8.
35. Screiber Collection, No. 455.
36. Above, page 100; Towner 1957, 32.
37. Cat. No.: M168'51.
38. D'Oench 1990, 320 — 321.
39. *ibid.*, 323.
40. Towner 1957, 32, and plate 67B.
41. Delhom Collection, Cat. No.: 65.48.DC.EPy.S590.
42. Ray 1973, plate 31e.
43. *ibid.*, 41.
44. For example, Towner 1957, plate 82B.
45. Liverpool Museum, Cat. No.: M2308.
46. Greenwald 1979.
47. Wedgwood MSS: E.18878-26 and E.18880-26.
48. Buten 1980, 28 plate 10.
49. For example, Towner 1978, 153 plate 80B.
50. Lockett & Halfpenny 1986, 84 no. 102; Williams-Wood 1981, 187, plate 114.
51. Reilly 1989 I, 237, plate 265.
52. I am grateful to Tom Walford for this information.
53. Hampson 1986, 33.
54. A pearlware teapot with an apparently identical print of *Juno* to that used by Greatbatch is illustrated in Seligmann 1975, 87; the manufacturer is not known.
55. Wedgwood MSS: 30137-30.
56. See Reilly 1989 I, 167 plate 134.
57. Barker 1989.
58. Sayer 1762.
59. Barker 1989.
60. A reference to pineapple ware in 1762. See Mallet 1967, 211.
61. Kaellgren 1986.
62. An example survives in the Victoria & Albert Museum.
63. Wedgwood MSS: 22359-30.
64. Price 1962, plate 150 nos. IIi, IVi and IVii.
65. Price 1959; Price 1962.
66. Wedgwood MSS: 22359-30.
67. Leith Hill Place Collection; see Farrar II 1903, 42.
68. Wedgwood MSS: E.26-18923.
69. Reilly 1989 I, 498.
70. Bemrose 1975.
71. Barker & Halfpenny 1990, 17.
72. For example, Keelings Road, Northwood, and Union Street, Hanley, both dating to *c.* 1765 — 1770, and both as yet unpublished. City Museum & Art Gallery, Stoke-on-Trent.

CHAPTER 7

CONCLUSION

This work has been able to describe only a proportion of the wares which may now be positively attributed to William Greatbatch. The sheer volume of excavated material makes a detailed treatment of all the types impossible, but the evidence derived from this material and its wider implications have been examined in depth.

The excavation of the Greatbatch site has brought William Greatbatch to the forefront of ceramic history today. Here is a potter whose family background is a mystery and who has been known to us only through his connections with Josiah Wedgwood. It is now clear, however, that Greatbatch has been vastly under-rated and that his importance in the 18th century North Staffordshire pottery industry has been largely ignored. This is hardly surprising when we consider the limitations of contemporary documentary evidence for Greatbatch's manufacturing career, both in its quantity and in its historical value. The most significant of the surviving documents span little more than two years, and leave eighteen years of his career a blank.

Greatbatch's correspondence with Wedgwood shows something of the nature of his early production, but this is no basis for an understanding of his production beyond these years. Only with the excavation of Greatbatch's factory waste tip have we had the opportunity to reach firm conclusions about this one factory's output over a period of twenty years, from its beginning until its eventual closure. Contemporary documents have their place in any ceramic research, but for detailed information about the pottery itself the evidence of such archaeological work is essential. With the site and extant pottery, we now have extremely detailed evidence for the changing nature and scale of production, and for technical and stylistic developments in a single factory at a time when the local pottery industry was undergoing a considerable transformation.

The place of Wedgwood in this transformation has been discussed at length and cannot be overlooked. He is all the more important in the present study as a yardstick against which to measure Greatbatch's own achievements. His immediate business dealings with Greatbatch are of interest, for in Greatbatch we have one of the many local manufacturers who were supplying Wedgwood with wares which he himself then sold on. The scale of this in-trading between manufacturers is rarely emphasised, but was a significant factor in local pottery production. Indeed, the business between Wedgwood and Greatbatch has been shown to be a two-way process, of the sort which was absolutely typical of the industry and which is adequately documented.

It is important, however, to take note of the high regard in which Greatbatch was held by Wedgwood. Greatbatch's employment at Etruria in the years following his bankruptcy was no act of charity on Wedgwood's part. He saw in Greatbatch a man of great ability upon whom he could depend, and the terms of his employment are such that he cannot be seen as a warehouseman, as has often been stated, but was clearly at Etruria in a capacity of some considerable importance. There is a strong possibility that Greatbatch was at Etruria as Wedgwood's general manager, a position which became vacant after the termination of the partnership between Josiah and Thomas Wedgwood in 1788. There is no record of any talented practical potter who might have succeeded Thomas Wedgwood as general manager of the Etruria works, with the exception of Greatbatch. He was well-known to Josiah, highly esteemed by him, and had a proven record of managing a successful manufacturing business over a period of twenty years.

Upon what, then, can Wedgwood's opinion of Greatbatch have been founded? The documentary sources give us little clue, but the pottery produced by Greatbatch, and identified through the excavation, tells of a manufacturer who reached, and maintained a high standard of production. It is impossible to know to what extent Greatbatch was an innovator, although we can see him responding to all new ceramic developments within a very short time of their introduction. Greatbatch's correspondence, and the high quality of his pottery point to a potter who clearly merited Shaw's praise for being a *general workman of first rate abilities*.

The Greatbatch site has provided us with a complete cross-section of the wares of a known 18th century pottery factory. The quantity of wasters recovered from a factory which was in production for twenty years could have been anticipated, but the range of pottery types found was a complete surprise. The documentary evidence hints at Greatbatch's varied output early in his career, but the excavation has shown that he was a manufacturer of considerable versatility. Greatbatch produced all those types which were current in North Staffordshire, with the exception of soft-paste porcelain, but it seems that he was not alone in doing so. Documentary sources attest to a degree of flexibility and versatility of the parts of many potters of the period, and recent archaeological excavations in North Staffordshire have emphasised this fact. The idea of manufacturers specialising in a limited range of wares appears to have little support from the available evidence. Greatbatch and his contemporaries clearly attempted to cater for every corner of the market, winning customers wherever possible. In a fiercely competitive industry, potters could not afford to be unnecessarily selective in what they produced.

The ways in which Greatbatch responded to the wider market are admirably demonstrated by the wares recovered. The chronological framework for the excavated wares enables us to see how the fortunes of the different types vary, a reflection of consumer demand. We see, for example, the early popularity of white salt-glazed stoneware and blackware falling off rapidly by about 1770. The enormous quantities of cauliflowers, pineapples and fruit basket wares produced during the 1760s represent the peak of popularity for elaborately moulded and brightly coloured wares in the rococo style. During the next decade, these give way to more simple, thrown creamwares which depend upon surface decoration. Over-glaze painted and printed decoration were widespread on Greatbatch's creamwares in the decade before his bankruptcy, while under-glaze blue painted decoration belongs exclusively to this period. As types of ware peaked and declined in popularity, so others were introduced. The 1770s saw Greatbatch producing the new pearlwares and canewares, the former reflecting the continuing fondness for things Oriental, while the latter is a marked departure towards the Neo-Classical taste. The chronological evidence for Greatbatch's wares allows us to place stylistic and technical innovations in a closely dated manufacturing context, an important aspect of this work which has implications for our understanding of all other pottery producers of the period.

Just how far we can use the evidence from a single production site to generalise about ceramic developments further afield is open to debate. Certainly no two factories can have been identical, either in the range of wares produced or in the techniques used. The industry has always been characterised by an idiosyncratic approach to production by individual manufacturers, and at the same time by constant cross-fertilisation of ideas. Greatbatch, too, would have influenced, and been influenced by his fellows, and elements of any one factory may be paralleled elsewhere. The evidence from the Greatbatch site is unique in its scale and in its variety, and it holds a potential for a much greater understanding of pottery manufacture in the 18th century. The importance of the evidence will increase as there come to be further points of comparison and contrast with other, similar groups of material. Only then, can we know exactly how typical or atypical was Greatbatch's production.

As a result of the excavation, we are now well-placed to identify Greatbatch's wares in collections and to assign accurate date ranges to them. Such identifications are based not only upon the discovery of marked wares, but upon a comparison of the details of vessels with the great body of excavated material. Moulded bodies, handles, terminals, spouts, knops and applied decoration may all be used together with a degree of confidence to support an attribution to Greatbatch. Evidence of this type is available for no other North Staffordshire manufacturer of the period: even Wedgwood's useful wares are less than perfectly understood, particularly during his earlier years of business.

The documentary evidence, such as it is, has traditionally been much used as a basis for attributing wares to Greatbatch. This volume has stressed repeatedly the dangers inherent in such an approach to the study of ceramics, and it is worth reiterating, at this point, that many of the past attributions to Greatbatch, made on the strength of the documentary evidence alone, are open to serious criticism. A situation of considerable confusion existed until recently, in which conflicting pieces of 'evidence', appearing irreconcilable, were distorted to fit the accepted 'facts'. This has happened to such an extent that the true nature of Greatbatch's production was quite unrecognisable. The absence of any link between the wares traditionally attributed to Greatbatch and the pottery excavated from his waste tip, has highlighted the shortcomings of superficial and subjective ceramic research.

Much as it has created a great deal of excitement about the wares of a single manufacturer, the Greatbatch excavation has had two other very important results. Firstly, it has brought ceramic research down to earth a little and has seen the beginning of a process of re-assessment — of the state of ceramic history, of the commonly held beliefs about manufacturers and their wares, and of what, ultimately, we can hope to learn from our source material. Something of the romance of looking at pottery may have been lost and the imaginations of over-enthusiastic individuals will have less scope to run wild, but this is no bad thing. Objectivity in any research is important, and a proper use of the available evidence is essential if ceramic history is to be taken seriously by a wider public. Secondly, it has redirected attention back to North Staffordshire potters other than Wedgwood, after several decades of obsession with the Yorkshire creamware potteries. It is ironic that many of Greatbatch's most characteristic wares have for many years been hailed as 'typical' of the Leeds Pottery, and that Greatbatch's involvement in their manufacture could only be seen in a Leeds context, so that some writers would have him working at Leeds, or else importing Leeds wares to Lower Lane for decoration. Not only are these hypotheses nonsense, and have been proven so, but, more importantly, they are quite simply not founded upon a single shred of evidence. This confusion is a situation from which ceramic history must be rescued.

We return to Greatbatch who, we can claim, is now better known to us in his own right through his pottery than through any association with Wedgwood. We have shown that Greatbatch was an extremely versatile and talented potter and that his wares were of a quality comparable with that of most of his contemporaries. He is far from deserving the historical oblivion into which he had sunk and is at last able to get the recognition from collectors, scholars and ceramic enthusiasts which he had from his fellow potters. In many ways, however, this volume could have been about any one of Greatbatch's contemporaries who have become removed from the attention of the ceramic world simply because they neither marked their wares nor corresponded with Wedgwood. The works of these potters survive in museum and private collections, with no name now attached to them, and yet a single workman's trench in any one of the Six Potteries Towns could alter this situation dramatically. A chance discovery of factory wasters, or a carefully planned archaeological excavation undertaken at some future date, will eventually open yet another chapter in the story of North Staffordshire's industrial development.

Exterior of a Pottery.

FINIS.

BIBLIOGRAPHY

Adams, Elizabeth 1977	James Tidmarsh of Cobridge: Discovering the History of an Unknown Potter. *Northern Ceramic Society Journal* 2 (1975-6), 31 — 37.
Adams, Elizabeth 1986	Chelsea Fire and Aer. *Ceramics* 4, 94 — 97.
Adeney, John 1989	Incised and Impressed Decoration on Wedgwood. *Thirty-Fourth Annual Wedgwood International Seminar*, 103 — 124.
Aikin, J. 1795	*A Description of the Country from Twenty to Forty Miles Round Manchester.*
Allbut & Sons, J. 1802	*The Staffordshire Pottery Directory,* including *A Map of the Staffordshire Potteries 1802.*
Bailey 1781	*Bailey's Northern Directory.*
Barker, David 1984	18th and 19th Century Ceramics excavated at the Foley Pottery, Fenton, Stoke-on-Trent. *Staffordshire Archaeological Studies* 1, 63 — 86.
Barker, David 1988	William Greatbatch — New Light on 18th Century Ceramics. *Thirty-Third Annual Wedgwood International Seminar,* 11 — 19.
Barker, David 1989	A Potter's Amusement. *Ars Ceramica* 6, 35 — 40.
Barker, David forthcoming	A Group of Staffordshire Red Stonewares of the 18th Century. *English Ceramic Circle Transactions.*
Barker, David & Halfpenny Pat 1990	*Unearthing Staffordshire — Towards a New Understanding of Eighteenth Century Ceramics.* International Ceramics Fair and Seminar Exhibition Catalogue. City Museum & Art Gallery, Stoke-on-Trent.
Bemrose, Paul 1973	The Pomona Potworks, Newcastle, Staffs. Part I. Soft-paste: Its Production at Lower Street 1744 — 54. *English Ceramic Circle Transactions* 9 (pt. 1), 1 — 11.
Bemrose, Paul 1975	The Pomona Potworks, Newcastle, Staffs. Part II. Samuel Bell, his Red Earthenware Production 1724 — 1744. *English Ceramic Circle Transactions* 9 (pt. 3), 292 — 303.
Bickham, George 1743	*The Universal Penman.* (Facsimile edition by Dover Publications Inc. 1951)
Bidgood, Sheila 1985	The Universally Respected Mr. Potter. *Leeds Art Calendar* 96, 16 — 20.

Bidgood, Sheila & Walton, Peter 1990 — *Pots about People. Named & Dated Creamware & Pearlware 1760 — 1820.* Exhibition Catalogue, The Bar Convent Museum, York.

Blakey, Harold 1981 — Further extracts from the Sun Fire Insurance Policies. Guildhall MS 11.936. *The Northern Ceramic Society Newsletter* 42, 13 — 29.

Blakey, Harold 1990 — Some Staffordshire Potters in London. *The Northern Ceramic Society Newsletter* 79, 22 — 24.

Brears, Peter 1971 — *The English Country Pottery: its History and Techniques.* David & Charles.

Buten, David 1980 — *18th-Century Wedgwood. A Guide for Collectors & Connoisseurs.* Methuen.

Celoria, Francis 1976a — Techniques of Pottery-Making at Newcastle-upon-Tyne in 1765. *Science and Archaeology* 18, 20 — 24.

Celoria, Francis 1976b — Techniques of White Salt-Glaze Stoneware Manufacture in North Staffordshire Around 1765. *Science and Archaeology* 18, 25 — 28.

Chester & Mort 1796 — *The Staffordshire Pottery Directory.*

Copeland, Robert 1980 — *Spode's Willow Pattern & other designs after the Chinese.* Studio Vista.

Cox, Alwyn 1983 — Recent Excavations at the Swinton Pottery: White Salt-Glazed Stoneware and Creamware Pre 1785. *English Ceramic Circle Transactions* 11 (pt. 3), 232 — 255.

D'Oench, Ellen G. 1990 — Prodigal Sons and Fair Penitents: Transformations in Eighteenth-Century Popular Prints. *Art History* 13 (No. 3), 318 — 343.

Dossie, R. 1764 — *The Handmaid to the Arts.*

Dow, George Francis (ed.) 1927 — *The Arts and Crafts in New England 1704 — 1775.*

Elliott, G.W.E. 1981 — *Ceramic Manufacture in North Staffordshire, 1600 — 1760: A Study of Internal Developments and External Influences.* Unpublished M.A. Thesis (University of Keele).

Farrar, Katherine E. 1906 — *Letters of Josiah Wedgwood.* 3 Vols.

Faulkner, Frank 1912 — *The Wood Family of Burslem.* Chapman & Hall.

Greenwald, Vicki 1979 — Researching the Decoration on a Greatbatch Teapot: The Value of Research. *The American Wedgwoodian* 5 (no. 8), 238 — 241.

Haggar, Reginald G. 1951 — *The Masons of Lane Delph.*

Halfpenny, Pat. 1984 — Early Creamware to 1770, in Lockett, T.A. & Halfpenny, P. A. *Creamware & Pearlware,* 14 — 19.

Hampson, Eileen M. 1984 — Later Black Printing in Staffordshire, in Lockett, T. A. & Halfpenny, P. A. *Creamware & Pearlware,* 30 — 35.

Hargreaves, Thomas 1832 — *Map of the Staffordshire Potteries, & Newcastle.*

Haselgrove, Dennis & Murray, John 1979 — John Dwight's Fulham Pottery, 1672- 1978: A Collection of Documentary Sources. *Journal of Ceramic History* 11.

Holdway, Paul 1986 — Techniques of Transfer Printing on Cream Coloured Earthenware, in Lockett, T. A. & Halfpenny, P. A.: *Creamware & Pearlware,* 20 — 23.

Holdway, Paul forthcoming — 'Print with it the Glue Way' (from Sadler to Spode). *Thirty-fifth Wedgwood International Seminar* (1990).

Horne, Jonathan 1989 — *A Collection of Early English Pottery, Part IX.*

Horne, Jonathan 1990 — *A Collection of Early English Pottery, Part X.*

Kaellgren, C. Peter 1986 — From Silver Design to Ceramic Reality: An Earthenware Candlestick Copied from a William Kent Design. *American Ceramic Circle* 5, 89 — 95.

Lockett, T. A. & Halfpenny, P. A. (eds.) 1982 — *Stonewares & Stone Chinas of Northern England to 1851.* City Museum & Art Gallery, Stoke-on-Trent.

Lockett, T. A. & Halfpenny, P. A. (eds.) 1986 — *Creamware & Pearlware.* City Museum & Art Gallery, Stoke-on-Trent.

Lockett, T. A. 1986a — Problems of Attribution, in Lockett, T.A. & Halfpenny, P. A.: *Creamware & Pearlware,* 52 — 58.

Lockett, T. A. 1986b — The Later Creamware and Pearlwares, in Lockett, T. A. & Halfpenny, P. A.: *Creamware & Pearlware,* 44 — 51.

Luxmore, Chas. F. C. 1924 — *English Salt-Glazed Earthenware.* The Holland Press.

Mallet, John 1967 — John Baddeley of Shelton, Part II. *English Ceramic Circle Transactions* 6. (pt. 3), 181 — 247.

Mankowitz, Wolf 1953   *Wedgwood*. Batsford.

Meteyard, Eliza 1865   *Life of Josiah Wedgwood*. 2 Vols., London.

Miller, George L. 1987   The Origins of Josiah Wedgwood's Pearlware. *North-East Historical Archaeology* 16, 80 — 92.

Mint Museum, The 1982   *The Delhom Gallery Guide. English Pottery*.

Morley-Hewitt, A. T. 1954   Early Whieldon of the Fenton Low Works. *English Ceramic Circle Transactions* 3 (pt. 3), 142 — 154.

Mountford, A.R. 1971   *An Illustrated Guide to Staffordshire Salt-glazed Stoneware*. Barrie & Jenkins.

Mountford, A. R. 1972a   *Thomas Wedgwood, John Wedgwood and Jonah Malkin, Potters of Burslem*. Unpublished M.A. Thesis (University of Keele).

Mountford, A.R. 1972b   Thomas Whieldon's Manufactory at Fenton Vivian. *English Ceramic Circle Transactions* 8 (pt. 2), 164 — 182.

Niblett, Kathy 1984   A Useful Partner — Thomas Wedgwood 1734 — 1788. *Northern Ceramic Society Journal* 5, 1 — 22.

Noël Hume, Ivor 1970   The Rise and Fall of English Salt-Glazed Stoneware. *Antiques* (February 1970).

Parsons & Bradshaw 1818   *The New General and Commercial Directory of Staffordshire*.

Plot, Dr. Robert 1686   *The Natural History of the County of Staffordshire*.

Pitt, William 1817   *Topographical History of Staffordshire*.

Price, E. Stanley 1948   *John Sadler: A Liverpool Pottery Printer* (privately printed).

Price, Robin 1959   Some Groups of English Redware of the Mid-Eighteenth Century. *English Ceramic Circle Transactions* 4 (pt. 5), 1 — 9 and plates 1 — 6.

Price, Robin 1962   Some Groups of English Redware of the Mid-Eighteenth Century, Part II. *English Ceramic Circle Transactions* 5 (pt. 3), 153 — 168 and plates 150 — 161.

Ray, Anthony 1973   Liverpool Printed Tiles. *English Ceramic Circle Transactions* 9 (pt. 1), 36 — 66.

Reilly, Robin 1989 — *Wedgwood.* 2 Vols. Macmillan.

Sayer, Robert 1762 — *The Ladies Amusement: or, Whole Art of Japanning Made Easy.* (Facsimile edition 1959)

Seligmann, David 1975 — Two Ceramic Artists: William Greatbatch and David Rhodes. *Antique Dealer and Collector's Guide* (May 1975), 85 — 88.

Shaw, Simeon. 1829 — *History of the Staffordshire Potteries.*

Taggart, Ross E. 1967 — *The Frank P. and Harriet C. Burnap Collection of English Pottery in the William Rockhill Nelson Gallery of Art.* Revised Edition. Nelson-Atkins Gallery of Art.

Tait, Hugh & Cherry, John 1978 — Excavations at the Longton Hall Porcelain Factory. Part I. *Post-Medieval Archaeology* 12, 1 — 29.

Towner, Donald C. 1957 — *English Cream-coloured Earthenware.* Faber and Faber.

Towner, Donald C. 1963 — William Greatbatch and the Early Wedgwood Wares. *English Ceramic Circle Transactions* 5 (pt. 4), 180 — 193.

Towner, Donald C. 1978 — *Creamware.* Faber and Faber.

Towner, Donald C. 1980 — The William Greatbatch Site. *English Ceramic Circle Transactions* 10 (pts. 4 & 5), 266 — 271.

Tunnicliff, William 1787 — *A Topographical Survey of the Counties of Stafford, Chester and Lancaster.*

Victoria County History 1963 — *A History of the County of Stafford.* Vol. 8.

Walton, Peter 1976 — *Creamware and other English Pottery at Temple Newsam House, Leeds.* Manningham Press.

Weatherill, Lorna 1971 — *The Pottery Trade and North Staffordshire, 1660 — 1760.* Manchester University Press.

Williams-Wood, Cyril 1981 — *English Transfer-Printed Pottery & Porcelain. A History of Over-Glaze Printing.* Faber and Faber.

Yates, William 1775 — *Map of the Countie of Stafford from an actual survey, 1769 — 1775, engraved by John Chapman 1775.*

Young, Arthur 1769 — *Six Months Tour Through the North of England.*

Index

New Field Manufactory: 28, 59.

Ovens: 50, 105, 106, 118, 126-128, 139.
Oxides
— use in colours: 16, 17, 128, 129, 243.

Packing, packers: 108, 145, 146.
Palmer, Humphrey: 96, 264.
Peat, John: 81.
Pearlware: 24, 167.
Pineapple ware: 20, 97, 98, 112, 113, 136, 165, 259, 260.
Placing: 54.
— biscuit: 122-125.
— flatware: 136-138.
— glost: 123, 132-139.
— salt-glaze: 143, 144.
Plates: 136-138, 177-182.
Plaster of Paris: 18, 112, 114, 115, 117, 118, 121.
Pomona works: 15.
Porcelain, soft-paste: 13, 19, 108, 129.
Portland House: 59.
Pratt, William: 84.
Press-moulding, pressers: 108, 112-115, 117, 121.
Prices: 49, 50, 51, 52, 54.
Printing
— development and techniques: 21, 22, 101, 141-143.
Printed subjects
— Admiral Keppel: 100, 234, 235.
— Arms of the Society of Bucks: 239, 240.
— *Aurora*: 100, 233, 234.
— Captain Cook: 100, 228, 234.
— *Cybele*: 100, 234.
— Exotic Birds: 226.
— Flora: 224, 225.
— The Fortune Teller: 100, 236, 240.
— Harlequin & Columbine: 100, 232, 233.
— *John Wesley*: 223, 224.
— *Juno*: 100, 234, 240.
— A Lady and Gentleman in a Garden: 100, 233.
— *Lord Cornwallis*: 237, 238.
— A Man of War: 100, 234, 235.
— Minerva: 239.
— The Prodigal Son series: 100-102, 229-232.
— *Success to British Arms*: 237, 238.
— Tea Party: 228.
— *Telemachus*: 239.
— *The XII Houses of Heaven*: 77, 100, 101, 236, 240.
— Venus and Cupid: 227.
— The World with Sun, Moon and Stars: 100, 233, 234.
Prodigal Son, The: 100-102, 229-232.
Profiles: 77, 115-117.

Queensware: 15, 21, 24.

Radford, Thomas: 28, 100-102.
Red earthenware, glazed: 11, 15, 17, 19, 82, 122, 165, 271, 272.
Red stoneware: 17, 19, 49, 82, 83, 92, 93, 106, 119, 165, 187, 192, 261, 264-268.
Redware: see Red earthenware and Red stoneware.
Red Works, The: 41.
Reeded ware: 165, 185.
Rhodes, David, & Jasper Robinson: 22, 204.
Robinson, Jasper: see David Rhodes.
Robinson, John: 23.
Rouletting: 119, 177, 187, 254.

continued on inside front cover

SHELTON HALL

CAULDON CANAL

CAULDON PLACE

Lime kiln

Noahs Ark Inn
Harts Hill
CLIFF VILLE

Lock

Toll Gate

Trent Hay

Lodge
Brick Bank
Field Cottage

SHELTON

Shelton Wharf

PENKHULL

STOKE UPON

Vale Street

Hanley Road

Liverpool Road

Wharf

TRENT

Fenton House

Fenton Manor House

THE MOUNT

Honeywall

Church

National School

Mill

NEWTOWN

PENKHULL

Stoke upon Trent Poor House

STOKE HALL

Wharf

● Thomas Whieldon

Wharf

Chap

Bow

BOOTHEN VILLA

Newcastle Canal

River Trent

Mill

GREAT

NEWKEE

Brick

Mill

Stoke Lodge
Oak Hill
Boothen
Toll Gate

TOWNSHIP

Mole Cop

✝

'Map of the
Staffordshire Potteries,
and Newcastle'
by Thomas Hargreaves,
published in 1832

Fenton Mill

Sideway

Brick Bank

Black Lion

Little Sideway

Lime Kiln

Mill

Hanford Bridge
Church
River Trent
Parsonage

1 mile